D1535003

# Africana-Melanated Womanism

# Africana-Melanated Womanism:

*In It Together*

Edited by

Clenora Hudson (Weems)

**Cambridge
Scholars**
Publishing

Africana-Melanated Womanism: In It Together

Edited by Clenora Hudson (Weems)

This book first published 2022

Cambridge Scholars Publishing

Lady Stephenson Library, Newcastle upon Tyne, NE6 2PA, UK

British Library Cataloguing in Publication Data
A catalogue record for this book is available from the British Library

ISBN (10): 1-5275-8564-6
ISBN (13): 978-1-5275-8564-5

To Our Heavenly Father; My Mother and Father (Mary and Mathew Pearson); My Daughter and Entire Family; My Mentor, Dr. Richard K. Barksdale; Friends; Colleagues and All Africana People. Special Tribute to Dr. Wilfred Samuels (1946-2020), my Co-author of *Toni Morrison* (1990); Noble Laureate, Toni Morrison (1931-2019)—"And the Legacy Lives On!"

# TABLE OF CONTENTS

Foreword ............................................................................................ x
*Dean Deborah Jackson, DMin*

Preface ............................................................................................... xv
*Clenora Hudson (Weems), PhD; Gretel Thornton, Dissertator*

Introduction .................................................................................... xix
*Molefi Kete Asante, PhD*

**Part I: Theory: Africana-Melanated Womanism**

The Significance of an Authentic Africana Womanism Paradigm:
Collectivity and Interconnectedness for Social Justice .............................. 2
*Clenora Hudson (Weems), PhD*

Contrastive Analysis of Africana Womanism, Black Feminism
and African Feminism ............................................................................ 27
*Ama Mazama, PhD*

Africana Womanism as an Antidote to Mainstream Black Feminisms .... 43
*Mark Christian, PhD*

**Part II: Securing Our Legacy and Mission via Africana Texts**

Reclaiming Africana-Melanated Women: The Future of Africana
Family/The Power of the Media ............................................................. 59
*Marquita M. Gammage, PhD*

Our Children, Too, Need Models: A Letter to Aunt Daisy—
The Spirit of the Africana Womanist ...................................................... 80
*Alice Faye Duncan*

Africana Womanism: The Importance of Religion & Politics
in Africana Life ..................................................................................... 86
*April C. E. Langley, PhD*

Nobel Laureate, Toni Morrison: Model Africana Womanist Literary
Crusader for Social Justice .................................................................. 101
*Clenora Hudson (Weems), PhD*

**Part III: Moral Responsibility & Generational Wealth—An Africana
Womanism Perspective**

Pre-Africana Womanist, Ida B. Wells-Barnett: Embodiment of Africana
Womanism Principles .......................................................................... 113
*Charles Williams, PhD*; *Hilda Booker Williams, EdD*

From Public/Private Schools to the Academy: *Africana Womanism—*
Interconnectivity and the Africana Family ............................................ 128
*Tammy S. Taylor, Dissertator*

Today's Civil/Human Rights Movements: Africana Men & Women
Together—Against Racism & Emmett Till Continuums in a 5-Step
Solution .............................................................................................. 150
*Clenora Hudson (Weems), PhD*

Social and Racial Justice in Teacher Education: An Africana
Womanist Mandate............................................................................. 163
*Lasana D. Kazembe, PhD*; *Tambra O. Jackson, PhD*

Call "Mama": God, Family and the Un-Masked Authority of Black
Motherhood ........................................................................................ 178
*Debra Walker King, PhD*

Conclusion........................................................................................... 201
*Clenora Hudson (Weems) and Veronica Adadevoh*

Epilogue.............................................................................................. 205
*S. Renee Mitchell, EdD*

Afterword ........................................................................................... 207
*James B. Stewart, PhD*; *Anne Steiner, PhD*

Abstracts............................................................................................. 211

About the Book................................................................................... 222

About the Editor and Contributors ......................................................... 223

Appendix (Africana-Melanated Womanism Sample Syllabus).............. 225

Textbooks and Course Materials ........................................................... 227

Index...................................................................................................... 233

Praise for the Book ............................................................................... 240

# FOREWORD

## *DEAN DEBORAH JACKSON, DMIN*

The year 2020 will be remembered in history as one of catastrophic events. COVID-19, a previously unknown and presently incurable novel virus, gripped the world, leaving millions infected and over 1 million dead, with national economies devastated in the United States alone. The economic impact of the pandemic at its peak reached an alarming unemployment percentage of millions. While initial immediate stock market losses were recovered, the disparity between "the haves" and "the have nots" increased. The wealthiest individuals saw their earnings and portfolios grow. The poorest found themselves unemployed or underemployed, and with insufficient relief, struggled just to survive.

2020 is also a year of racial reckoning. Amid an extremely polarized political climate, the stresses of our lives were taxed and stretched, as we watched marginalized people suffer. We witnessed escalating and renewed attacks on black and brown bodies at the hands of law enforcement with the shootings of George Floyd, Breonna Taylor, Rayshard Brooks, Daniel Prude, Sean Monterrosa, Justin Howell, Jamel Floyd, James Blake, and too many others whose stories remained untold. In response, people took to the streets worldwide, led often by younger generations, the millennials, who used social media as an effective and powerful tool for communication and mobilization. We also saw rage. For those most marginalized, it was the rage of an anger that had no outlet and no relief. Years of oppression burst forth, angry and raw. Rage was also on display by extremists and supremacists, who fanned and fomented hate, unable to accept the demographic shift that will leave the United States as a minority country in less than 30 years.

Is there a way out of the morass that has left us fractured, distressed and despairing? I believe that there is, and this way is found in the theory and praxis of Africana Womanism. Our times demand a way forward that is both healing and restorative. A focus is required that helps societies function inclusively and holistically to ensure that all are served, and none are left behind. As scholar, author, and leader, Dr. Clenora Hudson (Weems) brilliantly demonstrates, Africana-Melanated Womanism speaks to our most urgent needs as a society, and this work provides a necessary and instructive hope for such a time as this.

Africana Womanism is the antidote to our ills because it represents a model through which we can operate in the world, providing a grounded sense of self, an esteeming and nurturing sense of others, and an uplifting focus on the world that is restorative. First conceptualized and articulated by Hudson (Weems) over 30 years ago, the encompassing 18 characteristics of the **Africana Womanist** speak to:

- **Who she is** – Self Naming, Self-Defining, Spiritual, Whole.
- **How she functions** – Mothering, Family Centered, Nurturing, Genuine in Sisterhood, Male Compatible, Respectful of Elders.
- **How she is viewed** – Respected, Recognized, Strong, Authentic.
- **How she works in the world** – Flexible Role Player, Adaptable, Ambitious, In Concert with Male in the Liberation Struggle.

The approach is complete and holistic. Because the Africana Womanist is self-named and defined, she is secure in her sacredness and rooted in her sense of self. A world that is stressed and distressed gains a sense of calm and assurance in her because of her way of being. But do not mistake this for self-aggrandizement. Relationally, she is mothering and nurturing. She cares for her family, is inclusively considerate of men and women, and she respects others, particularly elders. These relational ways of being demonstrate the love of others as a primal concern, along with self, and provide a positive template for living in the world.

The Africana-Melanated Womanist is strong, yet authentic in her dealings for which she is recognized and respected. The respect that she commands provides her with the space and ability to function flexibly in the world. She can lead, but just as important, she can follow. She is adaptable, but ambitious for the causes in which she engages. And, because she is inclusive, she functions in concert with men in the struggle for liberation of her people. These generative characteristics garner value and as such, she is well regarded by others.

Collectively, these attributes are critically important. We are living in a society that has lost its footing, as our actions across spectrums are self-serving and exploitative. To break this cycle, we need the paradigm which can be found in the Africana Womanist, for she, like the woman described in *Proverbs* 31:10, "is worth far more than rubies." Consider, for example, enslaved women of African descent in the United States. These women cared for the slave owner's children and households with the kind of love and nurture they provided for their own, as they were, after all, children. During the Reconstruction Era/post enslavement, African

American women came together to promote expanded rights for African American men as well. In fact, Fredrick Douglass solicited their support, with the assistance of Frances Watkins Harper and Maria W. Stewart, and succeeded in securing Sojourner Truth, thereby contributing to the ratification of the 15th Amendment to the Constitution in 1870, giving Black men the right to vote. And Black women, too, jubilantly rejoiced at the celebration of this great achievement for African Americans on the whole, even as they remained somewhat disenfranchised as women. Through the twentieth-century, countless African American women whose names have been lost to history, sought to lift others as they climbed for better opportunities. From their example and work, they fostered a culture of care that saves communities. If we would only glean from their experiences, we would extrapolate a robust and working theory of Africana Womanism. If we would learn from their actions, we would understand the supporting praxis methodologies. Hudson (Weems), and the gifted scholars with whom she collaborated in putting forth this important volume, has succeed in crafted an ideal model for success.

This collection of writings first situates an Africana Womanist paradigm as expansive and all-encompassing contextually, superseding previous theories. Theoretically, feminism believed itself to serve as an inclusive framework to articulate the lived experiences of women. However, in practice, its application excluded the experiences of Africana women. Feminism also sought an independence from and exclusion of male participation that Africana Womanism does not promote. Womanism, a term and definition coined by Alice Walker in the Introduction to her collection of essays, *In Search of Our Mother's Gardens,* sought to demonstrate greater inclusivity. However, to suggest that a "Womanist is to feminist as purple is to lavender" is to offer a sub-optimized definition where the shortcomings of one construct are foisted on that which was to be expansive, thus, causing this new construct to similarly fall short. Africana Womanism supersedes these definitions because this construct lays the groundwork for an inclusive human interconnectedness that strives to overcome racial dominance for all, while unapologetically asserting the equality for Africana people. This is the theoretical foundation.

But how, then, do we live? This body of work secondly applies theoretical principles to exemplars, thereby demonstrating effective functioning in the world. We can look to leaders like Ida B. Wells-Barnett, the anti-lynching Crusader for Social Justice, to understand how her life models the Africana Womanist theory that has been codified for our good, as she represents an unmistakable embodiment of these prized characteristics. We also see the model of Africana-Melenated Womanism through the writings of Toni Morrison, Nobel Laureate and author of the

Pulitzer Prize-Winning novel, *Beloved*. She provided context to the story of Africana people so that the world could better understand the multifaceted experiences of a people with depth, history, and a future. These women, aligned with the characteristics of Africana Womanism, show us how to be in the world.

Then Hudson (Weems) and these notable scholars expand our understanding of a praxis model by applying the learnings to various relationships and contexts. Our children, for example, experience the Africana Womanist as "Mama": a nurturer, provider, and protector. Her innate mothering abilities serve to shape the lives of the children in her care, ensuring their educational growth, instilling a love for God and others, and positioning them for success. Because she is a spiritual being, we experience the Africana Womanist as one with an unshakable faith in God. She sees in herself and others the divine actualization that results from being made in the image of God. As such, her faith enlivens her political stances to rail against oppression, and champion that which is just and right. Moreover, her faith demands equal sacrifice in our economic policies so that all could have what is needed and could then contribute to the well-being of the community in equitable ways.

But wanting to truly demonstrate that we are "In It Together," Hudson (Weems) and others demonstrate the durability of this Africana-Melanated Womanist model by tackling topics that speak to our present moment. We need, for example, to understand the violence of Whiteness and how it too often seeks to champion its dominant and dominating role in the lives of black and brown people. By exposing this violence, society can be positioned to leverage the characteristics of Africana-Melanated Womanism to overcome "privilege" and realize the rich benefits of true cultural diversity. As Africana Womanism calls for authenticity, we also need to see and celebrate authentic reflections of Black lives in the arts so that they might supplant the erroneous and harmful tropes that continue to manifest in society and motivate harsh and hostile responses to black and brown bodies. And finally, we need to understand where we go from here by revisiting the ongoing struggle of Africana people for ultimate human survival, mourning the continuation of "the Emmett Till Continuum," an identification designator coined by Dr. Hudson (Weems) in the 1990s, now referencing yet other brutal and senseless murders, like an Ahmaud Arbery and countless others, being prepared for how best to move forward.

Yes, 2020 will be remembered for its catastrophic events, but such occurrences have the power to help us seek innovations that dismantle oppressive systems and reconstruct ways of being for mutual benefit and societal good. It is with this hope that I embrace Africana-Melanated Womanism as a guiding model. Africana Womanism provides both the rigorous theory and validated praxis that withstands the test of time, is applicable across contexts, informs our lived experiences, and enables us all to fully realize ultimate liberation. This is the promise of God and as we remain "in it together," we will press on, as James Weldon Johnson "Lift Every Voice and Sing," the National Black Anthem, call for, "till [our] victory is won!"

# PREFACE

## *CLENORA HUDSON (WEEMS), PHD* AND *GRETEL THORNTON (DISSERTATOR, AUBURN U)*

The role of the Preface for a book is to share a somewhat personal backdrop of the author relative to the project. It gives life and texture to the subject, and, moreover, unveils the contributing factors that have brought the work to full fruition. This particular piece, written by both the editor of this book and her mentee, takes on a broader task, as it relates the commitment of the author and her chosen contributors in a collective initiative for both scholarship commonalities and for the growth and protection of the Africana community, thereby rendering a more complete story of the life of Africana people, in general, in their quest for eternal peace and freedom in a world that continues to deny them their rightful place in society.

Following the authors of the Foreword – written by *Dean Deborah Jackson*, who sets the tone and the mission; the Preface by *Dr. Clenora Hudson (Weems)* and *Gretel Thornton*; and the Introduction, written by *Dr. Molefi Kete Asante*, conceptualizer of Afrocentricity, who explicates an overall African-centered perspective, necessary and thus, presented in all the chapters – this volume closes with the Epilogue, by *Dr. S. Renee Mitchell,* and the Afterword, by *Dr. James B. Stewart* and *Dr. Ann Steiner*, who collectively render their assessment, validating that Africana-Melanated Womanism is, indeed, a worthy and much-needed authentic paradigm for the salvation of the Africana community. All the chapter authors diligently crafted masterful contributions to this three-part-volume, exploring many thought-provoking questions on the dilemma of the entire Africana family, men, women, and children, from an authentic family-centered, Africana Womanism perspective. As they expound upon controversial issues, they focus on how the theory of Africana Womanism best addresses burning questions today, relative to their specific diverse areas of expertise, as historians, philosophers, social scientists, anthropologists, administrators, and literary critics. The following is an overview of issues we have collectively taken on for debate.

In Part I, the first three Africana scholars – *Dr. Clenora Hudson (Weems)*, *Dr. Ama Mazama,* and *Dr. Mark Christian*, in their seminal chapters on the overarching theme – Theory: Africana-Melanated Womanism – lay down the foundation, wherein we witness their intellectual and private soul debates. Their primary mission is to distinguish between Africana Womanism and alternative female-based theories, keeping in mind at all times that the community and culture out of which they emerge represent a defining factor in identifying the most authentic paradigm for Africana people.

Part II, Securing Our Legacy and Mission via Africana Texts, offers important dialectics between Africana-Melanated Womanism and Feminisms, and by extension, Womanism, wherein interpretative, creative, and research-based readings of Africana texts are executed for deeper interpretations of life. This category explores the application of theory to texts, wherein, we observe the intellectual process of the following: *Dr. Marquita M. Gammage*, Black women stereotypes in the media; *Alice Faye Duncan*, Africana Womanist as model for our children; *Dr. April C.E. Langley*, an Africana Womanist perusal of the significance of religion and politics in Africana life; *Dr. Clenora Hudson (Weems)*, presents Nobel Laureate Toni Morrison as Model Africana Womanist Literary Crusader for Social Justice. This was the 2021 Keynote Address for 50th Anniversary of African American Studies at the U of Iowa, where Africana Womanism was, in fact, birthed in 1988 during my 1st semester at my Alma Mater.

Finally, Part III, Moral Responsibility and Generational Wealth, gives us rich insights into the nature and experiences of a people profoundly endowed. It opens with a co-authored chapter by *Drs. Charles* and *Hilda Williams*, in a veneration of the model Africana Womanist Social Justice Crusader, Ida B. Wells-Barnett; *Tammy S. Taylor* follows with her position relative to merging the Public and Private Schools with the Academy (colleges and universities) wherein she highlights the interconnectivity of the Africana family on all fronts; *Dr. Clenora Hudson (Weems)* offers a 5-Step Solution to End Racism, culminating in a true model case today of Generational Wealth for Blacks; *Dr. Lasana Kazembe,* and *Dean Tambra O. Jackson,* together, construct a pathway for our youths, our future leaders, who must have workable tools for mastering our new world. Finally, *Rev. Dr. Debra Walker King* takes us on a powerhouse, hallelujah sermon that ultimately leads to a glorious victory, a long-awaited moment wherein all could be right with the world, as God ordained that we rejoice and go forth.

If we seek real truth, we will have a deeper understanding of the physical and spiritual dynamics of both us and the other, so much so that we can leave with "the reasons why and the answers to and the people who and the places where and the days when," (Margaret Walker, "For My People," qtd. in *Call and Response*, 1159). All is reflected in the Conclusion, co-authored by *Dr. Clenora Hudson (Weems)* and *Veronica Adadevoh,* wherein we have a glimpse of how far we have come, up to the unlimited possibilities for Blacks today, who are long overdue true social justice. Herein lies invaluable information, reiterating the significance of Generational Wealth for Blacks, spelled out in solid details by a highly accomplished Black female businesswoman. Of course, the insightful endorsements by *Dr. Chike Akua, Laura Faith Kebede, Dr. Alveda King & Dr. Zifikile Makwavarara* confirm the value of this volume.

In the tradition of passing the legacy on to the next generation, I now pass the narrative to my mentee, *Gretel Thornton*, who will relate how she fits, as a doctoral student, into this overarching narrative of Africana people in search of answers, relative to who we really are, and what our role as teachers/professors and students need be for the ultimate salvation of our families and our future generations.

## II. The Mentee:

When I first arrived at my prestigious rural southern university to begin my PhD journey, many women and men of all ethnicities were exclaiming to me that Black Feminism was my home, and that all I wanted to do, everything I wanted to be, and every conundrum that I had ruminated upon thus far could be instantaneously solved if I just pledged my allegiance to the Flag of United Black Feminism. While I questioned this, after a while, I had almost been converted. Still, I could not completely force myself to believe in a theory that did not support how I actually felt. I knew all that was stated to me about the comfort that would be allotted to me as a Black Feminist was a fallacy, that almost everything that they were rapping to me was flawed in a way that had been obscured by the constant reanimation of this theory that did not take into account the Black Male bodies that were piling up in the streets, prisons, graveyards, and schools. How could Black Feminism as my main paradigm or theoretical framework aid me as an educator, boldly confronted with the reality faced by countless Black males who were, are, and will be discarded from education and western society like socks with holes? How could I tailor my research to help me as a Black female educator to understand how Black males are perpetually vilified and treated as brutes in American classrooms? I asked myself these questions every time I witness the assassinations of Black males in classrooms, who, at some point, may be added among those countless Black male victims outside of the classroom. Under another tree that celebrates the wholistic contours of the Black family, I have, hence, decided to seek my shade, comfort, and shelter. That other way of thinking is Africana Womanism, consisting of an interconnected unit including all of us, which naturally includes the plight of the Black male as a very important part of that family.

I had seen her picture (Dr. Clenora Hudson (Weems)) on the internet, the one who created this alternative paradigm, and revisited it many times throughout my years in undergrad. I kept seeing those eyes that spoke directly to me, until it got so bad that one day, I just had to email her, and just pray that she would respond. Well, I emailed her and heard nothing from her for five weeks. Maybe it was too long, I thought, as I went on and on, detailing my thoughts and experiences as a Black woman at a predominately white institution. Then, one day an email popped in my inbox, explaining to me how she had been busy working on her new book. Since that day I have felt at ease to look out the blight of African Americans from not this all-exclusory gender vantage point, but now, with a chance to view our various positionalities from 10,000 feet in the air view. Africana Womanism/Africana-Melenated Womanism offers us a chance to look down on us all, women, men, and children, and ponder ways to conceivably liberate us at last.

The book you are about to read was born from someone who has not followed the lead of others, but who struck up a new band and played a new song. My words are not to be mistaken as shade thrown at other Black women from other camps. They are not constructed to call out anyone. The words that I speak bring forth the notion that not all Black women lots are essential for all, assumed to be representing all. Understandably, there are others who view this world differently and I am simply telling you how it is for me as one of many: My heart, and my spirit, and my research have all found their home in a paradigm curated by a woman whom I am blessed to call my friend, my mentor, and my sister in the liberation struggle for all Africana people. As a young single mother from Atlanta, with four kids, it has taken me so long to find a place that I could feel comfortable with that does not make me forget about my male counterparts. Whether you love Black men and boys platonically or romantically, as members of the Black community, we must develop a way to ensure the survival of us all, not just our women and our girls, but our male cousins, uncles, brothers, friends, husbands, boyfriends, and Daddies. I can attest that Africana Womanism is the way to do that, to place the focus back on the Black family. We are together in this "thang"—Women, Men, and children! I thank Dr. Hudson (Weems) for another way of looking at our lives as a unit, interconnected as individuals with collective concerns about the survival of our people. And as we continue to deal with the varied issues in our lives as Africana people, we must prioritize race, class, and gender, truly Africana womanist in action.

# INTRODUCTION

## *MOLEFI KETE ASANTE, PHD*

It is possible for one to build a house without a blueprint; this is done often enough that we do not condemn people for doing so. However, to plan a project that will have consistency, uniformity, art, design, and positionality in relationship to other ideas, it is best to have a theory that provides a model for construction. This has been the idea behind or in front of the work of our most important intellectual leaders. They have tried to give us, after deep reflection on our condition, and situation, which is different, the necessary tools for designing our liberation. Clenora Hudson (Weems) has seen that it is essential that we not follow in the path of those who would lead us to our mental death. She has proclaimed by virtue of her deliberate search for a way forward through the fog, very useful highway markers for those who are seeking to reach the light. What this volume represents is a huge sign that there are now more people than we know who are on the path with her, following the patterns and models that she has given us in her provocative and enlightening books, articles and public presentations.

Clenora Hudson Weems has taken the bold step of bringing together an impressive array of intellectuals devoted to the idea of Africana Womanism that she pioneered in the 1980s as a powerful tool to explicate the relationship between African people with an emphasis on the black women and men in a way that was different from the role played by white feminists. In effect, Hudson (Weems) made several important advances. She gave us a way to theorize about the role of women and men in a way that modeled the African American culture. In fact, Hudson (Weems) provided a language of Afrocentric perspective to relationships, gender, and spheres of influence.

This work is a demonstration of her philosophy of complementarity because she has men and women writing and they are all pointing their works in the same direction. An idea founded upon the principle of African agency sits at the entrance to Africana Womanism. It is this idea that is being stood up each day as we reclaim our history and traditions and seek to connect our scholarship to the values and cultural inheritance we have been left. It is not that we seek to tear down, but rather to build up, and sometimes that means that debris has to be removed. I am pleased that the editor has devoted her life to this issue.

Hudson (Weems) was influenced by her important interview and discussions with Toni Morrison, which was invaluable, as she and her co-author were invited to write the first full-length critical study of the works of the Nobel Laureate, Toni Morrison, in the mid 80s, published in 1990. Morrison was one of the first black women to publicly discuss what black women in general really think about the women's liberation movement in a 1971 article appearing in *The New York Times Magazine.* Taking Morrison, a step further, as an Afrocentrist, Hudson (Weems) knew that any answer to the issues of gender and sex had to deal with African culture. What Hudson (Weems) wanted to do and what she did was to explore how race and culture impact issues of gender. She has given us a paradigmatic turn that has used the lives of ordinary Africana women as the concrete basis for analysis and potentialities. It is not that Africana womanism is a branch of white women feminism, but rather that Africana womanism is itself an autonomous system of examining culture and gender. Black women are not white women, and the commonality of their sex does not dictate the way they see gender. It is possible that they may have similar ideas, but there is a long stretch between the way the mistress of the plantation saw gender and the working woman in the cotton fields saw gender and relationships.

All theoretical advances result when we have critically assessed how other theories operate in the arena of our subjects. In this volume Clenora Hudson (Weems), the leading and founding theorist of Africana Womanism, has demonstrated the important dimension of scholarship that has often been ignored. I call this the community relationship where scholars seeking to establish academic solidarity with each other and with the subject agree to participate in a common project. We have seen that many scholars in this volume have followed the leadership of Professor Hudson (Weems). I think this is true because she has openly sought to invite some of the most well-known scholars to write for this project.

There will be much interest in this work and students and professors will learn from the essays and analyses brought by scholars who are deeply involved in questions surrounding the discourses about women and men, about iconic female writers, matriarchy, resistance to patriarchy, and the elevation of reciprocity. This volume should be seen as a definitive statement of the Africana Womanism community of scholars; I salute Professor Hudson (Weems) and her cohort of intellectual compatriots.

# PART I:

# THEORY:
# AFRICANA-MELANATED WOMANISM

*"Africana-Melanated Womanism:  I Got Your Back, Boo"*

Don't you know by now, girl, we're all In It Together!
Family-Centrality--that's it; we're going nowhere without the other
That means the men, the women, and children, too,
Truly collectively working—"I got your back, Boo."

*Racism* means the violation of our constitutional rights,
Which creates on-going legal, and even physical fights.
This 1st priority for humankind is doing what it must do,
Echoing our 1st lady, Michelle—"I got your back, Boo."

*Classism* is the hoarding of financial privileges,
Privileges we must all have now in pursuit of happiness.
Without a piece of the financial pie, we're doomed to have a coup.
Remember--protect the other—"I got your back, Boo."

*Sexism*, the final abominable sin of female subjugation,
A battle we must wage right now to restore our family relations.
All forms of sin inevitably fall under 1 of the 3 offenses.
Africana Womanism, "I Got Your Back, Boo," corrects our common senses.

**Clenora Hudson (Weems), PhD**
Dedicated to All Africana Women, FEB 2009

# 1

# THE SIGNIFICANCE OF AN AUTHENTIC AFRICANA WOMANISM PARADIGM: COLLECTIVITY AND INTERCONNECTEDNESS FOR SOCIAL JUSTICE

## *CLENORA HUDSON (WEEMS), PHD*

The Importance of Africana Womanism to Africana Studies/Africology cannot be overstated. Among its many virtues is its role as an important corrective to the continuing tendency to marginalize the experiences of Africana women and minimize their roles as active agents in the ongoing liberation struggle. Consequently, Africana Womanism is enabling Africana Studies/Africology to realize its full potential as a guiding beacon in the global battle to claim the natural rights of *all* people of African descent. (Stewart and Mazama, Foreword in *Africana Womanism* xiii).

The above quotation offers an overriding assessment of the significance of Africana-Melanated Womanism – a terminological, rather than conceptual evolution of Africana Womanism – to Africana people, particularly in academia, as well as in the Africana community. The sentiments and assessments of Dr. James B. Stewart and Dr. Ama Mazama, co-authors of the Foreword to *Africana Womanism: Reclaiming Ourselves* Fifth Edition (Routledge 2019), represent the critical charge and recommendations of two well-established respected academicians, strongly endorsing the theory of Africana Womanism, based upon solid and sound research. These scholars, the former – Past President of The National Council for Black Studies, Professor emeritus and Vice Provost (ret.) at Penn State U, and the latter – Afrocentric Guadeloupe scholar, Associate Professor at Temple U, and managing editor of the *Journal of Black Studies*, both assess the theory of Africana Womanism.

In substantiating their position, the editors of a major Black Aesthetics Anthology, *Call and Response: The Riverside Anthology of The*

*African American Literary Tradition*, published by one of the nation's leading publishers, Houghton-Mifflin, assert the following endorsement:

> The first African American woman intellectual to formulate a position on Africana womanism was Clenora Hudson-Weems, author of the 1993 groundbreaking study *Africana Womanism: Reclaiming Ourselves*. Taking the strong position that Black women should not pattern their liberation after Eurocentric feminism but after the historic and triumphant woman of African descent, Hudson-Weems has launched a new critical discourse in the Black Women's Literary Movement." (Patricia Hill, et al, *Call and Response*, 1811.)

Indeed, Africana Womanism is new and significantly different, thus, according to Dr. Delores P. Aldridge, the Grace T. Hamilton Professor of Sociology and founding Chair of the Department of African American Studies at Emory University,

> Hudson-Weems' paradigm frames ideas about Africana women in an authentic way that differs from all other gender-based theories. Moreover, it demonstrates that women in Africana/Black Studies are critical thinkers . . . Her model, with its own label, has set forth to explain a given set of ideas. Both older and younger scholars can emulate such labeling by developing new models, laying claim to them as they position themselves to continue the tradition of African women as critical theorists (Aldridge, Foreword to *Africana Womanist Literary Theory* xii-xiii).

Much like Dr. Aldridge and the editors of *Call and Response*, Dr. Adele Newson-Horst's critique ultimately counters the established practice and mindset on the part of mainstream thought within the Academy. Perceptively, she concludes that

> In the last few decades, feminism and Black feminism have gained such a stronghold in the Academy that the activities of most all of the important women writers have been stamped as feminist enterprises. While feminism provides a refreshing alternative to patriarchal hegemonic discourse, it is nevertheless inadequate to account for the numerous and varied works produced by Africana women. . . . the inherent contradiction, an ahistorical impulse, in defining a Black tradition and a theoretical and preoccupation as feminist, commands that a distinction be made between feminist impulses and feminism. (Newson-Horst 359)

Her statement came from her interpretation of "*Mama Day*: An Africana Womanist Reading" in *Contemporary Africana Theory, Thought and Action: A Guide to Africana Studies*. The literary critic challenges the pervasive propensity in the Academy to obtrude feminist theory upon

Africana literary texts. The problem here is that feminism as a theoretical concept represents practices and opinions that are generated from a Eurocentric reality that lacks the "lived" experiences of Africana people, as it was named and created by white women based upon their lives and needs. Because an authentic terminology designed for Africana women is also important, it is needed in order to make an authentic interpretation of the lives of Africana people. Therefore, while feminism, a female-centered concept, reflects the particular needs of white women who are primarily concerned with elevating themselves as equal to their male counterparts, Black women, on the other hand, are necessarily concerned about the destiny of their entire family, as men, women, and children are indisputable victims of racial injustices in a world of racial dominance. Thus, Africana Womanism, a family-centered concept that aims at empowering the entire Africana family, rather than the female-centered concept that centers its energy on female empowerment, has taken on the responsibility and duty of naming and defining Black women, two of 18 cornerstones of the Africana Womanism paradigm.

There is no need to look outside of ourselves to explicate our lives, which Dr. Hudson-Weems validates in a seminal chapter, "The African American Literary Tradition" in *The African American Experience* (2001). She contends that embracing feminism for Black women lacks rationale:

> Most women outside and some inside academe have found the terminology problematic, since any and all brands of feminism see female empowerment as their collective priority. Alice Walker attempted to offer a solution to the dilemma with her label womanist. Unfortunately, her term and definition of womanist in the short introduction to her collection of essays, *In Search of Our Mother's Gardens: Womanist Prose* (1983) as "a black feminist or feminist of color . . . Womanist is to feminist as purple to lavender" was insufficient. (Hudson-Weems 135)

Rather than accept the theory of the dominant culture, "feminism," Dr. Hudson-Weems initiates a more appropriate theoretical framework from which to interpret Black life, Africana Womanism, tailored to meet the demands of the Africana family via an authentic paradigm reflecting our everyday lives on all fronts. Naturally commanding the cooperation of the whole family for our ultimate liberation, here we stand, "In it together," resolute against the unjust practices of racism. Since it is apparent here that Africana women require another term to define who they really are, as they are not easily persuaded to use a terminology and definition that are incompatible with their true selves, they object the unfamiliar, though they may not at that time have an alternative name/definition for themselves.

Demonstrating the global presence of Africana Womanism as an authentic Africana family-centered paradigm, wherein the collectivity of men and women is, indeed, salient, the theory shows its long-standing applicability to Africana people in Africa. This truth resounded at the First International Africana Womanism Conference, hosted by the U of Zimbabwe in 2010:

> Dr. Itai Muhwati—then Chair of the Department of Literature and Languages, now Dean of Faculty—and his colleagues coordinated the grand event. Hundreds of presenters and attendees came from not only universities throughout the continent of Africa, including several universities throughout Zimbabwe, the U of South Africa and the U of Botswana, but from universities in the United States as well, including California State U-Dominguez Hills, the U of Oklahoma, Delaware State U, the U of Missouri, and so on. Moreover, participants outside of Academia were represented as well, such as the Honorable Joice Mujuru, Vice President of the Republic of Zimbabwe, who delivered the Opening Welcome. . . Men and women alike [came] to discuss our destiny as African people and what we needed to make our quest a reality. (Hudson-Weems, *Africana Paradigms* 6)

In 2012, an edited volume of select papers from the event was published.

Four years later, we witnessed a perceptive article by a South African journalist, Gracious Madondo, in *The Southern Times: The Newspaper for Southern Africa*, wherein she expounds on the question as to "Why Africa Relates to Africana Womanism." Here, she highlights the male-female co-existence, dating back to pre-colonialism in Africa: "Unlike the Western rooted feminist approach to literature . . . Africana womanism speaks of male and female compatibility, where men and women co-exist together without conflict" (Madondo, 2018). She realizes that "the real cause of inequalities in Africa [is] colonialist patriarchal tendencies," hence, concurring with Pan Africanist, Dr. Molefi Kete Asante (Madondo). Dr. Hudson-Weems' analysis, too, goes back to African antiquity, thus, according to Dr. Asante in his Afterword to her second Africana womanism book, *Africana Womanist Literary Theory*, "Hudson's Africana Womanist thought has the perfect approach to gender issues in Africa as compared to American Feminism." (138). It should be here noted that Dr. Asante, who coined the term and refined the paradigm of *Afrocentricity*, makes a clear point that we as Africana people, too, have the right to name and define ourselves, as well as how we relate to each other. He further states that "Africana Womanism is a response to the need for collective definition and the re-creation of the authentic agenda that is the birthright of every living person" (138). As the first call for Africana Womanism, initiated by Dr. Hudson-Weems, had already appeared in *The*

*Western Journal of Black Studies* in "Cultural and Agenda Conflicts in Academia: Critical Issues for Africana Women's Studies" (1989), Asante's assertion renders a strong affirmation of what Africana Womanism offered. The on-going debates surrounding the call for an authentic paradigm for Africana women as writers and activists, indeed, validated the theory.

Africana Womanism, then, within the Afrocentric arena, makes its contributions to Afrocentric discourse via naming and defining Africana women according to their true nature and at the same time in explicating the importance of family centrality and positive male-female relationships for an "interconnected" existence and a collective pursuit for securing our birthright to abundance and happiness. According to Dr. Ama Mazama,

> Clenora Hudson-Weems coined the term Africana Womanism in 1987 out of the realization of the total inadequacy of feminism and like theories (e.g. Black feminism, African womanism, or womanism) to grasp the reality of African women, let alone give us the means to change that reality. (400)

That reality includes the riff between Africana men and women, commonly called "the battle of the sexes," historically inauthentic in Africa before the advent of colonialism. In going back to African antiquity, one knows that such a mind-set is non-Afrocentric, for men and women then shared responsibilities, including even powerful positions of leadership, i.e. kings and queens, while at the same time, enjoying and appreciating traditional roles in society, with designated responsibilities accordingly.

To further support this demand for authenticity for Africana people, I coordinated a number of panels for national conferences in the mid-80s, during the early stage of refining this theoretical construct, including some plenaries, which included a few males as well, which launched the heated debates about this critical need to name and define ourselves.  These presentations during the inception of Africana Womanism as a paradigm commenced during the mid-eighties, up to the end of that decade.  The venues for these exciting occasions for national Black organizations included Boston for The National Council for Black Studies Conference, and Philadelphia for The African Heritage Studies Association Conference in 1986; New Orleans for The College Language Association Convention, and even the National Women's Studies Association Conference in Atlanta in 1987 at the historic Spellman College, and again for that organization the following year in 1988 at the U of Minnesota; also there was Detroit  for  Association for the Study of African American Life and History in 1988, and many more.  I was also invited to speak on this subject at many colleges and universities throughout the country for their Black History Month, as well as Women's History Month celebrations, including the University of Utah, Southern

Utah University, Indiana University, Winston-Salem State University, Texas Southern University, etc., all during the embryonic stage of Africana Womanism, even before its first book publication in 1993.

The receptivity of the new theory was, indeed, amazing, culminating in that first release, *Africana Womanism: Reclaiming Ourselves* in 1993. That very next year, 1994, Dr. Maria Mootry reviewed the book for one of the major publications for Black studies, *The Western Journal of Black Studies*. It opened up with a powerful summation of the emotional experiences of Africana women, culminating in a powerful written acceptance of this authentic paradigm:

> Rage, shame, guilt, anguish, indignation, celebration, affirmation—voices of Africana women have ranged up and down the arpeggios of emotion in response to racism, classism and sexism. Now comes a voice, cool and clear, rising above the chorus, offering not only lucid insights into the status of Africana women and their literature, but a blueprint to help us find a way out of confusion and despair. . . . The result, in the words of Professor Charles Hamilton, is 'an intellectual triumph." (Mootry 244)

Research documents the fact that feminism was not intended to represent and interpret Black life, and thus, the magnitude of the vast totality of Black women lives was not, nor could it be accurately and totally addressed and/or recorded within the white feminist theoretical framework. And the term Black Feminism was clearly limited, as it was an obvious extension of feminism, notably reflected in the terminology itself. Perhaps due to this, more positive responses to Africana Womanism continued to grow. Dr. Delores P. Aldridge, the unprecedented two-term President of the National Council for Black Studies, who had supported Africana Womanism from its inception in the 80s, wrote a book jacket endorsement of the 1993 publication of the first Africana Womanism book, *Africana Womanism: Reclaiming Ourselves*:

> This work is unquestionably a pioneering effort whose time has come. It provides an exciting and fresh approach to understanding the tensions existing among the mainstream feminist, the Black feminist, the African feminist and the Africana womanist. (Aldridge, 1993)

Later in her co-edited volume, *Out of the Revolution: The Development of Africana Studies* (2000), with Dr. Carlene Young, Dr. Aldridge invited me to write a chapter for it, which I titled "Africana Womanism: An Overview." In that publication, Dr. Aldridge' seminal chapter, "Toward Integrating Africana Women into Africana Studies," drew a comprehensive picture of the growing trend of the presence and the role of Black women in the evolution of the discipline of Africana Studies, wherein she asserted that "it is from this perspective of Africana Womanism that this discourse is developed" (*Out of the Revolution* 193). Four years later, in the Foreword to Hudson-Weems' *Africana Womanist Literary Theory*, she concluded her assessment of Hudson-Weems seminal work/theory as follows:

> In this twenty-first century, no less than in ages past, the need will be great for scholars to provide paradigms and critical theories for understanding society and its various aspects or forms – historical, cultural, literary, social, and the like. Scholars such as Hudson-Weems will be listed among those who have made a difference in the conceptualization, development, and promotion of the discipline of Africana Studies. Just as (Aldridge, Foreword, *Africana Womanist Literary Theory* xiii).

Dr. April Langley, Chair of the African American Studies Program at the University of South Carolina, who specializes in early Black writers, Pre-Emancipation Proclamation women writers/orators/activists in particular, uses Africana Womanism as a tool of analysis in her approaches to early Black literary texts. For example, in her article, "Lucy Terry Prince: The Cultural and Literary Legacy of Africana Womanism," appearing in a 2001 Special Issue on Africana Womanism in *The Western Journal of Black Studies*, for which I served as Guest Editor, she contended that

> It is Africana Womanism as originated, developed, and outlined by Hudson-Weems that enables a reading which restores and revises the African origins of the early African American writing. . . . the import of this critical paradigm for the earliest Africana writers is essential for recuperating what is "African" in early African American literature. (Langley 158)

Dr. Daphne Ntiri, Professor and Director of Wayne State University, Another Chance, wrote a lengthy and informative Introduction to *Africana Womanism: Reclaiming Ourselves* in 1993. In assessing what she calls a "landmark pioneering treatise of Africana woman's realities," she closes with a very important quotation, headlined on the front-page cover story – "Beyond 'Bra Burning": [Africana] Womanism as alternative for the African Women," which appeared in *The Nigerian Daily Times* Newspaper on July 27, 1992. In reporting on Women of Africa and the African Diaspora International Conference, this publication also served as an endorser of the concept and, moreover, as a contributor to the globalization of the movement/theory, fully presented in its coverage:

> Personal and racial experiences . . . will be the factors responsible for the evolution of Africana Womanism. Therefore, legitimate concerns of the Africana Woman are issues to be addressed within the context of African

culture and history. Africana Womanists do not believe in "bra burning." They believe in womanhood, the family and society ("Beyond Bra Burning," 1992).

Africana men, too, strongly supported Africana Womanism, writing book endorsements, expressing their receptivity to the theory. For example, Dr. C. Eric Lincoln, Professor Emeritus of Duke University, asserted that

> Hudson-Weems' *Africana Womanism* sent unaccustomed shock waves through the domain of popular thinking about feminism and established her as a careful, independent thinker, unafraid to unsettled settled opinion. (inside jacket endorsement, 1993)

Dr. Talmadge Anderson, Chief Editor of *The Western Journal of Black Studies* and Professor at Washington State University, defined Africana Womanism as the embodiment of Black womanhood: "The work [*Africana Womanism*] captures the essence of the true meaning of black womanhood and resolves the classical debate relative to the prioritizing of race, class and sex in American society." (Inside jacket blurb, 1993).

Dr. Charles V. Hamilton, Professor of Political Science at Columbia U, who co-authored *Black Power: The Politics of Liberation in America*(1967) with Stokley Carmichael, a.k.a. Kwame Touré, succinctly advised that "This work is, indeed, an intellectual triumph. It is a product that not only must be read, but more important, be studies."

And finally, there was the book endorsement by Dr. Robert L. Harris, Jr., who reigned as Director of Africana Studies and Research Center at Cornell University before, during, and after the debut of *Africana Womanism*:

> In the triple marginality of black women, race rises above class and gender in this remarkable book. With it, a reunion, a much-needed healing, a human philosophy emerges for men and women of African ancestry and ultimately for all caring men and women. (Inside jacket blurb, 1993)

Notably, Africana men and women came together as one in support of the concept, as represented in *Africana Womanism*. In the Fifth Edition of the 1993 classic, Dr. Hudson-Weems added the following:

> The key to the true meaning of Africana Womanism is its mandate for inclusion of the whole family, men included, while highlighting also the very presence and role of the Africana Womanist in concert with her male companion in the ongoing cooperative struggle against racial dominance. Indeed, a cornerstone in the priorities of Africana Womanism, the race

> factor is primary in the scheme of things—race, class and gender—and, thus, must be properly placed within our own historical and cultural matrix. (Hudson-Weems, *Africana Womanism* 98)

Prior to the term, Africana Womanism in the mid-1980s, there was no existing name given for a new methodology that specifically addressed that critical need for a separate terminology, which does not include one that piggy backs off someone else's name and definition. The only existing names assigned to Black women, theoretically speaking, were Black Feminism, African Feminism, and Womanism, all clearly connected to Feminism, representing a procrustean approach, used perhaps to fit the acceptable concept of feminism. Of course, eventually Black women grew tired of accepting an alien paradigm and making their position fit the basic theoretical constructs of an inauthentic paradigm, and thus, began to step up, boldly challenging what was out there:

> While many other black women naively adopted feminism early on, because of the absence of an alternative and suitable framework for their individual needs as Africana women, more are reassessing the historical realities and the agenda for the modern feminist movement and have bravely stood firm in their outright rejection of it. (Hudson-Weems, "Africana Womanism" in *Out of the Revolution* 205)

Enthusiasm surrounded this paradigm, for the publication of its first book was only the beginning. Some 26 years after the 1st Edition in 1993, the reprint of that classic, the Fifth revised Edition, with a new section, Part III, with new chapters was released. (Routledge Press, 2019).

Below is a list of 32 Defining Quotes, representing only a few Black thinkers-activists, either anticipating or echoing this authentic persuasion, thus, suggesting a critical need for an Africana Womanism Paradigm. This can only be complete when Africana Womanists worldwide become fully aware of this theoretical construct with the realization that the theory was created with them and their families in mind:

## Defining Quotations:

1.  "The first African American woman intellectual to formulate a position on Africana womanism was Clenora Hudson-Weems, author of the 1993 groundbreaking study *Africana Womanism: Reclaiming Ourselves*. Taking the strong position that Black women should not pattern their liberation after Eurocentric feminism but after the historic and triumphant woman of African descent, Hudson-Weems has launched a new critical discourse in the Black Women's Literary Movement." (**Patricia L. Hill**, et al, *Call and Response: The Riverside Anthology of the Africana American Literary Tradition*, 1811.)

2.  "Africana Womanism is a response to *the need for collective definitions* and the re-creation of the a*uthentic agenda* that is the birthright of every living person." (**Molefi Kete Asante**, Afterword, *Africana Womanist Literary Theory,*138, 2004)

3.  "The Early Image of Women's Lib was of an elitist organization made up of upper-middle class [white] women with the concerns of that class and not paying much attention to the problems of most black women. . . . Too much emphasis is placed on gender politics." (**Toni Morrison,** *Time* 1971)

4.  "Among its [Africana Womanism's] many virtues is its role as an important *corrective* to the continuing tendency to marginalize the experiences of Africana women and minimize their roles as active agents in the on-going liberation struggle." (**Ama Mazama** and **James B. Stewart**, Foreword to 5th Edition of *Africana Womanism*, 5th Edition, xiv, 2019)

5.  "Hudson-Weems bravely takes the bull by the horns, confronts the Eurocentric avalanche of words on questions of gender, and puts forward the Afrocentric point of view." ('**Zulu Sofola**, Foreword in *Africana Womanism,* xii.)

6.  "In short, "feminist," in the modern sense, means the empowerment of women. For women of color, such an equality, such an empowerment, cannot take place unless the communities in which they live can successfully establish their own racial and cultural integrity." (**Bettina Aptheker,** "Strong Is What We Make Each Other" 3)

7.  "The national liberation of the Black South African is a prerequisite to her own liberation and emancipation as a woman and a worker." (**Ruth Mompati** in Ntiri's *One is Not a Woman, One Becomes* 112)

8.  "Black women and white women are not the same. Black women & men have shared racist oppression & still share it. We have

developed joint defenses & joint vulnerabilities to each other that are not duplicated in the white community." (**Audre Lorde**, *Sister Outsider*, 118)

9. "Hudson-Weems, having engaged in serious scholarly research on these matters [African heritage and gender question], dares to challenge the Eurocentric status quo. For the first time, the African position on gender issues is fearlessly presented with a global spread . . . " (**'Zulu Sofola**, Foreword in Hudson-Weems' *Africana Womanism*, Fifth Edition, xi.)

10. "The feminist has no exclusive on gender issues." (**Hudson-Weems,** *Africana Womanism.*)

11. "While feminism provides a refreshing alternative to patriarchal hegemonic discourse, it is nevertheless inadequate to account for the numerous and varied works produced by Africana women. . . . consider[ing] that the masses of Africana women do not identify themselves as feminists." (**Adele S. Newson-Horst** in *Contemporary Africana Theory, Thought and Action,"* 359, 2007)

12. "Women who are calling themselves black feminists need another word that describes what their concerns are. Black feminism is not a word that describes the plight of Black women." (**Julia Hare**, "Feminism in Black & White," in *Black Issues in Higher Ed.*15)

13. "As models and blueprints for the framework of their theory, therefore, when Africana women come along and embrace feminism, appending it to their identity as Back feminists or African feminists, they are in reality duplicating the duplicate" (**Clenora Hudson- Weems**, *Africana Womanism*, 5th Edition, 13-14, 2019; 1993)

14. "The current academic fad phase is 'intersectionality,' as if those of us in Africana discourse never considered the myriad of issues encountered by our communities. "Race," class and gender, and the prioritization therein, have always been key issues for comprehending *Africana Womanism.*" (**Mark Christian**, Afterword, *Africana Womanism* 131)

15. "When the Black feminist buys the white terminology, she also buys its agenda." (**Clenora Hudson-Weems,** *Africana Womanism* 25-26.)

16. "Clenora Hudson-Weems coined the term Africana Womanism in 1987 out of the realization of the total inadequacy of feminism and the like theories (e.g. Black feminism, African womanism, or womanism) to grasp the reality of African women, let alone give us the means to change that reality." (**Ama Mazama**, 400-401, 2001)

17. "Thus, while the Africana womanist writer should not make blanket justifications for the failures, frustrations, undesirable behavior and financial predicament of some of her menfolk, she is not expected to abandon them or badger them [which] inevitably ends in an unjustifiable and relentless lashing out at men in general, thereby sentencing them to perpetual verbal and emotional castration by their women." (**Clenora Hudson-Weems,** *Africana Womanism* 51-52.)

18. "This novel advocacy solidifies the commonality of political and socio-economic goals, gives legitimacy to our claim for equality, demonstrates clarity of mission and purpose in our Africanness, and adds originality to the collective voice of Africana women." (**Daphne Ntiri**, Introduction in *Africana Womanism* 4.)

19. "We need our own Africana theorists, not scholars who duplicate or use theories created by others in analyzing Africana texts." (Hudson-Weems, "Africana Womanism and the Critical Need for Africana Theory & Thought," (**Clenora Hudson-Weems**, *Contemporary Africana Theory, Thought and Action* 79.)

20. "Woman's cause is man's cause: [We] rise or sink together, dwarfed or godlike, bond or free." (**Anna Julia Cooper,** *A Voice from the South* 61)

21. "Personal and racial experiences . . . will be the factors responsible for the evolution of Africana Womanism. Therefore, legitimate concerns of the Africana Woman are issues to be addressed within the context of African culture and history. *Africana Womanists do not believe in 'bra burning.' They believe in womanhood, the family and society.*" (*The Nigerian Daily Times*, July 27, 1992.)

22. "We as Africana people must decide for ourselves who we are and what our agenda need be. Africana people must engage in identifying our own demands, beginning with self- naming and self-definition, so that we can better focus on what it will take for us to realize total human parity." (**Clenora Hudson-Weems**, "Self-Naming and Self-Definition" in Nnaemeka's *Sisterhood* 451.)

23. "Many women authors try to suggest that the self-definition, self-determination, & centering that she has articulated is really a part of some feminist movement. Those writers have found the Afrocentric ideas & concepts developed in Hudson-Weems' Africana womanism significant &, therefore, have sought to appropriate them without proper attribution. I believe that this exists because they do not want to admit that their concepts were first conceived in the writings of the Africana womanist school. (**Molefi Kete Asante**, Afterword in *Africana Womanist Literary Theory* 138.)

24. "No longer should African agency be examined, explained, and enhanced via postmodernist analyses. We, therefore, require such a blueprint [*Africana Womanism*] as here presented, one that is both effective and resolute in its attempt to dislodge the continued domination of white European intellectual canons in the Academy." (**Mark Christian,** Afterword in *Contemporary Africana Theory, Thought and Action* 2646.)

25. "Africana Womanism liberates the enslaved and distorted African cultural space and draws pedagogically nourishing perspectives on African womanhood and gender that can be utilized by people of African descent in their attempts to deal with challenges affecting their existence." (**Itai Muhwati**, *Rediscoursing African Womanhood: Africana Womanism* xvii.)

26. "As we assess the needs of the global woman of color, that mission has now pulled back the layers to reveal a rainbow & myriad of colors, revealing & accentuating an already pre- existing, inclusive, & diverse paradigm, birthed from Africana Womanism and now extending to [Africana-Melanated Womanism." (**Aubrey Bruce,** *Africana Womanism* 93.)

27. "When those Africana women finish fighting the feminist battle and feminists have succeeded in realizing all their goals relative to female empowerment, the Africana woman will be left with the reality that she is both black and at the bottom." (**Clenora Hudson-Weems,** *Africana Womanist Literary Theory* 83, 2004)

28. "In the triple marginality of black women, race rises above class and gender in this remarkable book. With it, a reunion, a much-needed healing, a human philosophy emerge for men and women of African ancestry and ultimately for all caring men and women." (**Robert Harris**, Book Endorsement, 1993)

29. "Indeed, women need to broaden their struggle to go beyond female-centeredness and embrace, for example, a gender and family-centered perspective that tackles the human rights of the entire family." (**Itai Muwhati** et al in *Rediscoursing African Womanhood: Africana Womanism* xviii)

30. "In the last few decades, feminism and Black feminism have gained such a stronghold in the Academy that the activities of most all of the important women writers have been stamped as feminist enterprises. While feminism provides a refreshing alternative to patriarchal hegemonic discourse, it is nevertheless inadequate to account for the numerous and varied works produced by Africana women. . . . the inherent contradiction, an ahistorical impulse, in defining a Black tradition and a theoretical and preoccupation as

feminist, commands that a distinction be made between feminist impulses and feminism." (**Adele S. Newson-Horst** 359, 2007)

31. "[Men and women alike] advancing to a higher plateau, the relativity of an important all- inclusive paradigm considering crucial global issues on all fronts . . . actively engaging in the urgent struggle for human survival against the odds of *race, class and gender oppression, the cornerstone for prioritization for Africana Womanism.*" (**Hudson-Weems**, Foreword in *Rediscoursing African Womanhood: Africana Womanism*, xiii, 2012)

And the list continues. The Africana Womanists, and their male supporters, continuously grow, as the global Movement spreads wide its arms, welcoming and embracing an even broader and diverse constituency. Gracious Madondo closes her article, entitled "Why Africa Relates to Africana Womanism," with the word "amazing." Most recently, in *Black Livity China*, the editorial team, in the recognition of International Women's Day, recognized Hudson-Weems for her theory of Africana Womanism--"In the Words of Clenora Hudson-Weems"—acknowledging that "Africana Womanism recognizes the supreme value placed on family dynamics where Africana men and women work together for their mutual survival and benefit" (March 2020).

Below is a poem I wrote in February 2009, on a flight to the 2nd National Africana Womanism Symposium in Pittsburgh, PA. The poem highlights the prioritization of race, class and gender for Africana Women and their families. It also demonstrates how we stand proudly, collectively working toward the realization of our mission to truly prevail as a successful Africana people, always remaining as one, for, indeed, "WE'RE ALL IN IT TOGETHER!

*Africana Womanism: "I Got Your Back, Boo"* (FEB 2009)

Don't you know by now, girl, we're all In It Together?
Family-Centrality--that's it; we're going nowhere without the other
That means the men, the women, and children, too,
Truly collectively working—**"I got your back, Boo."**

*Racism* means the violation of our constitutional rights,

Which creates on-going legal and even physical fights;
This 1st priority for humankind is doing what it must do,
Echoing our 1st lady, Michelle—**"I got your back, Boo."**

*Classism* is the hoarding of financial privileges,
Privileges we must all have now in pursuit of happiness.
Without a piece of the financial pie, we're doomed to have a coup,
Remember--protect the other—**"I got your back, Boo."**

*Sexism*, the final abominable sin of female subjugation,
A battle we must wage right now to restore our family relations.
All forms of sin inevitably fall under 1 of the 3 offenses.
Africana Womanism, **I Got your back, Boo**, corrects our common senses.

The poem addresses the collective interconnectivity of Africana men, women and children, reflecting the prioritization of race, class and gender. Indeed, the race factor is the number one priority for Africana men, too, who have been deemed, ironically, the enemy of their female counterparts. Though many Black women have been led to agree with this notion, many are now reevaluating the scenario and coming to the realization that we love and need each other. Thus, I wrote a companion poem favoring Africana men:

*"Africana Womanism: I Want My Boo Back"* (FALL, 2021)

They say my Boo, ain't worth an ounce of fuss.
Our choice is ours; it's totally up to us.
We choose our destiny; it's all in tack.
**Collectivity**—"I want my Boo back!"

We're family, meaning all must stick together.
I need you; you need me; it's us forever.
No matter what, we're from the same authentic sack.
**Connectivity**—"I need my Boo back!"

Today it's anti-him; tomorrow it's me
The sister others will not let her be.
Remember, jumping ships presents a serious lack.
**Commitivity**—"I get my Boo back!"

That said, Collectivity, Connectivity and Community have always been key issues for Africana people, and for Africana Womanism, this position has held true, dating back to its inception in the mid-80s, which has been labeled "Interconnectedness." Hence, evoked here is the notion of Africana

Womanism's Interconnectivity versus feminism's Intersectionality, which could be viewed as Counterbalances, as opposed to Competitors. In the opening chapter of *Africana Paradigms, Practices and Literary Texts: Evoking Social Justice* (2021), I made a distinction between the two:

> To that end, Africana Womanism strongly reflects the "interconnectedness" of Africana men and women confronting all matters of race, class, and gender within the context of life experiences, beautifully meshed together like woven fabric, in this collective mission for global Africana survival. Quite different from the later creation of "intersectionality," which separates the parts in its analysis for sake of focusing, a separation and division from each other, interconnectedness has always demonstrated how all parts come together, and has held true for Africana people, dating back to African antiquity. This legacy must continue until true parity for all is realized. (Hudson-Weems, *Africana Paradigms* 7-8)

Early on in Toni Morrison's 1971 *New York Times* article, she makes the following assertion relative to the agenda of feminism within the context of the lives of Africana women:

> The Early Image of Women's Lib was of an elitist organization made up of upper-middle class [white] women with the concerns of that class and not paying much attention to the problems of most black women." (Morrison in *Radical Feminism*, 455)

Morrison is quoted from this same *New York Time* article, appearing in Wendy Harding and Jacky Martin's *A World of Difference: An Intercultural Study of Ton Morrison's Novels*, in which she asserts that "Too much emphasis is placed on gender politics" (61).

The Nobel Laureate observed the position of white women, which excluded the race factor. Named and designed for them, it does virtually nothing to resolve our concerns; however, it does offer some incentives for whites and feminist theory, in that it improves their image today as a means of updating and, moreover, enhancing inclusion, indeed, a political act. The question is how important is terminology, particularly relative to identity and the true level of struggle of Africana women and their families in today's conflicting society? Moreover, what is the real mission and true intent of the feminist versus the Africana womanist and how does the connotation of the concept of feminism exaggerate its denotation? These questions can be addressed via first considering the nuances of terminology. Both connotation and denotation here are one, interconnected, interwoven and interdependent upon each other for true meaning. Yet, despite inconsistencies and the inapplicability of the term *Intersectionality* for

Africana women, it has been widely embraced by many Black Feminists, African Feminists and even Womanists, thus, enhancing their popularity, though often questioned by many Black women including scholars.

According to Dr. Mark Christian, an Africana scholar from Liverpool, England, in the Afterword to the Fifth Edition of Hudson-Weems' *Africana Womanism: Reclaiming Ourselves* (2019),

> The current academic fad phrase is *intersectionality* as if those of us in Africana discourse never considered the myriad of issues encountered by our communities. Race, class, gender and prioritization therein, have always been key issues for comprehending *Africana Womanism*. (131)

He strongly proclaims and supports the long-existing presence of the prioritization of Race, Class, and Gender in Africana life, prominently reflected in Africana Womanism. Indeed, its true essence dates back to African antiquity wherein lies

> . . . the primacy of the centrality of family and the priority of race empowerment in the rich legacy of African womanhood and motherhood. [They descend] from a lineage of strong, proud African women activists and culture bearers, dating back to the advent of the colonization of Africa by Europe, notwithstanding African warrior queens in antiquity, [including] Queen Hatsphepsut (1505-1485 B.C.E.) of Egypt, Queen Nzingha (1583-1663) of West Africa [and] Queen Mother Yaa Asantewa (1840-1921) of Ghana. (Hudson-Weems, *Africana Womanist Literary Theory* 51-52)

Grounded in this reality, Dr. Christian also upholds the insistence upon prescriptive analyses of Africana life, history and culture, and, of course, Africana Womanism remains ever resolute in recalling African traditions.

In African cosmology, the term *nommo* is powerful, for as literary critic, Barbara Christian, whom I debated in a 1995 television interview, contends in her book, *Black Feminist Criticism*, that "It is through *nommo*, the correct naming of a thing, that it comes into existence" (157-158). Unfortunately, however, she fails to follow her own reasoning here of self-naming. Feminism, which was coined by and designed specifically for white women, with Black women nowhere on its agenda, is basically incompatible to Black women's lives. Yet some are still enameled with it, particularly with intersectionality, identifying with it and commanding acceptance of and regard for it as a fascinating methodology for defining who they are as well. Admittedly there is some improvement in the Movement, a striking contrast to what it was traditionally. Indeed, their issues and position, prevalent in this growing persona today, have shifted to a more inclusive posture. Therefore, intersectionality can only serve as a counterbalance to interconnectedness, the later coming first in explicating the priority of race, class, and gender for Africana women, and by extension, the entire Africana family. It can never be a replacement due to the complexity of how race, class, and gender, forced upon Black lives. Therefore, it must be factored into our lives of Blacks in particular in contrast to that of whites. Otherwise, we are left with the reality that "when you buy the white terminology, you also buy its agenda" (Hudson-Weems, *Africana Womanism*, 5th Edition, 25-26). This is a truism which speaks volumes to the importance of words and terminology and its interconnecting nature for properly addressing and explicating the whole. Hence, like interwoven fabrics of life, the Africana-Melanated woman (Africana-Melanated reflecting a terminological rather than a conceptual evolution) and by extension her family must stick together, less they risk being weakened or damaged if separated or broken apart, as in the case of feminism and intersectionality, separating to focus on one aspect at a time.

In the Academy, intersectionality has been widely accepted by the white population, highlighting Africana women, which has galvanized more Black women. However, it must be noted that these followers are a minority, for the true tradition of Black women has proven that Black women, in general, have never allowed white women to tell them what to do, which is why most Black women, particularly in the community, do not consider themselves feminists. In fact, their course of action has served as a Blueprint for white women, who have observed Black women as an integral part of the work force. White women's inclination, then, in a *somewhat* similar manner, express an interest in moving "from homeplace to workplace;" they also observed that Black women were outspoken, both features that they aspired to and thus, used as models, as they proceeded in their commitment to "break silence and find voice," in their growing pursuits for their own careers. Morrison, too, saw Black women as models for white women in the 80s:

> When you really look at the stereotypes of Black women, the worst you can say about them, that is once you disregard the vocabulary and the dirty words and deal with the substance of what is being said, it is quite complimentary ... What is being said is, that Black women are wonderful mothers and nurturers (mammies), that we are sexually at home in our bodies (oversexed), and that we are self-sufficient and tough (henpecking and overbearing). And isn't that exactly what every woman wants to be: Loving and nurturing, sexually at home in her body, competent and strong? (Morrison, *New York Time*, 1989)

Indeed, despite stereotypical descriptors/identities given to naming and defining Black women, they have remained the original blueprint for many.

Yes, intersectionality is a step in the right direction, expanding beyond gender issues alone, is quite appropriate in defining white women in their 3rd and even 4th Waves of Feminism today, evolving from gender-exclusivity to current inclusivity. However, it offers nothing new or positive for Africana women and their communities. Chapter 11 of *Africana Womanism*, Fifth Edition, "Africana Womanism's Race, Class and Gender: Pre-Intersectionality," notes that:

> Today, the current emphasis on the relativity of feminist activity, called "intersectionality," which was introduced by race theorist, Kimberlie Crenshaw in 1989, has enhanced the dominance of the application of the Eurocentric tool of analysis for Black life. Clearly this is not necessary, as an Afrocentric tool of analysis for Black life, particularly relative to Black women and their families, was already in place with the earlier advent of Africana Womanism. (Hudson-Weems 107)

Indeed, the positioning of the issues of race, class and gender in the general definition of intersectionality, as outlined in *Wikipedia*, suggests a conscious usage of the prioritization first established by Blacks, which strongly echoes the originality presented in Africana Womanism. Ironically, this new priority, referenced in modern feminist thought, makes it appear that the prioritization of the race factor for the family-centered Africana Womanism paradigm did not heretofore exist, thereby suggesting that this is a new phenomenon. To be sure, feminism here pulls all stops in saturating the media in every area to promote its new stance, although the Africana woman had been operating from an inclusive family-centered perspective, prioritizing Race, Class and Gender for centuries. Continuing the legacy in the 1st call for Africana Womanism in print, "Cultural and Agenda Conflicts in Academe: Critical Issues for Africana Women's Studies," appearing in *The Western Journal of Black Studies* (1989), later reprinted in *Africana Womanism*, 1993 and 2019, Dr. Hudson-Weems asserts the following:

> She realizes the critical need to prioritize the antagonist forces as racism, classism and sexism, respectively. In the final analysis, *Africana Womanism* is connected to the tradition of self-reliance and autonomy, working toward participation in Africana liberation. (Hudson-Weems 25)

However, apparently, some people need to be reminded of the fact of the new consideration of race, class, and gender for the feminist. In the purest sense, intersectionality represents a divide in the process of cutting between parts based upon different identities. In other words, rather than looking at Black women's concerns as a whole, it, instead, separates their issues in the process of addressing them. As it considers race, class, and gender, it should retain its origin order, since, after all, that order does, in fact, reflect their true order of priorities. Another distinction is that intersectionality focuses on the overlapping nature of discrimination of different races of the same gender, specifically the female, in a format that continues to treat the components separately. Hence, intersectionality has yet to integrate the parts, instead of treating them as separate pieces or entities.

Demonstrating the interweaving/blending together of the intricacies and complexities of race, class and gender, Sojourner Truth exemplifies her dilemma in her 1852 oration, "And Ain't I A Woman." Before she could begin to address the absurdity of female subjugation, she as a Black woman had to first get beyond the race factor and be respected as a human being, entitled to basic human rights. It was only after her humanness, the race fact, was addressed could she move forward to address the remaining obstacles. Thus, her resounding self-actualization query, representing that interwoven nature of race, class and gender, as parts of her identity, were, in fact, parts of the whole. Although she was a Black woman, who dared to come to the all-white women's convention in Akron, Ohio to voice her opinion on matters relevant to women, she should have been welcomed as yet another woman among the community of women. However, because she was Black, she was not welcomed, as her race prohibited her from being considered a true human being. It must be here noted that her race could not be separated from her gender, and hence, unlike the white woman, she was also not considered or given the privileges of a woman, solely based on race. Clearly her race and her gender were interconnected, never to be separated. This scenario also reflects Linda LaRue's assessment in 1976 in her article, "The Black Movement and Women's Liberation:"

> Blacks are oppressed, and that means unreasonably burdened, unjustly, severely, rigorously, cruelly and harshly fettered by white authority. White women, on the other hand, are only suppressed, and that means checked, restrained, excluded from conscious and overt activity. And this is a difference. (218)

This interdependence, characterizing the three key issues for the Africana Womanist, makes it impossible to separate the parts of one's basic nature, activities and experiences. The total represents the defining and joining together of the forces, an interconnected phenomenon, be it positive or negative.

Consider the June 1995 Supreme Court Decision on Affirmative Action Set Asides. The ruling, affirming the unconstitutionality of racially based Set Asides for all, including Black women, has the obvious propensity for deeming Black women to be Black first rather than gender, while gender-based Set Asides for white women were ruled constitutionally solid and sound:

> When those Africana women finish fighting the feminist battle and feminists have succeeded in realizing all their goals relative to female empowerment, the Africana woman will be left with the reality that she is both black and at the bottom. (Hudson-Weems, *Africana Womanist Literary Theory* 83)

Here again, the race factor remains the ruling factor, reflected in all levels of existence, from our pursuits in securing a positive, healthy and secure family-centered reality for the entire family, to our pursuits relative to our careers and our overall mind-set and state of being. In short, the fate of Black women is almost invariably determined by race first; our gender comes into consideration later, if at all. Thus, the prioritization of Race, Class, and Gender, strategically interconnecting in the narrative of Africana people, particularly Black women, yet reigns today, as it well it should, given the pervasiveness of racial dominance throughout the world.

That said, given the fact that the two terms, Interconnectedness, and Intersectionality, have some credence, my inclination is to respect both as valid within the constructs of their distinct historical and cultural matrix. That is to say that both could very well remain, since both facilitate and accommodate their own audience. Neither need be eliminated in order for the other to survive, for the needs of each individual group are obviously real. While both should be respected and allowed to exist freely, without fear that only one can exist, for the idea of absolute applicability of a paradigm for all – Feminism – can only be realized if all are on equal footage, that is if no one is experiencing racial dominance, which automatically puts the oppressed group at an added disadvantage. It is virtually impossible to address a single common obstacle when another or others have to be first corrected, i.e. race first. At the same time, for feminism and its various collective forms, its audience can certainly appreciate its concept and terminology, with, of course, the realization that their concept, including the intersectionality signifier, should not presume to represent all women, particular Africana women. That would surely force the Africana woman to subjugate her number one obstacle, racism, while the dominant culture is allowed to continue gender prioritization or exclusivity, though covertly so. In the final analysis, then, let's be clear that when the Black woman succumbs to this, she will ultimately be forced to admit that she is still "black and at the bottom." Moreover, it must be realized and acknowledged that Africana women should have that same right to name and define themselves and our movement as does the "privileged" other. Indeed, Africana women should not allow themselves to be relegated to the level of assimilation as an alternative as dictated by total domination. Africana womanist theory says "NO" to this position, which only forces them to embrace someone else's paradigm and priorities for mere penance—superficial acceptance, feigned political presence, power and legitimacy.

By now, more serious consideration for the call for the acknowledgement of the obvious pre-existence of "interconnectedness," associated with Africana Womanism for Black women, is to be respected in much the same way as my not deeming feminism non-existent. Thus, in *Africana Womanism*, Fifth Edition,

> While I am not calling for a replacement of traditional, established paradigms, such as feminism, etc., for they were, indeed, created out of the needs of a particular group [white women] that had legitimate concerns or issues that needed to be addressed, I am nonetheless proposing for a broadening of the body of criticism to include yet another perspective or paradigm, which is Africana Womanism, now evolving to Africana-Melanated Womanism (112)

Just as there is no one solution to all the problems of the universe, there is no one position for all the people of the world. We are diverse people of diverse needs, and thus, demand diversity in thought and action, as well as in color, ethnicity, and culture, including our philosophical and methodological preferences. In the final analysis, then, with reference to the historical function of the African American Literary tradition as a corrective for historical wrongs, dating back to American slavery, and the seminal role of slave narratives (like Olaudah Equiano or Gustavus Vassa, followed by Frederick Douglass, Harriet Ann Jacobs, Harriet E. Wilson and others), Africana Womanism, too, offers opportunities for correcting continuous racist wrongs—beginning here with the mis-naming and mis-defining of the Africana woman outside of her historical and current context. Indeed, *Interconnectedness* is more appropriate in assessing Black women's activities, although it does not rule out Intersectionality for the feminist. As we review the powerful presence of the Africana woman, in concert with her male companion throughout history, it becomes clear that there was a real need for properly naming and defining Black women, justified by the very fact that such a paradigm, independently and separately named and designed for all women of African descent, only came about when Africana Womanism hit the scene in the mid 1980s. Although it is a global concept and still rising, it must be here noted that Africana women worldwide still need to be more cognizant of its existence, thereby enabling us to better hand down our rich legacy of Collectivity and Connectivity for our ultimate victory.

# Bibliography

Anderson, Talmadge. Book Endorsement. *Africana Womanism: Reclaiming Ourselves*. Troy, MI: Bedford Publishers, 1993.

Aldridge, Delores P. Jacket Blurb. *Africana Womanism: Reclaiming Ourselves*: Troy, MI: Bedford Publishers, 1993.

Aldridge, Delores P. "Towards Integrating Africana Woman into Africana Studies" in *Out of the Revolution: The Development of Africana Studies*. Lanham, Boulder, New York, Oxford: Lexington Books, 2000, 191-201.

Aptheker, Bettina. "Strong Is What We Make Each Other: Unlearning Racism Within Women's Studies." *Women's Studies Quarterly*, 9:4 (Winter), 1981, 13-6.

Asante, Molefi Kete. Afterword. *Africana Womanist Literary Theory*. Trenton: Africa World Press, 2004, 137-139.

Carroll, Peter N. and David W. Nobel. *The Free and the Unfree: A New History of the United States*. New York: Penguin Books, 1977.

Christian, Barbara. *Black Feminist Criticism: Perspectives on Black Women Writers*. New York: Pergamon, 1985.

Christian, Mark. Afterword. *Africana Womanism: Reclaiming Ourselves*, 5th Edition. London and New York: Routledge Press, 2019.

Cowan, Connell and Melvyn Kinder. *Smart Women: Foolish Choices*. New York: Clarkson N. Potter, 1985.

Crow, Barbara A, Editor. *Radical Feminism: A Documentary Reader*. New York: New York University Press, 2000.

Hamilton, Charles V. Book Endorsement. *Africana Womanism: Reclaiming Ourselves*. Troy, MI: Bedford, 1993.

Harding, Wendy and Jacky Martin. *A World of Differences: An Intercultural Study of Toni Morrison's Novels*. London: Greenwood Press, 1994.

Harris, Jr., Robert L. Book Endorsement. *Africana Womanism: Reclaiming Ourselves*. Troy, MI: Bedford, 1993.

Hill, Patricia Liggins, et al, eds. *Call and Response: The Riverside Anthology of the African American Literary Tradition*. Boston: Houghton Mifflin, 1998.

Hudson-Weems, Clenora. "Africana Womanism: An Overview." in *Out of the Revolution: The Development of Africana Studies*. Lanham, Boulder, New York, Oxford: Lexington Books, 2000, 205-217.

Hudson-Weems, Clenora. "Africana Womanism: Authenticity and Collectivity for Social Justice" in *Africana Paradigms, Practices and Literary Texts: Evoking Social Justice*. Dubuque, Iowa: Kendall Hunt Publishing Company, 2021, 3-22.

Hudson-Weems, Clenora. "Africana Womanism: I Got Your Back, Boo," in *Africana Womanism: Reclaiming Ourselves*, 5th. Edition. London and New York: Routledge Press, 2019, 120.

Hudson-Weems, Clenora. *Africana Womanism: Reclaiming Ourselves*. Troy, MI: Bedford Publishers, 1993.

Hudson-Weems, Clenora. *Africana Womanism: Reclaiming Ourselves*, 5th Edition. London and New York: Routledge Press, 2019.

Hudson-Weems, Clenora. *Africana Womanist Literary Theory*. Trenton: Africa World Press, 2004.

Hudson-Weems, Clenora. *Contemporary Africana Theory, Thought and Action: A Guide for Africana Studies*. Trenton: Africa World Press, 2007.

Hudson-Weems, Clenora. "Cultural and Agenda Conflicts in Academia: Critical Issues for Africana Women's Studies" in *The Western Journal of Black Studies*, 13: 4, 1989, 185-189.

Hudson-Weems, Clenora. "The African American Literary Tradition" in *The African American Experience: An Historiographical and Bibliographical Guide*. Westport, Connecticut, London: Greenwood Press, 2001, 116-143.

Ladner, Joyce. Book Endorsement. *Africana Womanism: Reclaiming Ourselves*. Troy, MI: Bedford Publishers, 1993.

LaFond, Daisy. Jacket Blurb. *Africana Womanism: Reclaiming Ourselves*. Troy, MI: Bedford Publishers, 1993.

Langley, April. "Lucy Terry Prince: The Cultural and Literary Legacy of Africana Womanism." *The Western Journal of Black Studies*, 25:3, Fall 2001, 153-162.

LaRue, Linda. "The Black Movement And Women's Liberation." *Female Psychology: The Emerging Self*. Sue Cox, ed. Chicago: SRA, 9176, 216-25.

Lincoln, C. Eric. Book Endorsement. *Africana Womanism: Reclaiming Ourselves*.Troy, MI: Bedford Publishers, 1993.

Madondo, Gracious. "Why Africa Relate to Africana Womanism" in *The Southern Times: The Newspaper for Southern Africa*, July 19, 2018.

Mazama, Ama. "The Afrocentric Paradigm: Contours and Definition." *Journal of Black Studies* 31:4, 2001, 387-405.

Mompati, Ruth. "Women and Life Under Apartheid" in *One Is Not A Woman, One Becomes: The African Woman in a Transitional Society*. Daphne Williams Ntiri, editor. Troy: MI: Bedford, 1982.

Mootry, Maria. Book Review in *The Western Journal of Black Studies*. Volume 18, Number 4, Winter 1994, 244-5.

Morrison, Toni. *Times*, 1989.

Morrison, Toni. "What the Black Woman Thinks about Women's Lib." *New York Times Magazine*, August 1971, 63.

Newson-Horst, Adele S. "Gloria Naylor's *Mama Day*: An Africana Womanist Reading" in *Contemporary Africana Theory, Thought and Action: A Guide to Africana Studies*. Trenton: Africa World Press, 2007, 359-372.

Ntiri, Daphne W. Introduction in *Africana Womanism: Reclaiming Ourselves*, 5th Edition. London and New York: Routledge Press, 1993; 2019, 1-8.

Stewart, James B. and Ama Mazama. Foreword in *Africana Womanism: Reclaiming Ourselves*, 5th Edition. London and New York: Routledge Press, 2019, xiii-xv.

The Editorial Team. *Black Livity China*. "In the Words of Clenora Hudson- Weems," March 2020

# 2

# CONTRASTIVE ANALYSIS OF AFRICANA WOMANISM, BLACK FEMINISM AND AFRICAN FEMINISM

## *AMA MAZAMA, PhD*

### *The Political and Epistemological Stakes*

In many ways, a contrastive examination of Africana Womanism, Black Feminism and African Feminism harks back to the poignant question posed by Molefi Kete Asante (1987: 181): "How can the oppressed use the same theories as the oppressors?" Asante was in effect suggesting that this was not possible because theories, far from being neutral and falling from the sky, are very much informed by the cultural values and ideological leanings of those who produce them. Therefore, as an example, those who are keen on conflict will produce conflict theories. Those who have a materialistic worldview will produce materialistic theories. Likewise, racists will produce racist theories. There is no neutral ground for, as Asante reminds us, we all stand somewhere. Thus, for an oppressed group to use theories produced by their oppressors is, at best, self-defeating and a form of self-sabotage.

Furthermore, and quite importantly, European theories have been major weapons in the intellectual and mental warfare waged against African people. Expected to accept European interpretations of reality as "universal" and "objective," African people have often unconsciously and unwillingly found themselves in a state of "conceptual incarceration," which has only furthered their subordination to Europeans and prevented them from freeing themselves from the grips of Eurocentrism.

African thinkers often experience malaise while attempting to apply European theories to their reality. However, instead of rejecting European theories as politically dangerous and culturally incompatible with the African reality, some, like Fanon, have suggested that European theories, in particular Marxism, should be "slightly stretched" (1961) to accommodate the African experience. Others have proceeded to add the word "Black" or "African" as prefixes to European theories or bodies of thought and knowledge, as if the mere adding of the word "black" or "African" would automatically entail a major epistemic transformation and make the theory in question relevant to and compatible with the experiences and needs of African people. Yet, as James Stewart cogently noted, there is no guarantee that this could ever be the case (1992). Indeed, while the focus may become the African experience, the perspective remains fundamentally European since the theory itself is of European origin, that is, laden with European cultural assumptions and biases. Such is the case of Feminism for example.

## *Feminism*

Feminism is often described as having occurred in three waves (Javaid & Zubair, 2012). The first wave of feminism reportedly began in the United States in 1848 as white women started rebelling against their political disenfranchisement and male property status. Indeed, white women were deemed unworthy of political participation due to their alleged inferiority on all levels. Feminism thus began as a Suffrage Movement which ended in 1920 when white women finally gained access to the right to vote.

It may seem surprising that it took so long for white women to secure participation in the political life of their communities. However, even a cursory survey reveals that in Western societies, characterized as they are by patriarchy (Diop, 1981), women have often been and continue to be treated with much cruelty and contempt. Physical violence, including rape, is rampant. In addition to physical abuses, political marginalization has remained common. It was only in 1976, for example, that Portuguese men allowed their women to vote. Given that voting is the primary mechanism for political participation, one gets the full measure of white females' political disenfranchisement in Portugal, and elsewhere among Europeans. And although they are no longer politically invisible and irrelevant, very few white women have managed to climb to the highest levels of political office, such as the presidency or prime ministry of their respective countries. The United States is yet to allow a woman to become president, for example. The presidency is jealously guarded by white males. To this, one must add the significant and pervasive pay gap that still exists between Western men and women, with men making about 20% more than women with equal qualifications.

Also, an examination of the religious sphere demonstrates most clearly that white women are still looked down upon by white men since they are considered unworthy of reaching the highest positions, such as that of priestess, cardinal, or pope. Only a white man can pretend representing white people's god (also a male) on Earth. As a result, white women are ipso facto excluded from the performance of the most sacred liturgical acts. This comes as no surprise since, after all, women were taken out of the European "holy trinity." This deletion reveals quite clearly white men's hostility and contempt for their women. This negative attitude is at the very heart of Christianity for, is it not true that Eve, the so-called original woman, was responsible for bringing sin and death into the world? Is it not also true that she was created from one of Adam's ribs and that women were ultimately created to keep company to men and serve them? (Wolgemtuh & Gresh, 2019). One can therefore not be surprised by the cruelties inflicted onto white women by their men. It might be worth remembering that from the time beginning at the end of the European Middle Ages up to the end of the 19th century, hundreds of thousands of women were judged, tortured, burned live, hung, accused of having sold their soul to the devil or of having murdered scores of children by sucking their blood, etc. (Federici, 2004). The children of the "witches," especially female children, were forced to attend their mother's public execution and witness her most painful demise. White men's savagery toward their women was simply appalling!

Those barbaric treatments also extended to what came out of white women's womb, their children. Indeed, for a very long time, white children were considered burdens and denied any ontological and legal status. During the Roman Empire, under the Pater Familias doctrine, and before the adoption of Christianism, infanticides were common. Fathers had absolute power over their children – even the power to deny them life. During the European Middle Ages, although it was no longer permissible to kill children, beating and torturing them was still permitted, so despised were white women and their offspring.

It is quite understandable, therefore, that white women would seek to address and put an end to the abuses they have suffered at the hands of white men for so long, hence feminism. While there is currently little consensus on a widely accepted definition of feminism, it seems clear enough that gender is feminism's main category of thought, and that its organizing principle is the need for women to identify and dismantle male oppression -although, as we shall see below, things have been complicated by post-modernism's questioning of fixed categories like "woman" or "man." Feminism, like Marxism, is a conflict theory since it postulates that the relationship between men and women is antagonistic, and that it is through fighting that women can hope to redress inequities. Thus, culturally and historically, feminism is fundamentally a European project launched by white women to free and protect themselves from white males' mistreatments.

The second wave of feminism began in the 1960s in the wake of the Civil Rights movement, with white women now expanding their grievances and seeking equality with men in the legal, political, social, and economic spheres of life. "Sexual liberation" was also high on their agenda, and this second wave is frequently referred to as the "Women's Lib" movement.

This second wave was typically led by white middle-class women who, while decrying male oppression, continued nonetheless to participate in the construction and imposition of whiteness as normative. Indeed, filled with typical white arrogance, these feminists insisted on the universality of the white female experience -with male oppression becoming the definitional attribute of femaleness around the world. White women, leading the fight against male chauvinism, positioned themselves as the "big sisters" of melanated women, showing the way to women's emancipation from male oppression, with the right words and concepts to name the plight of all women. Women's experiences around the world were homogenized and presented as uniform, that is, following the European model. What applied to white women applied to all women.

This ethnocentrism/racism annoyed many African (and other) women who had invited themselves or had been pushed into the feminist discursive realm. Again, instead of moving away from something that did not concern them since it was not created by them and for them, these women were seduced or convinced by Eurocentrism' pseudo-universalist claims and proceeded to make room for themselves into a profoundly European conceptual edifice by creating "Black Feminism" in the Diaspora and "African Feminism" on the Continent. The irruption of melanated women onto the feminist scene, along with the demand for recognition placed by non-heterosexual individuals, initiated feminism's third wave in the early 1990s.

## *Black Feminism*

Black Feminism has largely become equated with intersectionality, a term coined by the black feminist legal scholar Kimberlé Crenshaw in 1989. Crenshaw operationalized an idea that had been around for quite a while, that is, that black women were not oppressed simply due to their gender but also because of their blackness and, for many, because of their class status. Thus, intersectionality was a response both to male chauvinism and white feminists' systematic negligence of racial and socioeconomic factors. While there is no consensus on the precise genealogy of Black Feminism, the creation of the Combahee River Collective, along with the work of black female activists such as Deborah King, Frances Beal and Ana Julia Cooper, are often cited as intersectional/Black feminist precursors (Nash, 2019: 9). The Combahee River Collective, for instance, operated in Boston between 1974 and 1980. This collective was created by a group of black lesbians who were dissatisfied with the racism they encountered within the feminist movement, as well as the male chauvinism that was present in the Civil Rights movement. Few thus explains the advantages of intersectionality/Black Feminism for Black women:

> Black feminism allows a creative space where, according to one's own social location or station in life, Black women can "legitimately" place a foot in two or more realities—what one individually and/or collectively may perceive of what it is to be "Black" and what it is to be a "woman" simultaneously. Black women exist within an intersectionality matrix. An intersectionality matrix is a specific location where multiple systems of oppressions simultaneously corroborate and subjugate to conceal deliberate, marginalizing ideological maneuvers that define "Otherness." (2007: 455)

The intersectional idea, although originally created by Black feminists, and which suggests that one individual/group may inhabit several sites of oppression at the same time, and that the corroboration of those multiple and simultaneous oppressions creates a unique experience for that individual/group, soon became extremely appealing to a large number of scholars across a wide disciplinary spectrum (e.g., sociology, economics, political science, psychology, law, etc.). However, its success and novelty have also contributed to the vagueness and ambiguity of the theory, with inconsistent definitions and usages. Hill Collins & Chepp (2013) note, for instance, that intersectionality is understood differently by those who use it, with some claiming that it is a theory, a theory of identity, a theoretical contribution, a theoretical paradigm, a perspective, a concept, a type of analysis, a methodology, an analytic perspective, a research paradigm, a measurable variable, a type of data, or simply, according to others, something one personally experiences. Yet, as also suggested by Hill Collins & Chepp (2013), the practitioners of intersectionality share a number of assumptions, such as the interrelatedness of systems of oppression and the relationality of systems of power. However, the feature that deserves much attention here, for the sake of this contrastive analysis of Black Feminism and Africana Womanism, is the pervasive influence of post-modernism and its rejection of any unified identity on intersectionality.

Post-modernism has been engaged in a project of deconstruction and radical doubt, leading its proponents to the conclusion that the world being in constant motion, there can be no absolute truth or certainty (Madan, 1989). As an anti-foundationalist paradigm, post-modernism objects to any grand generalizations, but argues instead that the subject is a process that cannot be defined, and that identity is, by definition, complex, fluid and ever-changing. Post-modernism is thus an anti-essentialist paradigm, denying as it does the very existence of discrete and fixed units of analysis such as gender, race, or class. The influence of post-modernism has been tremendous. In the field of Women Studies and feminism in particular, it has led to the emergence of what may very well be a fourth wave, labeled by some "Post-Feminism," and which questions the very category upon which feminism used to be built, i.e., gender (Javaid & Zubair, 2012).

Post-modernism also called into question heterosexuality and became critical of "heteronormativity." This trend of thought has led to the emergence of theories such as "Gender Theory," which denies the biological basis of gender, as well as the emergence of a new obsession with "sexual orientation," now a major social identity marker in Western societies – with multiple and competing practices all presented as increasingly acceptable: zoophilia, pedophilia, homosexuality, bisexuality, transgenderism, asexuality, sologamy, childlessness, etc. That intersectionality has been deeply influenced by Post-modernism is made most obvious by Hill Collins & Chepp's following statement:

> Intersectionality's focus on relationality, multiplicity, complexity, and social boundaries has helped to recast gender beyond narrow definitions of woman and has shifted attention to the complex, relational boundaries that construct our understandings of masculinity and femininity. (2013: 6)

In addition to questioning gender as a valid category of analysis, post-modernism also insists that power is everywhere, and that all social relations are ultimately power relations. In other words, individuals and groups may at times be oppressed, and yet, at other times and in different circumstances, be oppressive. According to this line of thinking, then, there are no oppressors or oppressed per se, since we all share the ability to experience oppression but also privileges due to our multiple "intersocial locations" (Hill Collins & Chepp, 2013). According to this line of thinking, history is an endless play of domination, and post-modernism has become, in many ways, a convenient way to evade political questions altogether (Madan, 1993). For African people, who experience discrimination and vexations on a daily basis, post-modernism makes it impossible to talk about ourselves (since race is not a stable category), let alone talk about our oppression and ways to liberate ourselves from the deadly grips of white racism and domination.

While I am sure that not all black feminists may have agreed to this, the fact remains that Intersectionality's post-modern bend pushes Black Feminist scholars toward not only a blurry if not shaky sense of identity as African women, but also toward interdisciplinarity and bridge-building with other people/groups with whom they might share some span of oppression. In other words, Intersectionality pushes them in the direction of dilution and integration – a danger that many of them fear and resent. In her recent book on Black Feminism, Nash (2019: 117) shares this fear commonly expressed by many Black Feminists, as she writes that, "It has become commonplace for black feminists to proclaim the death of black feminism itself, to announce that the field's future is in peril because its visionary work has been stymied." The impact of institutionalization, and its taming effect, along with the pervasive appropriation of Black Feminism's main paradigm, Intersectionality, by European disciplines, is indeed a major source of anxiety for many Black feminist scholars.

Hill Collins & Chepp, on the other hand, actually marvel at the possibilities created by this new sense of diffused identity for "democracy":

These new conceptions of identities and communities can broaden our understanding of political allies and effective political partnerships. Rather than organizing along single systems of power (e.g., either gender or racial oppression) or single issues (e.g., either HIV/AIDS activism or welfare reform) or on behalf of a single community (e.g., either gay activists or single mothers), intersectional approaches to coalition building enhance democratic possibilities by expanding definitions of political allies, political identities, and political communities. (2013: 25)

This optimistic approach is greatly tampered, nonetheless, by the persistence of white racism and white attempts to continue to dictate and destroy the lives of African people, not only in the West, but also in Africa. As if this was not enough, some Black feminists, seduced by Queer Theory, have gone even farther in their repudiation of any sense of a definite identity and became Queer. Queer theory was developed by white scholars who, working within the paradigmatic confines of post-modernism and post-structuralism, focused on identifying and contesting the discursive and cultural markers found both within dominant and marginal identities and institutions which prescribe and reify "heterogendered" understandings and behavior," to propose instead a different conceptualization of sexuality, one which sought to replace socially named and presumably stable categories of sexual expression with a new fluid movement among and between forms of sexual behavior" (Cohen, 1997: 438).

Thus, once again, some Black women found themselves satisfied with simply repeating what their white conceptual masters had conceived. Read for example Charlene Carruthers' proud pronouncement: "Queer, as I am defining it here, represents a continuum of possibilities outside of what are considered normal sexual or gender identities and behaviors. Affirmation of queerness creates possibility outside the norm. (…). And in more ways than one, blackness is inherently queer" (2018: 23). I fail to understand what is so radical or revolutionary about thinking of blackness as inherently non-normative? Such a view is based on the implicit and disturbing acceptance of whiteness as the norm from which one attempts to deviate in the name of radicalness and for the sake of revolution, but whiteness remains the norm nonetheless by which difference (e.g., blackness) is evaluated and defined. Such a stance brings us back again and again to Asante's poignant question: How can the oppressed use their oppressors' theories and expect to liberate themselves? Just like Hill Colins & Chepp, Carruthers also reassures us that, "Organizing through a BQF [black queer feminist] lens is inherently collaborative and not antagonistic to other radical feminisms or liberatory politics and practices. It specifically honors Black feminists and LGBTQ liberation movements" (2018: 11). Is it our quest for white validation and white allies that makes us so pleased with being white people's "Other" or "Queer"?

It is refreshing that on the continent at least, African women have exercised greater caution and not fallen wholeheartedly for Eurocentric conceptual traps.

## *African Feminism*

Indeed, nowhere, perhaps, have the awareness of and dissatisfaction with the European facture of Feminism been expressed more clearly and stridently than in Africa, for a number of reasons. Confronted with persistent Western colonialism and neo-colonialism, African women could/cannot ignore the dangerous implications of embracing wholeheartedly feminism and its prioritization of gender as the main axis of struggle. Fighting against African men while Europeans continue to rule their societies, disrupt their lives and destroy their children's future, might not necessarily appear to be the wisest or most urgent move. In addition, the Western model of female liberation was/is not appealing to many African women due to its incompatibility with African cultural values, which, prior to the introduction of colonialism to Africa, upheld collectivity among African men and woman, thus, constituting family-centrality, indeed, major cornerstones for Africana Womanism. According to Gracious Madondo in "Why Africa relates to Africana Womanism,"

Gender inequality is caused by social institutions and organisations which suppress women's economic and social rights. In Africa, the harmony between sexes was mostly affected by changing political agendas. It is therefore without doubt that gender inequality in Africa owes its legacy of colonialism. (*The Southern Times*, July 27, 2018)

Therefore, the implicit imposition of European women's agenda and ideals as universal is/was also deeply resented by some. That white women were contributing to the further Eurocentric and racist reification of African women, under the guise of feminism, did not escape them either. The Indian feminist, Mohanty, while calling for the "decolonization" of feminism (as if such an exercise was possible), expressed the objection of many melanated women to the problematic construction of the "Third-World woman." This Western feminist construct that claimed to capture the reality of melanated women around the world, was/is less than flattering: "This average Third World woman leads an essentially truncated life based on her feminine gender (read: sexually constrained) and her being "Third World" (read: ignorant, poor, uneducated, tradition-bound, domestic, family-oriented, victimized, etc.). This, I suggest, is in contrast to the (implicit) self-representation of Western women as educated, as modern, as having control over their own bodies and sexualities and the freedom to make their own decisions" (Mohanty, 1991: 22).

African women's distrust for feminism and its agenda is thus profound. Leslie-Ogundipe, for example, laments over the fact that "… many of the African female writers like to declare that they are not feminists, as if it were a crime to be a feminist. These denials come from unlikely writers such as Bessie Head, Buchi Emecheta, and even Mariama Ba." And when there is African feminism, it, according to Gwendolyn Mikell (1997) "differs radically from the Western forms of feminism with which we have become familiar since the 1960s." According to the same author, "Western feminism" and "African feminism" have markedly different origins: While feminism in the Western world grew out of bourgeois individualism and struggle against patriarchal oppression, in Africa, feminism owes its birth to women resisting European domination and influences over African culture. Western and African feminism also have different foci: While European feminists have been concerned with individual control over reproduction, with a growing rejection of procreation as a form of servitude accompanied with an insistence on the freedom to adopt the sexual orientation of their choice, African feminists have, on the other hand, remained steadfast in their embrace of natality and heterosexuality, while being preoccupied with issues of personal and community daily survival and fight against imperialism. This divergence of focus has led many African feminists to be greatly annoyed with white feminists' imposition in African women's affairs, as noted by the French feminist historian Catherine Coquery-Vidrovitch, when she writes that "Anglo-Saxon women's clumsiness has long irritated African women's movements, which have reproached them for meddling …" (2018: 209). Yet, Coquery-Vidrovitch is pleased to report how, "Socially and politically, [African] women are starting to find their way. Recent changes have sometimes taken place at lightning speed. Today's women are vigorous, creative and full of promise." She continues that African women " … are just becoming aware of what is at stake for them, of their struggles and constraints …" (2018: 200). To this condescension one must oppose that African women, unlike European women, have historically experienced much greater respect and have played much more significant roles in their societies. It is no secret that, "A woman in Egypt could be head of state, religious leader, businesswoman, medical chief. She could bequeath her property to whomever she wanted, she could marry the man of her choice, she had access to means of contraception… And then, "Pharaoh," it is the couple: the king and the great royal wife, who is not a first lady dealing only with charity, far from it! The queen was at the head of diplomacy, spoke several languages… The girls were as educated as the boys" (Jak, 2019). Likewise, later in other parts of Africa, "Women's contributions as spiritual healers, mediums, and leaders were most often related to fertility and reproduction. With the intricate interconnection between marriage, family, children, and agricultural production, it was evident that women were at the center of local politics and economics, and they were not relegated to marginal positions outside of public activity. Their religious responsibilities were central to family health and the continuation of their communities" (Sheldon, 2018: 89). Addressing specifically the anthropological attributes of African supreme divinities, the same author comments that, "In nearly every case, the creator was clearly gendered as female, was considered both male and female, or was perceived as beyond gendered. Such beliefs were deeply imbedded in peoples' spiritual systems, and they further indicated the importance of matrilineal social structures." Thus, rather than being dismissed as inherently "bad," women in Africa occupied a central and dignified place in social life. Let us turn briefly to Shona culture and history as a compelling illustration of the place occupied by women until quite recently, and still today, but to a lesser extent.

## *The Case of the Mashona*

According to the Shona worldview, both worlds, spiritual and mundane, are organized around three similar and fundamental units: the family, the clan, and the nation. In the invisible world, there are spirits that specifically operate at the level of the family (*midzimu yepamusha*), the clan (*mudzimu wedzinza* or *mhondoro*) and the nation (*mudzimu wenyika*) (Maenzanise, 2009).

Likewise, Shona society recognizes leaders of the family, the clan, and the nation. Their primary duty is to protect and restore, if need be, the well-being of their community. In order to do so, they may have to follow instructions received from the spirit world, via mediums, and carry out prescribed instructions, for protection, propitiation or expiation sake. Indeed, spirits, regardless of their position in the spiritual hierarchy, that is, be they clan or family spirits, and even Mwari (the Supreme Divinity) itself, choose individuals with whom they will share their recommendations and messages to be delivered to the living. Such mediums are known as *masvikiro* (sing. *svikiro*). Masvikiro are seen as being above other human beings, for they have supernatural intelligence and insights that are not readily available to common people. Some masvikiro operate at the family level. In that case, the svikiro is a member of a particular family lineage who is mounted by an ancestral family spirit to convey to the remaining members of the family their ancestor's wishes and instructions. Quite importantly, chiefs are installed by masvikiro, who are guardians of that significant position on behalf of the people.

Other masvikiro operate at the higher level of the clan and serve as mediums for the powerful mhondoro spirits. They are recognized and respected as major sources of social and spiritual authority and are charged with the task of performing the rituals necessary to protect and restore their community's balance and integrity. Mhondoro spirits can also convey Mwari's messages to the living.

Quite interestingly for the purpose of this discussion, while both men and women can serve as family and clan masvikiro, only a woman can serve as Mwari's medium – at least this was the case in 19th century Shonaland, before British attempted takeover and disruption of Shona social and cultural mores, causing great mental dislocation. All sought this female oracle's advice on all important matters. This may very well be the case because Shona consideration for women, especially as mothers, is quite high. The universe itself is conceived as feminine. In Shona society, before it was disturbed by European colonialism and patriarchy, there was no aspect of their community's life over which Shona women did not exercise power and authority. Not only were women keepers of important shrines, but they also assumed key political positions within the family and community. This unmistakably points to the fact that in the Shona worldview women were not perceived as afflicted with some essential degradation but were seen as comparable to men. The critical sociopolitical role and importance of women is made most clear by Nehanda's place in Shona society and history. Indeed, Nehanda, a highly respected Shona Mhondoro spirit associated with rain and fertility, of the land and otherwise, is credited for having played a major role in the First and Second Chimurenga – the nationalist fights again British colonialism in the 19th and 20th centuries, eventually leading to the birth of Zimbabwe. Today, Nehanda is revered by most Zimbabweans as the mother of their nation (Charumbira, 2015).

It is therefore not surprising that African women's own experiences did not necessarily support the view of women as naturally oppressed and socially suppressed by men, for, as South African journalist, Madondo, asserted, "Africa before colonialism had better gender parity." ("Why Africa Relates to Africana Womanism," 2018). Clearly, African women who wished to embrace feminism, had to twist and "stretch" feminist discourse in order to adapt it to their own reality. Thus, according to Mikell (1997: 168),

> Although indebted to the global feminist movement, African feminist discourse takes care to delineate those concerns that are peculiar to the African situation. It also questions features of traditional African cultures without denigrating them, understanding that these traditional features might be viewed differently by the various classes of women. (168)

In an attempt to avoid that African feminists' preoccupations and views be altogether subsumed under feminism, Leslie-Ogundipe (1997) even suggested a different name, "STIWANISM," which stands for "Social Transformation Including Women in Africa," which rather emphasizes social equality between men and women as the ultimate objective. Although Leslie-Ogundipe's proposal was not adopted, the question she raised is a critical one, i.e., the imperative of naming oneself and defining one's agenda instead of adopting someone else's name and program of action. That question lies at the very heart of Africana Womanism.

## *Africana Womanism*

Africana womanism is a theory developed about 30 years ago by scholar Clenora Hudson-Weems to deal with African women's issues from an Afrocentric perspective. At the heart of the Africana womanist theory lies the assertion that a true understanding of the nature of the relationship between African men and women requires a thorough understanding of and grounding in African culture and historical experiences. In fact, Hudson-Weems coined the term *Africana womanism* in 1987 out of the realization of the total inadequacy of feminism, and like theories (e.g., black feminism, African womanism, or womanism), to grasp the reality of African women, let alone give them the means to change that reality" (Mazama, 400).

Having noted the discomfort of many African diasporic and continental women with feminism, Clenora Hudson-Weems writes that, many of the African women who adopt feminism, "do so because of feminism's theoretical and methodological legitimacy in the academy and their desire to be a legitimate part of the academic community." Yet, feminism, under all its forms, but especially Black feminism, "is extremely problematic" and "invites much debate and controversy among today's scholars and women in general" (1993 and 2019: 11). To begin with, Hudson-Weems holds that self-naming and self-defining are critical aspects of the liberation struggle that African people worldwide are or should be engaged in. In that regard, the label "feminism," which stems out of Europe, is simply unacceptable. It signifies an abdication of one's agency as an African woman, coupled with the implicit acceptance of being named and defined by Europeans – a long-standing and major discursive weapon against African people's sanity and best interest. As mentioned above, simply adding "black" or "African" to feminism does not entail any epistemic transformation. Moreover, it is humiliating for African women to use the term "black feminism," or "African feminism," for it acknowledges the fact that they are simply trying to fit into and appropriate something that was never theirs to begin with, but that was imposed on them as universally relevant by white women's arrogant ethnocentrism.

In addition to the thorny question of self-naming and self-defining, there are three other problems with the adoption of feminism by African women. Feminism, Hudson-Weems correctly argues, is fundamentally a European phenomenon. As such, it is loaded with European metaphysical principles, such as the problematic and conflictual relationship between the genders, with men seen as the primary enemies of women. Such an antagonistic view of men is understandable in the context of white male hegemony and the subsequent relegation of white females to inferior and subordinate status in their own societies. Furthermore, feminism as it developed in the 1880s, was blatantly racist. The feminist movement, which started as a white women's suffrage movement, was initially concerned with the abolition of slavery and social equality for all, irrespective of race, class, or gender. However, it eventually became quite conservative at the time of the ratification of the Fifteenth Amendment, which granted voting rights to African American males but not to white females. For these reasons, Hudson-Weems argues, feminism does not and cannot reflect the beliefs or interests of African women. She points out in particular how, historically and culturally, African women do not apprehend African men as their enemy. Instead, Hudson-Weems insists on the necessary complementarity of males and females always posited by African culture as an imperative for the continuation of life itself.

The third objection to the adoption of a feminist agenda by Africa women is political. Can African people, Hudson-Weems asks, afford to be divided along gender lines although both African men and women face the same evil of white supremacy? Would it not be in our best interest, as a people subjected to relentless racial attacks, to fight together against our common enemies, i.e., white males and white females? Instead of focusing on building bridges with imagined outsider allies, and embarking further on the path of European deliquescence and decadence, would it not be wiser to invest our energy into strengthening and protecting our families and communities? Hudson-Weems writes, "If one considers the collective plight of Africana people globally, it becomes clear that we cannot afford the luxury, if you will, of being consumed by gender issues" (*Africana Womanism,* 1993 and 2019: 17).

Hudson-Weems recognizes that there are issues plaguing the relationship between African women and men, and she addresses this in the following two remarks: On one hand, such issues have often been the result of living in a racist and highly patriarchal society, creating at times unhealthy behaviors and attitudes in African women and men; on the other hand, due to their lack of institutional power in a highly racialized and racist society such as the United States, African men have never been in the position to oppress African women to any great extent. Thus, instead of being pushed further toward Europe by feminism, intersectionality, queerness, etc., Hudson-Weems proposes that we embrace Africana Womanism, a theory that stems from African culture and focuses on the very unique experiences and needs of African women:

> Neither an outgrowth nor an addendum to feminism, *Africana Womanism* is not Black feminism, African feminism, or Walker's womanism that some Africana women have come to embrace. *Africana Womanism* is an ideology created and designed for all women of African descent. It is grounded in African culture, and therefore, it necessarily focuses on the unique experiences, struggles, needs, and desires of Africana women. (*Africana Womanism,* 1993 and 2019: 15)

In conclusion, the development of Africana Womanism as an alternative to Eurocentric theories, is undoubtedly an extremely important step toward African epistemological and cultural decolonization. The work ahead of us is tremendous, but Africana Womanism certainly places us on the right path, the path back to ourselves, so that we can recover our sanity, integrity and self-respect.

# Bibliography

Asante, Molefi. (1987). *The Afrocentric Idea*. Philadelphia, Pa: Temple University Press.

Carruthers, Charlene. (2018). *Unapologetic: A Black, Queer, and Feminist Mandate for Radical Movements*. Boston: Beacon Press.

Charumbira, Ruramisai. (2015). *Imagining a Nation: History and Memory in Making Zimbabwe*. Charlottesville: University of Virginia Press.

Cohen, Cathy. *Punks, Bulldaggers and Welfare Queens: The Radical Potential of Queer Politics? GLQ* (1997). 3 (4). 437–465.

Coquery-Vidrovitch, Catherine. (2018). *African Women: A Modern History*. New York & London: Routledge.

Crenshaw, Kimberlé. "Mapping the Margins: Intersectionality, Identity Politics, and Violence Against Women of Color." *Stanford Law Review*. 43. 1991. 1241-99.

DeMoss Wolgemtuh, Nancy & Dannah Gresh. (2019). *Lies Young Women Believe*. East Peoria, Il: Versa Press.

Diop, Cheikh Anta. (1981). *Civilisation ou Barbarie?* Paris: Présence Africaine.

Fanon, Frantz. (1961). *Les Damnés de la Terre*. Paris: Maspéro.

Federici, Silvia. (2004). *Caliban and the Witch: Women, the Body and Primitive Accumulation*. Brooklyn, NY: Autonomedia.

Few, April. "Integrating Black Consciousness and Critical Race Feminism Into Family Studies Research." *Journal of Family Issues*. Volume 28 (4). April 2007. 452-473.

Hill Collins, Patricia & and Valerie Chepp. Intersectionality. The Oxford Handbook of Gender and Politics. *Edited by Georgina Waylen, Karen Celis, Johanna Kantola, and S. Laurel Weldon*. 2013. DOI 10.1093/oxfordhb/9780199751457.013.0002.

Hudson-Weems, Clenora. (2019). *Africana Womanism. Reclaiming Ourselves*, Fifth Edition. London & New York: Routledge.

Jacq, Christian. "Interview on Ancient Egypt." *Le Parisien Magazine*. July 19, 2019.

Javaid, Sundus & Zubair, Shirin. "Searching for a third space at the intersections of Postfeminism and postmodernism: Lessing's (Meta) Narrative of free women." *Kashmir Journal of Language Research*, 2012, Vol.15(1). 43-60.

Madondo, Gracious. "Why Africa Relates to Africana Womanism. *The Southern Times: The Newspaper for Southern Africa*, July 27, 2018.

Maenzanise, Beauty. (2009). Ritual and Spirituality among the Shona People.

Hopkins, Dwight N., and Marjorie Lewis (eds). *Another World Is Possible: Spiritualities and Religions of Global Darker Peoples*. Routledge, 2009. 183-189.

Mann, Susan Archer & Huffman, Douglas. "The Decentering of Second Wave Feminism. *Science & Society*." Volume 69 (1). January 2005. 56-91.

Mikell, Gwendolyn. *(*1997). *African Feminism. The Politics of Survival in Sub- Saharan Africa*. Philadelphia, Pa.: University of Pennsylvania Press.

Mohanty, Chandra Talpade. (1991). Under Western Eyes: Feminist Scholarship and Colonial Discourses," in *Third World Women and the Politics of Feminism*, ed. Mohanty, Russo & Torres, 51–80.

Nash, Jennifer. (2019). *Black Feminism Reimagined: After Intersectionality*. Durham, NC: Duke University Press.

Ogundipe–Leslie, Omolara. "The Female Writer and Her Commitment." *African Literature Today*, 15. 1987. 5–13.

Sarup, Madan. (1993). *An Introductory Guide to Post-Structuralism and Postmodernism*. New York: Harvester Wheatsheaf.

Sheldon, Kathleen. (2017). *African Women. Early History to the 21st Century*. Bloomington, In: Indiana University Press.

Stewart, J. (1992). Reaching for higher ground: Toward an understanding of Black/Africana Studies." *The Afrocentric Scholar*, 1(1), 1–63.

# 3

# AFRICANA WOMANISM AS AN ANTIDOTE TO MAINSTREAM BLACK FEMINISMS

## *MARK CHRISTIAN, PHD*

Africana Womanism, as articulated by Dr. Clenora Hudson-Weems, offers a refreshing and sanguine perspective on the overall empowerment of women, while not diminishing the role and/or partnership of Africana males. A caveat to the reader, women are literally most naturally the 'makers of men' who owe their lives to them. Let there be no confusion, this author is both an admirer and advocate for the empowerment of all women wherever they be in this complex, unpredictable, and unfair world. That stated, the focus here is on the role and importance of Africana Womanism within the paradigm offered by Hudson-Weems (2020) in relation to it offering a more optimistic perspective in relation to the empowerment of global Africana communities.

This chapter will probably be deemed controversial. It covers the issue in what could be considered loosely described as "mainstream Black Feminism," that currently proliferates within the confines of academia, masking itself in righteous anger and finding misogyny in all things that matter, especially black male lives. Moreover, it appears to be sweeping all other ways of thinking about gender relations aside, and this bodes for a rather problematic scenario because it largely goes by without critique. In other words, if one is not ingratiating oneself to Black feminisms (plural because the Black feminists find it difficult to even define the term), it can mean one is advocating patriarchal society and misogyny. As incredulous as this may seem, it is rather evident in academia, especially in the era of 'Me-Too-ism' that tends to cancel out anyone who stands erect within the context of Black manhood. Crucially, this chapter intends to focus on Africana Womanism, as espoused by Hudson-Weems (2020). It is a paradigm of gender relations that offers the distinct empowerment of Black women of African heritage, while allowing her male counterpart to live in harmony and equality. It is not idealistic to think of a woman and a man of African heritage experiencing equilibrium in their lives. Nor does this mean there should solely be focus on the relationship between an Africana woman and her male counterpart – that in itself would be myopic and self-defeating from the premise of this chapter.

In other words, to try and explain briefly, James Baldwin and Lorraine Hansberry were friends and creative geniuses who derived from the African American experience to share their profound insights on what it was to be human in a world that detested their humanity – largely because of their cultural heritage. The fact that Baldwin was gay and Hansberry was a lesbian/bisexual remains for this author irrelevant – which most probably to the current Black Feminist queer theorist will no doubt incur blasphemy. Yet for this author, Baldwin and Hansberry informed about the life of the mind in relation to the social reality of racism, and their private lives may have come out in some of the work that they produced, depending on one's reading. But they both wrote to share through their minds, it appears to me, specifically for the African American experience. Indeed, when one reads Baldwin or Hansberry, there is not an exclusion of the heterosexual because these African American writers were not about exclusion. There is nothing in their work that bleats on and on about homophobia and misogyny within the African American experience. Rather, there is an acknowledgement concerning the deeply rooted inhumanity that has engendered via a white supremacist system that hurts us all. Now, of course, this is what the author of this chapter takes from a reading of Baldwin and Hansberry, for example, in *The Fire Next Time* and *A Raisin in the Sun* respectively.

In a recent biography on Lorraine Hansberry, Perry (2018) writes about the friendship between Baldwin and Hansberry and adds in Nina Simone – whom she describes in the modern academic parlance as "queer" and a good friend of both, making them a trio of queers. Again, the news of Nina Simone being queer neither surprises nor interests this author because it is her private life. It seems in this "modern day of queering" that the sexuality of the artist overrides all else, the obsession with this seems to be an increasingly popular phenomena within academia. Highlighting the queer over the artistry is another implicit form of separating the heterosexual community from celebrating the artist. After listening to Nina Simone for over forty-years and not knowing her sexuality does nothing to separate my love for her and her music, this is something that seems to get lost when reading Black Feminists and queer theorists – there is an unexplainable but tacit point within Black Feminist writing that simply endeavors to exclude. Yet artists like Baldwin, Hansberry and Simone were not interested in excluding heterosexuals within their overall struggle to improve humanity – at least this is not the reading of this author. Perry states in relation to Baldwin and Hansberry, "The friendship that grew between Lorraine and Jimmy is storied. It was both an intellectual and soulful partnership" (Perry, 2018, 118). In other words, sexuality was no big deal; they loved each other in company and as soulful intellectual African Americans. They were fighting the same causes – ugly discrimination in all forms and the assault of Africana humanity.

In a noted essay by Audre Lorde titled, "The Master's Tools Will Never Dismantle the Master's House," she explains hers grievances as a Black lesbian scholar being excluded, apparently, in the proceedings within the context of a conference on Feminism held in New York City in September 1979. It is a rather short piece, four pages, given its prevalence in Black Feminist circles. Essentially, Lorde explained, "The absence of any consideration of lesbian consciousness or the consciousness of Third World women leaves a serious gap within this conference and within the papers presented here" (Lorde, 2000, 111). Two score and more years on, one could argue that Lorde's critique of white feminist-controlled academia has opened more avenues for perspectives that include queer theorists and other marginalized communities. Certainly, it seems currently in academia that there is a hegemony across liberal arts that embraces exactly what Lorde was then complaining about in 1979 – the exclusion of persons with her sexuality in conference proceedings.

Interestingly, Lorde's phrase has gained far more depth than what she first employed it for, because scholars in the field of Africana Studies also find such a term useful. The "master's tools will never dismantle the master's house" can be defined as there being no adequate use in employing the pedagogical and philosophical methodologies of mainstream academia that merely flow back to "old white men" who have largely disempowered people of color with pseudo-racialized theories and the spread in delusions of grandeur in regard to the supposed superiority of white European derived peoples over people of color. As ludicrous as this appears today, some of those ideas still hold sway with scholars who fail to see the efficacy in human oneness. Clearly, if this institutional racism is as systemic as most agree it is, then there is remnants of it still in the minds of some present day academics. It is rather absurd for those holding such views to be bold enough to defend them, but they do with relative gusto. Therefore, if the master's tools are no good for students of color to employ, that too, as an uncomfortable truth, needs to be espoused candidly. Too often in academia lip service is given to the notion of equal opportunity and fairness. Most know that this is illusory and has yet to be obtained; white racism has a silent edge, too, these days but it lurks in the minds of even the most liberal of scholars (Trepagnier, 2010).

Lorde continued, "…As women, we have been taught either to ignore our differences, or to view them as causes for separation and suspicion rather than forces for change." There is an appeal to white feminists to be more open in including Black lesbian perspectives in the structure of the conference under scrutiny. Lorde continues, "…Without community there is no liberation, only the most vulnerable and temporary armistice between an individual and her oppression. But community must not mean shedding of our differences, nor the pathetic pretense that these differences do not exist" (Lorde, 2000, 112). To be sure, Lorde is speaking about the necessity to accept difference *within* the context of women. She does not speak to the community of women and men. Her critique speaks to having a problem with being largely excluded within the context of what appears to be largely a white feminist conference, with a lack of papers reflecting the complexity and diversity inside women experiences. This is crucial for the discussion on diversity because it reveals there is more to women than a monolithic response to patriarchal oppression. For instance, Lorde shows interest in the lack of a diverse womanhood being articulated and that it fundamentally does not speak to her world of Black lesbianism. Lorde feels excluded within the context of a conference that is about women and this is instructive because diversity in higher education can be extremely limited in scope. Again, Lorde is not interested in addressing the need to "educate male ignorance" about the plight of her complex world; she sees that as a tool of the oppressor and in being "occupied with the master's concerns" rather than focusing directly, and only, on women in all their heterosexual and queer ways.

This is a legitimate perspective to hold for Lorde, and it is a point of view that appears to be holding sway in academia. However, if an issue is put forward for a Black heterosexual male, on the other hand, that is if one was to write forcefully for the empowerment of his kind, as Lorde does for her Black lesbianism, it is likely he would be deemed a misogynist. Yet one would never label Lorde a misandrist even though her prose is pretty powerful in the realm of discussing female-male issues within an anti-male framework. Indeed, there is actually no discussion in relation to men as her entire focus is on empowering a Black lesbian point of view within the overall feminist frame of reference. This is something that explains the problematic aspect of explaining gender within neat operational boxes. Human experience is rather messy, as there is not one female point of view, as Lorde professes, nor is there a one male outlook. This should be commonsense that there abounds different perspectives within women studies, and beyond, but it seems improbable to find such common ground when Black Feminists appear to speak only to a misplaced anti-Black male agenda within patriarchy. One way to address this or get beyond this impasse is to comprehend more convincingly that the system does not really care as long as it appears that Black Feminists are aiding in the division of Black lives. This could be deemed a cynical response, but the proof appears rather ubiquitous. Today in higher education, for example, Black Feminism and queer theory abounds to the exclusion of other points of view in the African American and broader Africana experience.

What is happening is rather sad, so if Audre Lorde were alive today, she would most probably be pleased in some sense with some progressive change for her points of view, but disappointed in other ways with the lack of progress in terms of women of color not holding more power than they precariously possess. She would not care too much about men, whatever their ethnicity, because they are all in a sense oppressors from reading her essay. Is this acceptable? Maybe, as long as other points of view are aired within the context of the Africana global scene. True diversity of thought is in allowing all points of view to air, and this author is one hundred per cent against the growing "cancel culture" across campuses that do not allow, for example, far-right conservative thinkers to speak. All scholars should be allowed to air their views within an academic setting and then be critiqued within the same arena. Let students learn from opposing views rather than stifling some scholars in favor of others. This is a major problem on today's university and college campuses; there is too much political correctness without critical thought.

Africana Womanism, on the contrary, does not focus on eliminating men from the empowerment of women, neither does it limit the scope and breadth of women while doing so. The Black Feminists, and more lately aligned with queer theorists, tend to oppose Africana Womanism as Stewart and Mazama point out in the Forward of the latest edition of *Africana Womanism*: "In developing and articulating Africana Womanism, Hudson-Weems has confronted opposition from both White and Black feminists" (Stewart and Mazama, cited in Hudson-Weems 2020, xiii). The Black Feminists, as argued via Lorde, tend to ignore any attempt to bring a holistic approach to the problems encountered by the entire Africana experience. Maybe this is a legitimate concern of women of African heritage to tell 'herstory' at the expense of all due to the fact that history often ignores their experiences.

Even the renowned and important scholar-activist, Angela Y. Davis recounts how the history of African American women was largely left out in terms of the recounting of life under enslavement by historians. What she may have overlooked in that this is how the entire field was largely controlled by white historians, and that those of African American heritage most often spoke to the experiences of women. Clearly not as well as Davis and others would want, but that again is due to the fact that, arguably, not until the 1970s and beyond did women appear on the scene to write and publish in the field of historical scholarship. Davis' book *Women, Race & Class* was first published in 1981, and it offers an insightful account from a Marxist perspective on the experience of African American women from enslavement through to the 1970s. It is a marvelous book that does not engage entirely in male-bashing, with some accounts on how African American males have been maligned – specifically chapter eleven 'rape, racism and the myth of the Black rapist.' Yet, and rightly so, there is a focus on the experiences of African American women.

Davis (1983) predates the notion of 'intersectionality' which is a tediously ubiquitous term in academia presently. Basically, the idea of feminism was once solely concerned with the experiences of white women and not particularly concerned with 'race' and class issues (Hudson-Weems 2020, 106-112). Clearly, then the notion of 'intersectionality' is simply a new fad for Black Feminists and queer theorists to employ but, in fact, before "intersectionality," writers have most often combined multiple ways in explaining the historical reality of racism, sexism, and classism – along with a myriad of other forms of discriminatory practices. However, with the current crop of Black Feminist perspectives having an impact that could be deemed rather negative toward males, it is important to not lose sight of the fact that what they are offering is often problematic for the entire Africana world.

What is salient, and it is something Hudson-Weems (2020) fully comprehends, is in the fact that women have more than a right to speak to issues that directly impact their lives, past, present and future. However, what she offers is far more than the average Black Feminist account, which is often akin to white feminism in black face. That is, the bottom line always for Black Feminists is in espousing that all men are oppressors, and do not need to be discussed within any legitimate context other than as the *sexist oppressor.* To be sure, this is *part* of the life between men and women, but surely it is not the all and end of men-women relationships. If so, what a negative reality, and what role in this situation can be laid at the feet of women themselves? After all, have they not been the principle raisers of African American boys to men since at least the 1970s, maybe longer? Of course, this is playing devil's advocate because there should be no blame on the destruction of the African American family passed solely to either Black men or women, given the historical trajectory of enslavement, segregation, and second-third class citizenship. The breakdown of the Africana family should be an issue that is solved and reconstructed by the entire community, young and elder, women and men. Instead of pointing the finger at one another, it would be more efficacious to find ways to bring all parties together. Just as Hudson-Weems (2020,

134) advocates, there should always be room for "genuine sisterhood in concert with male in the liberation struggle" without any hierarchical partnering – only in shared responses to the needs and aspirations of what is best for positive growth and development of the family and its broader community.

Now, before the Black Feminist queer theorist points the finger, this does not mean there is no room for other relationships and family structures. It simply means that men and women should be encouraged, in all complexities, to work together in harmony for the constructive good of the Africana community. Even the renowned bell hooks (1995) speaks to the problematic aspect of some Black Feminist perspectives, asserting that the "Contemporary feminist movement has had little positive impact on black life in the United States... Ironically, more black women are just beginning to embrace narrow notions of feminism (i.e., the idea of woman as victim, man as oppressor/enemy)" (hooks 1995, 62). Well, hooks was writing from her book *Killing Rage Ending Racism* some twenty-five years ago, and it is sad to state here that the majority of Black Feminist writers continue to peddle the 'narrow notions of feminism' in academic works, adding for a more unified or partnership with queer theory. Indeed, actually it would be a good thing for all concerned if hooks could explain the less narrow aspects of Black Feminism because in my three decades in academia, one has merely encountered the narrow. Fortunately, Hudson-Weems had earlier expounded on this male-female equation in *Africana Womanism*, but from a more historical perspective in explicating the dynamics of the Black woman and the absence of the "battle of the sexes" as being a White, not Black phenomenon:

> First, the Africana woman does not see the man as her primary enemy as does the White feminist, who is carrying out an age-old battle with her White male counterpart for subjugating her as his property. Africana men have never had the same institutionalized power to oppress Africana women as White men have had to oppress white women. (*Africana Womanism*, 1993, 2019; 25, 15, 1st Edition, 5th Edition respectively)

Earlier still, in the mid-1980s, beginning with her presentations at National Black conferences, which culminated in her 1989 publication in *The Western Journal of Black Studies*, Hudson-Weems asserted the following in "Cultural and Agenda Conflicts in Academia: Critical Issues for Africana Women's Studies":

> Historically, Africana women have fought against sexual discrimination as well as race and class discrimination. They have challenged Africana male chauvinism, but have stopped short of eliminating Africana men as allies in

the struggle for liberation and family-hood. (*Africana Womanism,* 1989, 1993, 2019; 185, 21, 35, *WJBS,* 1st Edition, 5th Edition respectively)

Perception can often cloud reality, especially within the context of diversity. The author was on panel at the diversity conference held by the City University of New York in March of 2017, like Lorde back in 1979, which was a marginalized panel concerning the experience of faculty of color men surviving in higher education. Hence, the author endeavored to explain that there is a dire need to confront the shallowness of diversity initiatives in the current form and to consider how "race" has been relegated to insignificance compared to the superficial and ambiguity of the phrase "intersectionality" – a term that simply considers the obvious in taking into account numerous factors of discrimination: gender, sexuality, class, disability, body image, and so on till it becomes an exhausting exercise and litmus test in diluting legitimate protests concerning racialized issues in society, because 'race' and ethnicity needs to be recognized as a primary factor (Fitzgerald 2017).

 If one focuses, for example, on 'Black male heterosexual demise in academia,' one can be deemed by diversity pundits as being too narrow in scope – so again one is marginalized by the hegemony of the day in academia. Now, if instead the paper would be titled 'Black queer theory' the paper would most likely be applauded and the speaker acclaimed within diversity circles. To emphasize the point, James Baldwin is currently a celebration in academia; he is lauded (rightly so) as a visionary, yet the exploitation of his homosexuality is both out of context with the man himself and diversionary to his major and constant critique of white supremacy. But it seems that one cannot succeed within mainstream academia without such exploitation of a thinker and his or her attributes. Maybe soon there will be a revival of Richard Wright and his foray into Marxism, but right now 'diversity' is all about the queering of society.

In point of fact, a recent study by Charlene Carruthers (2018) exemplifies the current academic scene in liberal arts and the social sciences. Carruthers's book is titled, *Unapologetic: A Black, Queer, and Feminist Mandate for Radical Movements* and is salubriously endorsed by the likes of Cornel West, Robin D.G. Kelley, Barbara Ransby and others from the "Black Lives Matter" organization. In the Preface Carruthers states,

> I am one of the many who have taken up that responsibility [the history of African American liberation struggle] in my generation. Since 2013, I have steered the growth and development of BYP100 (Black Youth Project 100), one of the most prolific and integral Black liberation movement organizations who believe that a Black freedom movement is possible in

our lifetime and that it must be Black, queer, and feminist. (Carruthers 2018, xvi)

Clearly, if this is the way forward for the Black liberation struggle, it raises some problematic issues. If a movement *must be* 'Black, queer, and feminist,' what does this say about the millions of heterosexuals? We are to simply follow the lead? Is this not a tad fundamentalist in scope? Should it not also be an inclusive movement that critiques the very idea of a label that demands one follows this or that ideology? Maybe there is a frustration combined with a naïve boldness among such thinkers, but the support from the 'radical left' (who all occupy very lucrative positions in the Ivy League) will allow Carruthers the space to keep on, keepin' on, regardless of the myopic scope of her endeavors. When anything 'radical' comes in a 'must be' context, it sends the wrong message. But the queer theorists, on the other hand, if nothing else, have a strong foothold in academia. And if anyone raises an iota for concern for such a narrow Black radical liberation movement, as this author is doing, he or she is summarily labelled homophobic and banished from having papers read at conferences led by them. In other words, one is set upon by the every-growing 'cancel culture' that pervades the halls of academia – very worrying, indeed.

Dialogue certainly needs to increase between those who feel excluded and marginalized in society and academia, and that includes both Black heterosexual males, and Black authentic traditional females. If anything is to be gleaned by the recent blatant murder of George Floyd at the hands of police in Minneapolis (May 25, 2020), and if *all* Black Lives *truly* Matter (Ransby 2018), then this chapter will be considered legitimate in raising concern for the continued subjugation of Black males throughout society and in academia who just happen to be, by no fault of theirs, Black first and heterosexual. Black males by and large do not hold power over Black women; indeed, given the current situation across society, it is a rather strange notion. The lack of African American males in academia, for example, compared to African American women in the US is palpable. So before the reader picks up her pen to castigate the author, read closely the words of bell hooks: "To begin feminist struggle anew, to ensure that we are moving into feminist futures, we still need feminist theory that speaks to everyone..." (hooks, 2000, xiv). However, feminist theory that speaks to everyone has never appeared in my academic world, nor is it expected to, as various gender-based theories, like Africana Womanism, have been created by insiders with "lived" experiences to better address their particular historical and cultural needs and demands, if, of course, they are not influenced by or dictated to by those of the dominant culture, a too often proven reality. Also, as the wonderful African writer Chimamanda

Ngozi Adichie writes, "…Gender matters everywhere in the world. And I would like to ask that we should begin to dream about the plan for a different world. A fairer world. A world of happier men and happier women who are truer to themselves" (Adichie, 2014, 25).

Currently in the Africana world there are too many disgruntled and closed off from each other, men and women of color. To be frank, this is understandable because there are many initiatives in mainstream society that perpetuate divide and conquer techniques. Africana scholars need to be a little more aware of the historical legacy that white societies have created, ways to keep the majority of Africana communities at loggerheads. Some would argue that this is the way capitalism is structured in order to operate. There are always losers in this system, and the fifteen million African Americans mired in poverty and urban decline will catch hell more than other cultural groups. The high rates of police brutality and incarceration continue to blight these communities.

There are many Africana women scholars who give hope in aiding our communities across the globe. Scholars like Hudson-Weems (1993, 2004, 2019) and Reid-Merritt (2000, 2002) offer a more holistic way in bringing Africana communities together. They are the scholars who should be read and read carefully by the younger generation. Sexuality should never be the foremost criteria for joining a Black liberation movement; that is ridiculous and narcissistic in tone. Is it old fashioned to expect sex to be left in the private domain? Is it old school to think of sexuality as something private? It seems not so these days, and if this is the way of the 21st Century for Black liberation, then it is headed for another breakdown in scope, vision, and productive gains. There is a great deal of hypocrisy in academia with many fake leftists pontificating 'radical this, and radical that' yet when one looks closely at the output, it boils down to a 'radical conference' whereby a back-slapping session takes place on the latest books published by, usually, Duke University Press.

One can become cynical after thirty years in academia (Christian 2017, 2012), but if there is anything to learn from it all, it is in the fact that humanity is a contradiction, and appearance often does not meet with reality. There is too much romanticism over, say, the Black Panthers, and/or Angela Davis and her wonderful Afro from the 1960s. But she, too, has spent her life speaking Marxism while living in Capitalism. Her work in breaking the chain of prison incarceration is commendable, but there are problems when one looks deeper at the Black feminist approaches that implicitly down her 'brothers' in the struggle. There are hypocrites in all walks of life, but none come worse than the present crop of 'black radical feminists' who destroy anyone who utters criticism of their myopic analyses. The back-slapping radical lefties in academia do not come close to Malcolm X or even Martin Luther King, Jr. in putting their lives on the line. Most of them hide in Ivy League positions being well-paid and staid in analysis. The Black Feminists are heading this pack while being supported on the back of newly published academic books by the old guard so-called Black Radicals. If it was not unutterably sad, it could be humorous – an oxymoron.

There is an antidote required for this malaise in the current form of Black Feminism, the work of Hudson-Weems (2019) pulls Africana women from the clutches of white feminism and brings us back in line with an Ida B. Wells-Barnett, a Fannie Lou Hamer, or an Ella Baker, the last one being an advisor, organizer and supporter of an all African American youth college group, SNCC (Student Non-Violent Coordinating Committee), led by Howard University student, Stokely Carmichael in the 1960s. On the 1960s, and Dr. Martin Luther King, Jr. the author witnessed one of the so-called radical Black feminists giving a presentation on the Civil Rights Movement, and who was telling a younger generation how Dr. King refused to go on the Freedom Rides, and thus, was implying that he was a coward. She failed to state that Dr. King was jailed twenty-nine times, stabbed nearly to death, had his house bombed, was consistently threatened all his public life, and finally assassinated at the age of 39. Now, does that sound like a cowardly man? The Black feminists are being rather clinical in pulling down the Black male leaders as they usurp the narrative of the Civil Rights era with calls of sexism and the invisibility of women leadership due to the sexism of Black male leaders.

One of the themes goes this way: they argue that women who were leaders did not get the kudos they deserved. But one could state the same about many men who did not get the kudos they deserved. They tend to put down Dr. King as 'not the only leader' during his era, and then bring out the names of women who should get more kudos, Ella Baker, Fannie Lou Hamer, Jo Ann Robinson, Daisy Bates, Constance Motely Baker, Septima Clark, to name a few of the usual suspects. This is all fine, but the context of sideling and diminishing Dr. King in the process is rather unacceptable. The fact that Coretta Scott King kept his legacy alive speaks volumes of her; she was a brilliant woman in her own right, as was Betty Shabazz, the wife of Malcolm X. Yet many Black Feminists find ways to belittle them, along with the Black Panther male leadership. It is rather tedious, and unnecessary to pull up women and put down men. What does that do for future generations? It is detrimental and unnecessary. For example, who knows of Reverend George W. Lee (1903-1955) who was assassinated in Belzoni, Mississippi in May of 1955, murdered by white supremacists for organizing African Americans to vote. This was three months before young Emmett Till was murdered in Money, Mississippi, but Reverend Lee is largely forgotten. What do Black Feminists state about this? Indeed, one could argue that for every woman activist lost in history, there is a male standing by her too, and this is not to diminish the fact that sexism existed and continues to exist just as racism does. Or what about Esau Jenkins (1910-1972) who could be described as an entrepreneurial activist, again someone who is largely forgotten for all his good work in South Carolina during the height of segregation. The point is today's scholars should be building up, not knocking down Dr. King and others who led, bled, and died for African American liberation. Let those who are not guilty of sin, cast the first stone. To be sure, there are many unsung heroes and heroines within African American history in relation to the Civil Rights Movement.

Africana Womanism is still marginalized because the hegemony of Black Feminism in academia holds sway with white liberals due to its practice of dividing men and women. White liberals are rather adept at keeping their racism silent (Trepagnier 2010; Kimmel and Ferber 2017); and the history of white people lets us know that there is an underlying aspect to white culture that reeks of white supremacy, and this has been a mainstay in the history of Europe and its expansion into the so-called 'New World' some five hundred plus years ago (Painter 2010). There is a history of racism and discrimination that goes far deeper into the recesses of society whereby women and men of color require knowledge and partnership of all kinds in order to improve the impact on contemporary society. The present situation bodes very poorly with the issue of Black Feminism and the queering, only, of African American protest leadership. That is a recipe for disaster and not because of anything other than a narrow conception of the African American experience. Moreover, there needs to be more critique without canceling out those who criticize the limitations in the vision of African American leadership.

The publication of this text is very important because Africana Womanism needs to be heard, studied, and comprehended for its more comprehensive and empowering factors for the African American experience and beyond in the global Africana community. According to Columbia University Political Scientist, Dr. Charles V. Hamilton, "This work [*Africana Womanism*] is indeed an intellectual triumph. It is a product that not only must be read, but more important, be studied" (Book Endorsement, 1993). Black Feminism does not speak authentically to the African American experience largely because it is borrowed conceptually from a culture of white feminism that failed drastically to empower women of color. If Audre Lorde can critique its lack of flexibility for the Black lesbian world she occupied, then it is legitimate to state it does not meet with the needs of Africana Womanism that was created by Hudson-Weems

(2019). There is a paramount need to expand the knowledge of women of African heritage and to bring that knowledge into the realm of her brothers, nephews, uncles, fathers and male allies. Globally there is a treasure trove of women's writings we can now access (Guy-Sheftall 1995; Busby 2019), and there is a need to combine such scholarship with that of Africana Womanism. This then, if disseminated, shall prove to be efficacious to the overall Africana global experience who need more connection, not fragmentation, in order to forge positive and broad impactful communities. Crucially, Africana Womanism is the antidote to the rampant flight to an unqualified and misrepresentative Black Feminism.

# Bibliography

Adichie, Chimamanda Ngozi. *We Should All be Feminists.* New York: Anchor Books, 2014.

Baldwin, James. *The Fire Next Time.* London: Penguin, 1964.

Busby, Margaret. ed. *New Daughters of Africa: An International Anthology of Writing by Women of African Descent.* New York: Amistad, 2019.

Carruthers, Charlene A. *Unapologetic: A Black, Queer, and Feminist Mandate for Radical Movements.* Boston, MA: New Beacon Press, 2018.

Christian, Mark. "From Liverpool to New York City: Behind the Veil of a Black British Male Scholar Inside Higher Education." *Race Ethnicity and Education.* 20 (3) (2017): 414: 428.

Christian, Mark. ed. *Integrated but Unequal: Black Faculty of Predominately White Campuses.* Trenton, NJ: Africa World Press, 2012.

Fitzgerald, Kathleen J. *Recognizing Race and Ethnicity: Power, Privilege, and Inequality, 2nd Edition.* Boulder, CA: Westview Press, 2017.

Hansberry, Lorraine. *A Raisin in the Sun.* New York: Random House, 1959.

hooks, bell. *Feminist Theory: From Margin to Center, 2nd Edition.* Cambridge, MA: South End Press, 2000.

hooks, bell. *Killing Rage Ending Racism.* New York: Penguin, 1996.

Hudson-Weems, Clenora. *Africana Womanism: Reclaiming Ourselves.* New York: Routledge, 2020 (Bedford Publishers, 1993)

Hudson-Weems, Clenora. "Cultural and Agenda Conflicts in Academia: Critical Issues for Africana Women's Studies." *The Western Journal of Black Studies* (Reprint in *Africana Womanism* 1993 & 2019; 33-42 & 21-27).

Kimmel, Michael S. and Ferber, Abby L. *White Privilege: A Reader, 4th Edition.* Boulder, CO: West View Press, 2017.

Painter, Nell Irvin. *The History of White People.* New York: Norton, 2010.

Perry, Imani. *Looking for Lorraine: The Radiant and Radical Life of Lorraine Hansberry.* Boston: Beacon Press, 2018.

Ransby, Barbara. *Making All Black Lives Matter: Reimaging Freedom in the 21st Century.* California: University of California Press, 2018.

Reid-Merritt, Patricia. *Sister Power: How Phenomenal Black Women are Rising to the Top.* New York: John Wiley & Sons, 1996.

Reid-Merritt, Patricia. *Sister Wisdom: 7 Pathways to Satisfying Life for Soulful Black Women.* New York: John Wiley & Sons, 2002.

Sheftall-Guy, Beverly. ed. *Words of Fire: An Anthology of African-American Feminist Thought.* New York: The New Press, 1995.

Trepagnier, Barbara. *Silent Racism: How Well-Meaning White People Perpetuate the Racial Divide, 2nd Edition.* Boulder, CO: Paradigm, 2010.

# PART II:

# SECURING OUR LEGACY AND
# MISSION VIA AFRICANA TEXTS

Combating the predominance of negative images of Blackness in the mass media, Black women's celebrations of Blackness in the media serve as a form of Black racial pride, while at the same time operating as advocates of Black cultural values as a means to empower Africana people globally. Implicit in the construction of celebratory images of Africana women and families in the media is the embracing of historical legacies, cultural phenomenon, and the African worldview system, working together to construct media that authentically reflects what it means to be African or of African descent. Moreover, how we are authentically identified, Africana Womanism, demonstrating the power of restorative justice in the media via recognizing the long-standing practice of authentic existence for the advancement of the Africana family, represents the authentic paradigm for Africana womanists and their families.

**(Marquita M. Gammage, PhD)**

# 4

# RECLAIMING AFRICANA-MELANATED WOMEN: THE FUTURE OF THE AFRICANA FAMILY AND THE POWER OF THE MEDIA

## MARQUITA M. GAMMAGE, PHD

### Establishing Culturally Conscious Media Ownership and Production

The public imagination of Black bodies has skyrocketed on screen, in social media and in music. Unfortunately, the representations of Blackness in the media have been inundated with anti-Black ideologies that marginalize the humanity and cultures of Africana women, men and children. (Gammage 2015; Allison 2016). Mass media has systematically reflected a white male patriarchal gaze, which is not surprising, given that the majority of the media industry in America is owned by wealthy white men. Within this lens, Blackness has been viewed on a spectrum on inferiority to whiteness, whereby Eurocentric ideologies define the human experience and juxtapose Black reality to white beliefs, values, and practices. (Parenti 1992; Gray 1995; Entman and Rojecki 2000; Gammage 2015) The resulting racist mythology of Africanness has yielded inaccurate memes, caricatures and stereotypes that have maintained a stronghold on the public perception of Black culture and Black families. Indeed, the persistent arrogance of whites has corroded the framing of Blackness while seducing the public into accepting the superiority of whiteness.

One very important fact surrounding the incomplete and thus, inaccurate presentations and portrayals of Blacks and Black life in the media is that whites predominate, not only as major financers and thus, financial benefactors of the productions, but more important, they monopolize the key positions in the making of films, including Black films, wherein lies why affirming messages of Blackness are not present in certain productions. Consider the following facts relative to the 1998 film adaptation of the 1987 Pulitzer Prize-Winning novel, *Beloved*, by the 1993 Nobel Laureate Toni Morrison:  Only 1 out of 5 Producers was Black; the Associate Producer; the Director and the Executive Producer were all white; 1 out out of the 4 Screenplay writers was African; both Film Editors were white; the Cinematographer was Asian; the Casting Director was white, and virtually all of the other key Crew Members were white. Other than Oprah Winfrey, African Americans were absent among this production crew.  Hence an authentic African American perspective was missing from the production of the film; which by in large may have compromised the genuineness of the storyline and the portrayals of the Black characters experiences and their cultural phenomenon.  Authenticity is a major cornerstone in the theory of Africana Womanism, thus the incorporation of Black cultural perspectives in film production of Black stories is necessary.

In a 1999 review of the movie in *The Western Journal of Black Studies* by Dr. Clenora Hudson-Weems, conceptualizer of Africana Womanism, and co-author, with Dr. Wilfred Samuels of the first full-length critical study of the works of Nobel Laureate, entitled *Toni Morrison* (1990),

> Morrison had stated years ago that her intentions in writing the book was to "rip that veil" to tell the whole story of slave life and to present the interior lives of the enslaved themselves. Together, these issues communicate the bigger picture, which unfortunately the movie sorely misses (Hudson-Weems, *"Beloved*: From Novel to Movie" 204).

Indeed, what is missing is the perspective and defining issues, cares and concerns of Black people, including our life-style and unique talent, i.e. the art of dancing, which the title character lacks in the movie. In the novel, however, she has master that talent, for her sister asks, "Where'd you learn to dance?"  Moreover, the character, Six-o is grosely misrepresented in the movie, whereas we have a fuller presentation of him in the novel:

> Sixo-o, too, who represents in the novel the profound love of Black men for Black women in his relationship with his "thirty-mile woman--for whom he has to travel thrifty miles to another plantation just to spend an hour with her—appears [in the movie] in a quick flash, with barely a name, barely a history. (204)

In the movie, we witness only a quick snap of a man hanging with a noose around his neck, assumed to be that of Six-o, denied in the movie real presence as the recipient of an important part of life in general—LOVE. Black movies, on the whole, do not emphasize Black Love.

Finally, there is the absolute omission of the poignant experience of another key character in this slave saga, Paul D, the significant other of Sethe, the mother of Beloved, who, after she is left without her husband, the father of her five children. Here again we witness the denial of the fuller picture of Paul D, his recounting his sexual exploitation during his time on a Georgia chain-gang which "made him tremble." Hudson-Weems offers a possible explanation for this omission, stating "that experience, the sexual exploitation of Black men by white men (guards), forces us to appreciate the commonality of the sexual exploitation of both Black men and Back women, used as receptacles for white pleasures during slavery" (204). Certainly, a conscious commitment to broadcasting the internal underpinnings of Blackness and how we experience our reality has been rejected from the movie-making process.

For Black women's portrayals in particular, standards of womanhood have been restricted to white feminist systems that further subjugate the Black women to a marginal existence. That is to say, the Black woman's image in the media have by in large existed within a racist and sexist context, limiting her possibilities and distorting her truths. (bell hooks 1992; Collins 2005; Gammage 2015; Allison 2016) Nonetheless, the media industry's control and ownership of the Black image have not gone uncontested. In fact, Black media creators and producers have purposely rebelled against this monopolization of Black stories calling for anti-racist policies and practices in the industry and society in general, and by systematically constructing more authentic representations of Black reality and culture.

Pushing back against the disenfranchisement of Black media producers, Black women's artistry reimagines the possibilities of Black individuals, families and communities. Fundamentally, the intentionality of culturally conscious representations is designed to sensitize the public to images more germane to Africana people's cultures and lived realities and move the public perception away from anti-Black ideologies of criminality and hypersexuality. Through the use of television and film media, independent media, and social media, the Africana woman media producers are reinvigorating media content with our stories told from our perspectives, serving as a fundamental precept to the reclamation of the Africana image in the media.

Black women's investment in the ownership of Africana media undertakes the activism and advocacy needed to dismantle the racist patriarchal dominance of the media. A new path of independence has been plotted and has allowed for Africana-melenated artist to control their creation and production of images of Blackness in the media. Black women owned media corporations, such as Harpo Productions—founded by Oprah Winfrey; ARRAY—inaugurated by Ava DuVernay; Issa Rae Productions—established by Issa Rae, and Cleo TV—owned by Urban One which was founded by Cathy Hughes, all having elevated the voices of Black storytellers from conception to marketing and distribution. These Africana women have been able to establish safe production spaces for creators of media content that seek to tell authentic Black stories. Shows including *Black Love* (2017-present), *Cleo Speaks* (2019), and *Queen Sugar* (2016-present) offer viewers diverse representations that explore the complexities of the Black experience.

Black women media producers, creators and performers, such as Issa Rae, are able to bring to life the experiences of Africana people in a way that is authentic and true to their current lives. Through Issa Rae Productions and Color Creative, founded by Issa Rae and Deniese Davis, Issa Rae has been able to establish new categories of Black media and generate opportunities for other artists, which has paid off significantly. Issa Rae's *Insecure* (2016-2020), a comedy-drama centering the experiences of young Black women as they navigate life, love, friendships, and careers, is highly acclaimed and has been awarded over 20 industry awards, including a 2019 Outstanding Comedy Series Award from Black Reel Awards for Television.

The success of these Africana-melanated women has catapulted the desire of the American public to see more wholistic and multi-dimensional representations of Black women and Black families in the media. There media productions have yielded high dividends and have been exceedingly awarded and applauded by audiences globally. Now, media broadcasting companies are more compelled to produce media content that speak to Black media consumers. However, Black women are not waiting on affirmation and buy-in from major production companies. Rather, Black women are reclaiming ownership of the creative and production process, thereby ensuring the advancement of Black stories from Black perspectives. In an interview at the Obama Foundation Summit with Theaster Gates on November 8, 2019, Ava DuVernay advanced this agenda in her discussion of her film distribution and resource collective company ARRAY:

> You know we tried to build our own systems of distribution and amplifying things so that we can rely on people valuing our stories at lot less, because they may value it today and not value it tomorrow; and that's not what we are building. We are building something that allows us to be prioritized and center in every moment in everyday of our lives. That's the institution

building that I am working on… and building our own pipeline. (DuVernay 2019)

DuVernay, like other Black female media producers, emerges like a breath of fresh air, restoring and proclaiming the beauty and value of Black stories. Through their ownership, Africana media creators have successfully distributed authentic narratives that reclaim Black family heritage, social justice-driven counter narratives, and have broadcast celebrations of Blackness.

## *Authentic Narratives that Reclaim Black Family Heritage*

Political figures, governmental agencies, literature and media have consistently unfairly represented Black families as nonexistent and dysfunctional. (Staples 1997; Sudarkasa 1997; Gammage and Alameen-Shavers 2019) The leading literature in the 20th century on Black families relied predominately on research applying Eurocentric methodological frameworks, such as the pathological paradigm which assessed the Black family using a middle-class white family model. This treatment of Black families ignored Black family cultural characteristics and instead penalized the Black woman for her role within the Black family system. White patriarchy and its by-product female subordination were standard rubrics applied when discussing Black families, despite the fact that white American family values differed significantly from Black families.

A classic example of this can be noted in Daniel P. Moynihan's report to the U.S. Department of Labor in 1965 entitled *The Negro Family: The Case for National Action*. In chapter four, *The Tangle of Pathology*, he applies a normative cultural approach whereby the Black family is evaluated in comparison to the middle-class white family. Here, Moynihan concludes that the Black family is pathologically dysfunctional because it fails to mirror that of the white male dominated family system. As a result, he classifies the Black woman as a burden to the Black family's ability to ascend into the American dream as she stands in direct opposition to the Black male assuming a position of dominance and control over the family. Un-affirming of the white patriarchal order, the Black woman in particular in the Black family was miscategorized as a matriarch and single-handedly blamed for the social and economic challenges faced by Black families in America, without a single account for the institutional racism that marginalized Black social, political and economic mobility.

This racist mis-categorization of the Black family has been used to rationalize the systemic public policy attack on Black women, which has framed the Black woman as an illegitimate criminally unfit "baby mama"—the welfare queen, and Black men as super-predator, absentee baby daddies. And the media has primarily reflected these same stereotyped sentiments. From impoverished welfare dependent portrayals to drug addicted caricatures, the media has overwhelmingly perpetuated racist typecasts of Blackness. The myths surrounding Black families were overly sensationalized in the media for centuries (Bennett 2010); however, culturally grounded Black media producers have endeavored to reclaim and take ownership of the Black family representations in the media as a form of restorative justice and Black cultural pride

Re-centering the authentic cultural practices of Africana families have served as a priority among Africana media owners and producers. In particular, Africana-melanated women in the media have intentionally devoted their creative works to producing culturally conscious Black family centered media content that both celebrates the beauty of African cultures and simultaneously challenges century old racist narratives of the dysfunctional Black family and community. Contemporary media imagery by Africana women engenders continuity between the cultural practices of African Americans and their aspirations, while at the same time highlighting the voices of Black media creators and artists.

Africana women such as Ava DuVernay, Issa Rae, Codie Elanie Oliver, and Stella Meghie use the power of the media to transform the way Black family stories are communicated. In 2019, Ava DuVernay contends that there exists a need to decompose the negative and problematic images in the media. She states:

> At Array we focused on the image, we focus on the cinematic image and the way in which the telling of story in a distorted way about all of us and who we are have really diminished us as people. The story telling is such a part, it's the crux of our belief about each other. The stories we've been told about each other. Right. And not just the stories pasted along and whispered between families and generations, but the way that the image has been used to really harm. To really portray certain people as thugs, certain people as lazy, certain people as frivolous, certain people as sinister; it's the stories that have done that, that have been kind of beaten into us through repetition over the years. And so, that's what we try to deconstruct and disrupt at Array. All of the systems around the story. (DuVernay 2019)

In abandoning the anti-Black racist ideologies that engulf the media, Black women are envisioning a newer more complete multifaceted depiction of Blackness for now and the future.

A noteworthy genre that illustrates the revolutionary stance applied in Black women's media is in the area of romantic love. New Black media chronicles Africana people's commitments to love and the interdependence of community while existing in a racist dehumanizing society. Previously, stories of Black love in the media have predominantly been limited to unhealthy unconsummated hopes for love. Joyous love was difficult if not impossible to imagine in media among Blacks romantic couples. Many romantic storylines would end with hopes of sweet fulfilling love; yet spend the majority of the screen time drowning in grief and sorrow with sprinkles of passionate love scenes. In their completed form, films such as *Baby Boy* (2001), *Love Jones* (1997), and *Jason's Lyric* (1994) were unable to fully actualize the establishment of Black love in a healthy and longstanding relationship. While each of the films are entitled to their own accolades within Black cinematic productions, their characters' potential for mature love was underdeveloped, given that they lacked personal traits to be a healthy partner in a relationship. For instance, Jody in *Baby Boy*—a drama detailing the immature romantic entanglements of a 20-year-old Black male, Jody—was portrayed as a self-centered childish male incapable of socio-emotional, financial, sexual or spiritual commitment to a single partner. Yet, by the end of the film he committed to Yvette, one of the mothers of his children, and their family. Ironically, the film did not allow time for the viewer to witness the carrying out of their new union. Prior to his revelation and commitment to his family, he did not display signs of fidelity, trust, nor commitment. Thus, the audience is left to wonder if Jody actually possesses the ability to maintain the relationship in a healthy and mutually fulfilling state. Similarly, in *Love Jones*—a romantic drama depicting the romance of two young African Americans, Darius and Nina—the characters are not represented as having the attributes of honesty, selflessness and commitment. Both Darius and Nina allow their pride and personal insecurities to override their willingness to love each other, and it is only when they momentarily put their egos aside that they chose love—and then the story ends. In both films the characters' display of selfishness compromises their ability to be committed partners in healthy relationships. Therefore, when they make the choice at the end of each movie to pursue love, we must question if love is actually possible and can it be sustained.

Not only are viable character traits missing in each of the storylines, but each must make major personal sacrifices in relation to family and/or their careers, as in the case of *Love Jones*. An illustration of this can be found in *Jason's Lyric*, a Black romantic drama set in an economically devasted community, engulfed in violence that tells the love story of Jason and Lyric. Both are surrounded by family drama and crimes that challenge the potential of their romantic relationship. For example, in order to pursue their relationship, both must sacrifice their relationships with their immediate family members, and both of their brothers are involved in violent crimes. Essentially, they must abandon the African cultural values of family and community in order to achieve love. While Jason struggles to commit to both love and family, he is torn and forced to decide to relinquish one, the family. In this struggle, he jeopardizes his safety and freedom and that of the woman he loves. In the end, Jason and Lyric lose their relationships with their families and must leave their community in an to attempt to build their own union. In each of these films, the characters are fractured, lacking essential qualities needed for healthy relationships.

Another important aspect of romantic relationships and marriage among Africana people is the role of family and models of marriage. (Chapman 1997; Franklin 1997) Illustrated in all three films is the lack of sustained healthy marriages. Only in *Love Jones*, one of Darius' friendships stories, include a married couple; however, their relationship is struggling and leads to the wife leaving their family home. Additionally, the sage advice of elders from the family and community is generally missing from the storylines. Lyric (*Jason's Lyric*) is left to solicit relationship advice from a friend who is in a toxic and dangerous love affair. Jody (*Baby Boy*) has his mother to turn to; however, he does not value her advice. as she has struggled to establish a lasting romantic relationship. The thread of tragic and unhealthy love has been woven throughout the representations of Black romantic couples, yet increasingly there has been an investment in transforming the narratives of Black love. Now, the possibilities of Black love are being reimagined outside of the racialized tropes of Black hypersexuality, violence and poverty. Alternatively, Black love is being imagined with depth and width, spanning beyond the confines of two wounded souls hoping for real love.

The 2020 romance drama, *The Photograph*, directed by Stella Meghie, who is also credited for the screenplay, conceptualized Black love among two mature, multifaceted adults, Mae Morton and Michael Block. The couple consciously step into love despite fears and uncertainty; and their hopefulness for love is realistic as its possibility is displayed in the film through another couple, Kyle and Asia. The established longstanding romantic relationship among two Black adults as a model for genuine healthy love serves as a reference point for the potential of genuine love. This is especially important for Mae, given that her immediate reference point for romantic love unfolds through her discovery of her mother and father's past romance. Mae worries that, like her mother she will allow her own fear to override her ability to love. To combat their doubts, both Mae and Michael seek the advice of family, friends, and elders to guide them in their journey for love. It is these examples, advice, and both Mae and Michael's willingness to step outside of their own comfort zone that allows them to experience love with each other.

In terms of television shows, in both *Queen Sugar* (2016-2019) and *Cherish the Day* (2020) Ava DuVernay unpacks the burdens of racism and classism and the impact of Black families and Black love. While her characters are not without flaws, it is the complexities of each character and their interactions with others that provide a richness to their relational experiences. These shows also have embedded within their storylines examples of committed loving relationships. *Queen Sugar* chronicles the family reunion of the Bordelon siblings—Charley, Nova and Ralph Angel, after the unsuspected tragic loss of their father. Within the television series there is a plethora of varying romantic entanglements that are explored and flushed out, and then reimagined. Violet, the aunt to the Bordelon siblings, and Hollywood's relationships serve as a grounding anchor for the younger adults and couples around them. While both characters have their own insecurities and flaws, the maturity of their love allows them to commit to marriage and a lifetime together. Both are willing to make personal sacrifices that do not compromise their own families and desires but instead helps fulfill the other's needs and aspirations. Ralph Angel and Darla's relationship comes full circle in its unfolding of the many layers of love— and given that the series is still going, it would not be surprising to see their relationship take a full 360 again. As for Charley, Nova and Ralph Angel, they are constantly challenged by each other and their family and friends to develop healthy loving relationships based in honesty and respect. While these relationships are not perfect, they do not need to be; instead they offer endless possibilities of love.

Apparent in both *Queen Sugar* and *Cherish the Day* is the presence of family and community, each demonstrating their investment in the romantic couples' journey for love. *Cherish the Day* (2020) is a new television series on the OWN network, created and produced by Ava DuVernay. The show uses single day storylines, for each episode, to disentangle the process of love for Gently and Evan. After a chance encounter at a library, Gently and Evan journey together on a rocky yet inspiring romance. Gently relies on the advice and support of the elders in her life, including her adoptive father, uncles and mentor, Miss Luma Lee. Their advice coaches her into making informed decisions that leads to her relationship and marriage to Evan. Likewise, Evan has the support and advice of his family and friends to aid him in his pursuit of love with Gently, although the advice he receives is discouraging at times. When the couple fails to heed the advice of their love ones, it is then that the couple's relationship comes to an end. When the couple reunite at a birthday party, it is clear that they still love each other, and the prospect of a rekindled love is presented. The series reimagines the struggles of love among Black couples and the endless opportunities for romance, love and devotion, while incorporating Black cultural values of communalism and familyhood. (Staples 1997; Sudarkasa 1997)

Presently, Black love have been overwhelmingly displayed through scripted and semi-scripted reality television shows. Through this medium Black love has been showcased as dangerous and toxic. Gammage 2015; Alameen-Shavers 2016) Departing from these unhealthy representations of Black relationships, Black women, using culturally authentic lens, seek to project truth to the lived realities of Black romantic couples. *Black Love* (2017-2020), created by Codie Elaine Oliver, highlights the unscripted honest and complex love stories of real Black couples. This docu-series sheds light on the intricacies of marriage among Blacks and the couples' willingness to be vulnerable and committed to love. Fantasy and toxic narratives of love are put aside for authentic discussions of healthy Black relationships, which have proven to be of interest to Black media consumers, as the show is now in its fourth season.

Indeed, the shifting projections of Black families and Black male-female relations by Black women media creators have changed the trajectory of the unidimensional narrative of Blackness, as they have clearly opted for the last of the "three distinct reactions to the dominant standard—acceptance, adjustment, and rejection," which is REJECTION (Hudson-Withers, "Toni Morrison's World of Topsy-Turvydom" 132). While racial tropes of Black families and Black love continue to be broadcasted in the mass media, these are no longer the singular narrative for consumers. Diversifying the media portrayals of Black families is proven to be viable and sustainable. The telling of our stories from our varied perspectives enhances the significance of our culture in our lives and affirms the need for the media to be more inclusive of Black voices and ideas. This is what Africana Womanism promotes—the prioritization of race and class, and gender, too, coupled with family centrality and positive male-female relationships, truly needed to be reflected in authentic Black love films as evidenced in life.

## *Social Justice Driven Counter-Narratives*

For decades the experiences of African Americans with the criminal justice systems have predominately been told from the vantage point of the American justice system, which has historically viewed and treated Blacks in America as criminal and as a threat to the American sovereignty. These media images have largely been created and produced by white Americans who have used the media to perpetuate America's racist views of Blacks. Early film productions such as *Birth of a Nation* (1915) produced by D. W. Griffith and adopted from Thomas Dixon Jr.'s novel, *The Clansman: An Historical Romance of the Ku Klux Klan*, depicted racist ideas about Black Americans, which framed Blacks as unintelligent, criminal and hypersexual, which helped rationalize the public brutality and attack on Blackness. This film set the stage for the cinematic criminal mistreatment of Africanness/Blackness on screen and is still applauded today.

Over the next two centuries, images of Blacks in American television and film continued to reinforce white racists supremacist propaganda that advanced anti-Blackness as the inherent culture of America. However, as Black media producers entered the industry, they began to challenge the stereotypes by generating more robust representations of Blackness. Unfortunately, many of these films and shows were drowned out by the industry, which was almost exclusively controlled by white men. While there was some marketing to Black media consumers, media representations in the late 20th century diverged very little from the stereotypical portrayals of the early 1900s. Instead, modernized images of Black criminality and hypersexuality emerged in the form of thugs, pimps, bitches and whores. (bell hooks 1992; Gammage 2015; Allison 2016)

The current demand for a more just and inclusive society in America has gave way for Africana media producers to create imagery that reflect the call for social justice. Africana-melanated women have taken up this challenge and have invested their creative energies in sharing and retelling the stories of Blacks in America who have been victimized and terrorized by law enforcement and the American criminal justice system. Ava DuVernay's LEAP initiative focus on changing the lens of the narrative for which police misconduct and brutality is framed shifts the media discourse to unearthing genuine narratives of Black experiences. Fighting systematic racism in the media, especially as it pertains to the representations of African Americans' encounters with the criminal justice system, works in conjunction with the social and political movements, aiming to dismantle the inherent racial injustice in America and affirm the rights and freedoms of Black people. The problematic white-centric depictions of Blacks as criminals in news media and mass media in general have bolstered the anti-Black perceptions that are deeply rooted in the American psyche. Self-representations, which depict the intimate human experiences of Black Americans with the cruel and unjust systems in America, directly interrogates the myth of justice in America and repositions how we think about justice for African Americans.

One such attempt can be observed in the revolutionary film *When They See Us* (2019) created by Ava DuVernay. The film retells the story of five Black and Latinx teens from the Harlem community in New York City, known as the Central Park Five, and their grotesque entrapment in the criminal justice system in America. Antron McCray, Kevin Richardson, Raymond Santana, Yusef Salaam, and Korey Wise were wrongfully convicted in 1989 for the assault of a white woman in Central Park. The politics and media coverage of the case applied the same racist tropes of the Black male as pathologically hypersexual and criminal and a threat to white womanhood, as broadcasted in the film *Birth of a Nation* (1915).

Post their exoneration, Ava DuVernay challenged herself and the media to retell the stories of each man and produce a counter narrative of their experiences with a social justice lens. The film shows the interconnectedness of the justice process and racial indifference for the rights and lives of Black Americans. The systemic process of racism is unpacked to reveal how the justice systems and its gatekeepers—the offices, attorneys, judges and juries—work collectively in upholding racist ideologies and disenfranchising the rights of the vulnerable Black populations. In the film the false assumptions about the youth's guilt is exposed through the lack of physical evidence connecting the youth to the case, and how they were forcibly coerced into admitting their involvement in a crime of which they were completely innocent. Let me be clear; the film did not apply a fantasy-based portrayal of the youth and their fight for freedom. It applied an historical and ethnographic assessment of evidence and experiences, including the auto-biographic stories of the youth and their families. Truth-telling in media-making elevated *When They See Us* from a simple biopic to a much-needed social justice counter narrative. Following the release and success of the film calls for further justice for the now adult men ensued in the form of holding the officers of the court accountable for their gross "miscarriage of justice"—to date, criminal charges have been filed against the prosecutors or officers involved in the case.

Counter narratives rooted in social justice more accurately contextualize the everyday inequalities and discrimination experienced by Black Americans. Often the voices and stories of Black women and men are eclipsed by racist practices and policies carried out by all levels of law enforcement. Capturing the historic legacy of African Americans and the American justice system, the documentary *13th* (2016) by Ava DuVernay chronicles the deeply embedded racism of the criminal justice system and its predatory nature that forces Blacks into the prison industrial complex. Evidence based social and political commentary guides the viewer through the long-standing racial targeting used to disenfranchise Blacks rights, and how these systems of oppression are commonplace in American law enforcement and the entire criminal justice system. Its release in 2016 came at a time when social movements on the part of the Black community, demanding justice in a system that has proven itself to be incapable of delivering justice for all Americans, particularly African Americans, were on a rise. The film echoed the concerns and critiques of the American criminal justice system as championed by the Black Lives Matter movement; therefore, the film became a form of media advocacy.

The hashtag #BlackLiveMatter was created in 2013 by Alicia Garza, Patrisse Cullors, and Opal Tometi as a conscious Black affirmation movement designed to expose and dismantle systems of oppression that marginalize the lives of Blacks globally. The momentum of the movement has led to local and national protest and legislative reform agendas.

The discourse and public sentiment surrounding the current Black Lives Matter protest questions the legitimacy of African American social movements and direct-action protest. Sparked after the murder of George Floyd, recorded on video, and the failure to bring criminal charges against the civilians who murdered Ahmaud Arbrey, and the offices who murdered Breonna Taylor, Black Lives Matter global protest of 2020 demands for the deconstruction of systemic racism in the criminal justice system by calling for the abolishment of state funding for police and the systematic restructuring of the criminal proceedings process. However, these protests have been accused of threatening the sovereignty of the nation. U.S. President Donald Trump has attacked Black Lives Matter—activities, calling it anti-American and destructive. As president, Trump operates as the national voice of America; thus, his rendering of the Black Lives Matter as illegitimate, counterproductive, and disillusioned, discredits and dismisses its perceived purpose, thus, validates public institutions and officials' failure to enact justice for the countless number of Black lives unjustly taken by America.

Black media producers have published counter narratives that attempt to disrupt this line of thinking about Black social movements and protest. *Selma* (2014) directed by Ava DuVernay, took a humanistic view of African Americans struggles for equality during the Civil Rights Movement and the 1965 voting rights march, led by Dr. Martin Luther King Jr. from Selma to Montgomery, Alabama. The biopic demonstrates the great personal sacrifices, both physical and socio-emotional, taken by African Americans in an attempt to improve and advance America as a nation. The patriotic nature of the march, as represented in the film, challenges the American perception of Black protest. The film grounds Black social movements in the duty and responsibility of citizenship to enhance the country.

Television dramas such as *Shots Fired* (2017), whose Executive Producer is Gina Prince-Bythewood, attempts to explore the civil unrest and cry for justice surrounding the unjust killings of Black men, women and children in America by police officers and the resulting failure of the criminal justice system to hold its law enforcement officials accountable. The one-time series portrays African Americans' legitimate distrust in the criminal justice system, still with their continued hopefulness for an equal, more just institution and nation. Thus, in the film we see the convergence of the legacy of institutional racism, as well as African Americans desire for justice and equality as citizens.

Likewise, *Queen & Slim* (2019), an American drama film, shadowing the pursuit of freedom by Slim and Queen after they protected themselves from the violence of a police officers, which resulted in their being considered cop killers, represents the fears and legacy of trauma experienced by African Americans every time they are pulled over by a police officer. Directed by Melina Matsoukas, *Queen and Slim* encompasses an empathic look at the vulnerability of Black bodies in America. Songs such as *I Can't Breathe* by H.E.R., speak to this same terrifying existence for African Americans. The lyrics state:

> Started a war screaming "Peace" at the same time
> All the corruption, injustice, the same crimes
> Always a problem if we do or don't fight
> And we die, we don't have the same rights
> What is a gun to a man that surrenders?
> What's it gonna take for someone to defend us?
> If we all agree that we're equal as people
> Then why can't we see what is evil? (H.E.R. 2020)

The criminalization of innocent beautiful Black bodies through the lens of law enforcement takes a haunting toll on African Americans and restricts their ability to enjoy the privileges and liberties of citizenship, which is yet to be fully granted. Paradoxically, white America is disconnected from this fear that entraps the African American. Therefore, media such as *Queen and Slim* demonstrates the impact of racism in America society on the African American experience and the responsibility of the nation to address these gross injustices.

Undeniably, social justice driven counter narratives serve to challenge and transform institutional racism and aim to dismantle the racist tropes and ideologies that cripple the American psyche, practices and culture. Through socially conscious revolutionary media, Black women are painting masterpieces that point us to the justice that African Americans seek daily and have been pursuing for centuries. These storytelling platforms give credence to the voices of Black women writers who seek to create authentic thought-provoking media that helps move the nation forward.

## *Broadcasting Celebrations of Blackness*

Combating the predominance of negative images of Blackness in the mass media, Black women's celebrations of Blackness in the media serve as a form of Black racial pride, while at the same time operating as advocates of Black cultural values as a means to empower Africana people globally. Implicit in the construction of celebratory images of Africana women and families in the media is the embracing of historical legacies, cultural phenomenon, and the African worldview system, working together to construct media that authentically reflects what it means to be African or of African descent. Moreover, how we are authentically identified as Africana Womanists, rather than being named outside of our cultural reality, demonstrates the power of restorative justice in the media via recognizing the long-standing practice of authentic existence for the advancement of the Africana family. (Hudson-Weems 1993, 2019; Gammage 2015)

Highlighting the historic legacies of Black women through the media, biographical cinematic productions aspire to recount the lived experiences, struggles and triumphs of extraordinary Black women. Black women have often had to experience life in America as the first and at times the only one of their race and gender. From entry into colleges, to traveling to space, and heading governmental agencies and major corporations, Black women have embarked on journeys that have placed them as the first African American woman, and often first woman to achieve accomplishments of these magnitudes. These women's stories have made their way onto the screen over the years, with films like *Hidden Figures* (2016), *Harriet* (2019), and *The Rosa Parks Story* (2002) that chronicle social advocacy and activism among Black women. Most recently, *Self Made: Inspired by the Life of Madam C. J. Walker* (2020), directed by Demane Davis and Kasi Lemmons, debuted on Netflix in February 2020 and narrates how a Black woman, whose parents were enslaved, became the first female African American self-made millionaire in the early 1900s. The film reinforces Black cultural and political principles of self-reliance and Black economic mobility that has been practiced by African Americans for decades. These were the exact principles promoted by the Black Panther Party and the Black Power Movement in the 1960s and 1970s and are part of the current Black Lives Matter movement of 2020.

Although met with controversy over the accuracy of the film, the film nevertheless was able to broadcast these principles as natural and necessary for Black Americans. The timing and relevance of the movie is what makes it even more important. Hence, its released came at time when Black activist have been advancing the economic support for Black owned businesses by Black consumers. In fact, in summer 2020 the Black community advocated for a month-long Buy-Black campaign commencing on June 19, 2020, through July 19, 2020. Promotions of Black consumers boycotts from shopping seasons and companies that fail to respect the humanity of Africana people are a part of the historic trajectory to uplift the Black community and the race. Thus, what *Self Made: Inspired by the Life of Madam C. J. Walker* provides is validation for Black economic self-reliance and the film reinforces the cultural values that have strengthened African Americans and have built Black wealth. The genius of the film is embedded in its indirect achievement of these very principles. While some have focused on the accuracy of Madam C. J. Walker's business practices, others have been able to gain knowledge of the usefulness and power of the Black dollar and Black businesses.

In an attempt to reinforce and fortify the significance of our contributions to the world and the human experience, Africana-melanated women media producers tell the stories of themselves, their mothers and grandmothers, their sisters and girlfriends. These self-representations unmistakably culminate in the affirmation of our humanity, cultures and experiences. Thus, storytelling is in and of itself a celebration of Blackness, for too long have Black women's stories gone unheard of by the general public and the world. African people are of an oral tradition, a storytelling tradition; which has served to past down family histories from generation to generation. Therefore, it makes sense that we use the media to tell our stories on a grand scale, becoming imprinted on the fabric of America and thus have the potential to become eternal.

Emboldened with the knowledge and strength of her heritage, Beyoncé has launched celebrations of her Blackness as a reclamation of her identity. As the most acclaimed Black female performing artist of the 21st century, Beyoncé has chosen to use the power of her celebrity to advocate for the just and humane treatment of Blacks through her art. In July 2020 she released *Black is King*, a musical film celebrating the wonders of Blackness globally and its impact on the world. In a 2020 interview on ABC's *Good Morning America* (GMA) Beyoncé explains the significance and purpose of *Black is King*. She states:

> My hope for this film is that it shifts the global perception of the word Black, which has always meant inspiration, and love, and strength and beauty to me. But *Black is King* means Black is regal and rich in history, in purpose and lineage. (Beyoncé)

The visual album illuminates the diversity of Blackness, its beauty and strength. From African clothing, hair styles and dance moves, to African cultural and spiritual phenomenon, the musical film marvels at the uniqueness and power of that which is Black. With songs like "Nile," "Brown Skin Girl," and "My Power," Beyoncé invokes the spirit of Africaness in a way that unapologetically affirms Blackness. In her song *Black Parade*, Beyoncé weaves together Black heritage, cultural pride, injustice and the power of social movements:

On fours, all black
All chrome, black-owned
Black tints, matte black
Walked by, my window down, let 'em see who in it
Crack a big smile (ding)
Go figure, me and Jigga, fifty 'leven children
They like, "Chick, how?"
I charge my crystals in a full moon
You could send them missiles, I'ma send my goons
Baby sister reppin' Yemaya (Yemaya)
Trust me, they gon' need an army
Rubber bullets bouncin' off me
Made a picket sign off your picket fence
Take it as a warning
Waist beads from Yoruba (woo)
Four hunnid billi', Mansa Musa (woo)
Stroll line to the barbeque
Put us any damn where, we gon' make it look cute
Pandemic fly on the runway, in my hazmat
Children runnin' through the house and my art, all black
Ancestors on the wall, let the ghosts chit-chat
(Ancestors on the wall, let the ghosts chit-chat)
Hold my hands, we gon' pray together
Lay down, face down in the gravel
We wearin' all attire white to the funeral
Black love, we gon' stay together
Curtis Mayfield on the speaker (woo)
Lil' Malcolm, Martin, mixed with momma Tina (woo)
Need another march, lemme call Tamika (woo)
Need peace and reparation for my people (woo)
Fuck these laid edges, I'ma let it shrivel up (shrivel up)
Fuck this fade and waves, I'ma let it dread all up (dread all up)
Put your fists up in the air, show black love (show black love)
Motherland drip on me, motherland, motherland drip on me (Beyoncé 2020)

Here, Beyoncé successfully promotes Black ownership, African spiritual systems and social justice advocacy. The story that unfolds is the story of the Black experience.

Empowering and motivating media that celebrates our Black pride, beauty, resistance and resilience is increasingly transforming how we, and the world, perceive our Blackness. Advancing the multidimensional layers of Blackness as glorious, Black women have also used social media hashtags like #MelaninPoppin, #BlackGirlMagic, and #BlackGirlsRock to advance the brilliance of Blackness. Seemingly the projections/suggestions of Dr. Mark Christian, over a decade ago in the Afterword to Hudson-Weems' edited volume, for securing total presence, is being played out:

> . . . We are now in an age of unsurpassed technological revolution. The next generation of Africana scholars [artists, producers, etc.] has the potential to become key players in providing the necessary knowledge needed to combat what could be deemed "technological racism" and the exclusion of Africana paradigms in mainstream cyberpsace. . . . Therefore, [we] will not only need to build on the works of the past generations, it will also entail having an input into the production of knowledge via Africana cyberspace debates and discourse for the next step for interpreting, preserving and actualizing Africana theory and thought in this new millennium. (Christian, Afterword in *Contemporary Africana Theory* 464-465)

This new wave of publicly displaying Black pride through media puts rich diverse representations of Africana-melanated people at the world's fingertips. Thus, we are beginning to transform the media into a tool that we can use for social justice advocacy and racial upliftment.

# Bibliography

Alameen-Shavers, Antwanisha. (2016). ""The "Down Ass Bitch" in the Reality Television Show Love and Hip Hop: The Image of the Enduring Black Woman and her Unwavering Support of the Black Man." In *Black Women's portrayals on Reality Television: The New Sapphire* edited by Donnetrice C. Allison. Lanham: Lexington Books.

Allison, Donnetrice. 2016. *Black Women's Portrayals on Reality Television: The New Sapphire*. Lanham: Lexington Books.

Bennett, Dionne. 2010. "Looking for the 'Hood and Finding Community: South Central, Race, and Media. In *Black Los Angeles: American Dreams and Racial Realities*. Edited by Darnell Hunt and Ana-Christina Ramon. New York: New York University Press.

Beyoncé (Director). (2020). *Black is King*. [Film]. Disney Plus.

—. *Beyoncé Talks 'Black Is King' Release*. ABC Good Morning America. Retrieved from https://www.youtube.com/watch?v=MoaGOHMMiY4

—. (2020). *Black Parade* [Song]. On *The Lion King: The Gift* [Album]. Parkwood, Columbia.

Collins, Patricia Hill. 2005. *Black Sexual Politics: African American, Gender, and the New Racism*. New York: Routledge.

Chapman, Audrey B. 1997. "The Black Search for Love and Devotion." In *Black Families* (3rd ed.), edited by Harriet Pipes-McAdoo, 273-283. Thousand Oaks: Sage Publications.

Christian, Mark (2007). Afterword in *Contemporary Africana Theory, Thought and Action: A Guide to Africana Studies*. Trenton: African World Press, 461-45.

Dash, J. (Director). (2002). *The Rosa Parks Story* [Film]. CBS.

Davis, D., Lemmons, K. (Director). (2020). *Self Made: Inspired by the Life of Madam C. J. Walker* [Film]. Netflix.

DuVernay, Ava. 2019. Places Too Often Hidden: Ava DuVernay in conversation with Theaster Gates. Retrieved from https://m.youtube.com/watch?v=4ly9Jp6RHhI

—. (Director). (2016). *13th* [Film]. Netflix.

—. (Director). (2014). *Selma*. [Film]. Plan B Entertainment, Harpo Productions, Ingenious Media, Pathé, Cloud Eight Films.

—. (Director). (2019). *When They See Us* [Film]. Netflix.

—. (Executive Producer). (2020). *Cherish the Day* [TV series]. Oprah Winfrey Network.

—. (Executive Producer). (2016-present). *Queen Sugar* [TV series]. Oprah Winfrey Network.

Franklin, John Hope. 1997. "African American Families." In *Black Families* (3rd ed.), edited by Harriet Pipes-McAdoo, 5-8. Thousand Oaks: Sage Publications.

Gammage, Marquita M. (2015). *Representations of Black Women in the Media: The Damnation of Black Womanhood*. New York: Routledge.

Gray, Herman. 1995. *Watching Race: Television and the Struggle for "Blackness."* Minneapolis: University of Minnesota Press.

Griffith, D. W. (Director). (1915). *Birth of a Nation* [Film]. D. W. Griffith Corp.

H.E.R. (2020). *I Can't Breathe* [Song]. On *I Can't Breathe* [Album]. RCA Records.

Holland, G., Charles, M. (Executive Producers). (2019-present). *Cleo Speaks* [TV series]. Cleo TV.

hooks, bell. 1992. *Black Looks: Race and Representation*. Boston: South Ends Press, 1992.

Hudson-Weems, Clenora. (2010). *Africana Womanism: Reclaiming Ourselves*, Fifth Edition. London and New York: Routledge.

Hudson-Weems, Clenora. "*Beloved*: From Novel to Movie." *The Western Journal of Black Studies*. Vol. 23, No. 3, Fall 1999, 203-204.

Hudson-Withers, Clenora. "Toni Morrison's World of Topsy-Turveydom: A Methodological Explication of New Black Literary Criticism." *The Western Journal of Black Studies*. Vol. 23, No. 3, Fall 1986, 132-136.

Lemmons, K. (Director). (2019). *Harriet* [Film]. Perfect World Pictures.

Matsoukas, M. (Director). (2020). *Queen & Slim* [Film]. 3BlackDot, Bron Creative, Makeready, De La Revolución Films, Hillman Grad Productions.

McHenry, D. (Director). (1994). *Jason's Lyric* [Film]. Polygram Film Entertainment.

Meghie, S. (Director). (2020). *The Photograph* [Film]. Universal Pictures.

Melfi, T. (Director). (2016). *Hidden Figures* [Film]. Fox 2000 Pictures, Chernin Entertainment, Levantine Films

Moynihan, Daniel P. (n.d.). "History—Chapter IV. The Tangle of Pathology." *U.S. Department of Labor*, 1 May. https://www.dol.gov/oasam/programs/history/moynchapter4.htm

Oliver, C. E. (Executive Producer). (2017-present). *Black Love* [TV series]. Oprah Winfrey Network.

Parenti, Michael. 1992. *Make-Believe Media: The Politics of Entertainment*. New York: St. Martin's Press.

Prince-Bythewood, G. (executive Producer). (2017). *Shots Fired* [TV series]. Fox Broadcasting Company.

Rae, I. (Executive Producer). (2016-present). *Insecure* [TV series]. HBO.

Singleton, J. (Director). (2001). *Baby Boy* [Film]. Columbia Pictures.

Staples, Robert. 1997. "An Overview of Race and Martial Status." In *Black Families* (3rd ed.), edited by Harriet Pipes-McAdoo, 269-272. Thousand Oaks: Sage Publications.

Sudarkasa, Niara.1997. "African American Families and Family Values." In *Black Families* (3rd ed.), edited by Harriet Pipes-McAdoo, 9-40. Thousand Oaks: Sage Publications.

Witcher, T. (Director). (1997). *Love Jones* [Film]. New Line Cinema.

# 5

# OUR CHILDREN, TOO, NEED MODELS:
# A LETTER TO AUNT DAISY—
# THE SPIRIT OF AN AFRICANA WOMANIST

## *ALICE FAYE DUNCAN*

Literature transforms human experience and reflects it back to us. In that reflection, we can see our own lives and experiences as part of the larger human experience. Reading then becomes a means of self-affirmation, and readers often seek their mirrors in books. (Bishop, "Mirrors, Windows & Sliding Glass Doors," ix)

**31 July 2020**
**Memphis, Tennessee**

Dear Aunt Daisy,

I am writing to you on my 53$^{rd}$ birthday. Cousin Tee called this morning with birthday wishes from Baltimore. She also called to check on your health during this dreadful pandemic and to reminisce about brighter days when your North Memphis home on Alameda Street was her childhood home, filled with love, laughter, and loads of sunlight, evocative of the 1979 classic disco by the R&B vocal group, Sister Sledge – *We Are Family!*

Cousin Tee went way-back to recall those years I would visit on weekends and throughout the summer when my mother was a graduate student and needed a babysitter. I was a bratty kid and Cousin Tee was an annoyed teenager, who somehow learned to stop my aimless chatter with books, my constant and very best friends. Tee used to banish me and my prattling to your sewing room, lined with cedar bookshelves. My irritation with being sent away never lasted long because somehow, between tattered Bibles and commentaries, the shelves contained dime store picture books, a set of illustrated encyclopedias, and a smattering of Dr. Seuss' classics, like *Green Eggs and Ham* and *Put Me in the Zoo*. As an emergent reader, the makeshift collection suited my ability and always captured my complete attention.

Speaking with Cousin Tee made me remember how quiet moments in your sewing room offered me exhilarating opportunities to hone my facility with language and words. If I was not reading books, I used the time alone to write little stories and poems on scrap paper that I pulled from your dining room table, which also served as a desk where you paid bills and wrote letters to family and friends.

Cousin Tee consistently achieved her mission, which was to make me hush or leave her alone to socialize in the living-room with her sweetheart—Wayne. They dated throughout high school. In my young mind, the kissy pair would abide in love forever. But Wayne was never one of your favorite people and as you hoped that ravishing romance did not survive the college years. Tee married Derrick, who kinda looked like Wayne. They had the same pecan complexion and Jimi Hendrix Afro. And while Cousin Tee assumed that I would certainly grow up to be literate, she never dreamed that my time alone in your sewing room would destine me to write books for Black children, who do not find their bright faces in the Dr. Seuss classics. Indeed, they, too, must see shining images of themselves in literature to strengthen their self-esteem.

Are you curious about the appearance of this letter in your mailbox? After all, it is not your birthday. And across your 100 years of living, you and I have never corresponded in this way. In the past, you have mailed me birthday and holiday greeting cards. And in the past for Mother's Day, I have mailed you a variety of fancy cards, always complimented with cash surprises. But never have we exchanged handwritten, heart-felt letters on stationary. You can blame the inspiration for this inaugural letter to you on Cousin Tee. She had said this morning that she had wondered if, at your age, you were still writing long-winding missives to your nonagenarian and centenarian relatives and friends. Neither of us knew if you were, but your penned reply will determine that answer.

Today as we spirited back in time. Tee remembered and talked about, in details, one famous letter you wrote to Cousin Jim Ella, who was still living in Toledo. It was the seventies. Tee said that you drafted the note in pencil. And with the indelible loops and swirls of your cursive script, for Jim's records, you listed our family tree, which spreads across the 19th Century from a Virginia slave plantation to the rural plains of West Tennessee, where Jim and you were born in Eads during the 1920s.

As Tee remembered reading your unsealed letter on the dining room table, I remembered festive Christmas dinners seated around that same mahogany table, crowded with kinfolk. The table was made for six, but you would extend the leaf and squeeze-in seven more bodies. When I was a child, your husband, Uncle Ed was dead, leaving you to sit at the head of your table with your favorite brother, my Grandaddy Hezekiah— seated on your right side. *We Are Family!*

During each Christmas dinner, the family eagerly listened as you described the devastation of losing your father to a heart attack, when you were just five years old. With each holiday, my ears picked-up more interesting family facts that were new to me. The greatest pain would reach your twinkling eyes when you remembered 1936, the year you quit the 11th grade because in the middle of the Great Depression, your mother, Bell, was a sharecropper, who needed help providing food and shelter for your baby sister, Evelyn, and you.

This story moved me the most. In your search for work, a white woman hired you to clean her home. Up until 1936, you had been a dedicated student at the segregated Fayette County Training School. By your own admission, you were a good student and a "terrible maid." So, the white woman took extra care to explain and demonstrate the fine skills and rituals of housekeeping, which she had observed from her pervious Black housekeepers. Her instructions shaped your destiny. You cleaned houses pass your 70th birthday. The Black maids were the real models that you could pattern your newly acquired skills after, assigned skills for many Black women, posing no competition to white women, who were privy to have such financially reasonable assistance.

You harbored no shame concerning your humble profession. Whenever you shared this personal herstory about your life, I remember your gratitude for employment, though your forfeited education was a hardened regret that lingered in your tone. And even at an early age, when I listened to your anecdotes about missing school to help your mama, I gleaned the implicit meaning. Love requires sacrifice and education is a priceless prize.

This morning as I ended my call with Cousin Tee, an urgency to write this letter rested on me. I know what you are thinking. Why waste time writing, when it is my daily task during this pandemic to prepare your afternoon meals and tidy your home where you live alone. My visit today will give us plenty of time to chat and chuckle like we did and still do today at your dining room table of frequent occasions. I can speak and share my immediate thoughts in person. But spoken words are ephemeral. Speech is temporary and fleeting. To write or publish an expression is to have and hold it as a permanent record. And what I want to say to you on my birthday is beyond blather about the weather. What I want to express is more urgent than the mind-boggling despair that has consumed my summer in the wake of the ravaging coronavirus and the lynching of George Floyd, who was murdered by Minneapolis police. I want to talk about the real you, Aunt Daisy, and what you represent for me and for all of us through the years. I want to talk about how you have lived your life, with a profound love for your family and the insistence upon sticking together, through thick and thin, always remembering that, no matter what, *We Are Family!*

As a particular revelation has captured my understanding, I am compelled to put these words to paper because tomorrow is not certain to arrive. And if it doesn't arrive, this letter will stand as proof that you, Daisy Wash Malone, lived your simple and conquering life as an Africana Womanist, both family-centered and in concert with your male companion. You would never define your existence in such terms. But it's true. As the Black mother of five children and wife to Ed Malone, you stood at his side as an equal helpmate and companion, in the true spirit of Dr. Clenora Hudson-Weems' "Africana Womanism." With meager wages from domestic work, you helped the Firestone factory worker, the love of your life, feed the family and purchase a sturdy home that remains a refuge of safety and solitude, even now. You Aunt Daisy, like a devoted Africana Womanist, not only mothered your children – Wes, Bell, Lou, Mack, and Tee – but the extended Black family, which you lovingly nurtured with an ever-present maternal fire. You shaped the physical and emotional development of nieces, nephews, and neighborhood kids, who grew-up eating from your table and listening to your stories about life in the country, where there was no electricity, no indoor plumbing, where Jim Crow ruled the land.

I want the record to show that as a beneficiary of your love and light, I received your gifts intellectually. But I also listened to you with my soul and spirit. My heart heard you clearly. And by the time I reached high school, your oral herstories had created a hunger in me to read books on the subject of segregation and the American Civil Rights Movement. My favorite authors by then were Mildred Taylor, Alice Childress, and Patricia McKissick. These Black women writers in particular inspired me to consider words as a viable profession.

It was during college that I began to really understand the magic of the dime-store picture books and Dr. Seuss classics in your quiet sewing room. Graduation was near. I needed a course of action. How would I use my words to make a living? What kind of books would I write? A variety of chance encounters and divine impressions helped me assess my place in the world. The Holy Spirit spoke to me. A dream was coming into view. After college graduation, I visited Alameda Street to share my lofty ambition. I said there was a demand on my creativity to write picture books that would allow Black children to see their majestic faces, too, on the printed page. You smiled brightly and said, "God is in the plan."

I was 23 years old. That was thirty years ago. And in the passing of time, I have published ten books that celebrate Black children, the joy of their Black lives, and the resiliency of their Black ancestry. In this letter, what I want to say for the record is that life is a circle, and "we're all in it together. Family-Centrality--that's it; we're going nowhere without the other" (Hudson-Weems, "Africana Womanism: I Got Your Back, Boo" 120). That is to say that all that you have given me is the gift that I am giving. And no virus or aberration of racial violence and terror can ever annihilate this beautiful, empowering thing – Black Love, for *We Are Family*!

I love you, Aunt Daisy.

Alice Faye

# Bibliography

Bishop, Rudine Sims. "Mirrors, Windows and Sliding Glass Doors" in *Perspectives: Choosing and Using Books for the Classroom*. Vol. 6, No. 3. Summer 1990.

Hudson-Weems, Clenora. *Africana Womanism: Reclaiming Ourselves*, Fifth Edition. London and New York: Routledge Press, 2019.

Sledge Sisters. *We Are Family*, Rhythm & Blues Disco. Nile Rogers and Bernard Edwards, Producers. New York City: Power Station, 1979.

# 6

# AFRICANA WOMANISM:
# THE IMPORTANCE OF RELIGION & POLITICS
# IN AFRICANA LIFE

## *APRIL C. E. LANGLEY, PHD*

Africana-Melanated women have long demonstrated their understanding that religion and politics operate in tandem. That is, they have simultaneously celebrated faith and spirituality through the sacred call to fulfill the secular demands for global, national, and local civic response to our shared struggles and triumphs. They have, in short, rigorously sought to make manifest a biblical mandate for a better world "on earth, as it is in heaven."i As such Africana women, who have all too often been mis-characterized or considered "the least of them"ii in this world, have labored to lift and liberate themselves and others, as they exercise free will and existential power in a myriad of contexts. Clearly, it's a bit more complicated for Africana women, because they are triply oppressed by racism, classism, and sexism—structures which systematically undermine their humanity. Rather than merely surviving under looming and ever-present threats of physical and metaphysical brutality, their socio-political religious work—historically and contemporarily—has and continues to make possible Africana women's ability to engage in the process of living and thriving, on their own terms.

For social justice workers like Tarana Burke, her faith represents the cornerstone of her activism. Religion is the ground on which she "stands in the gap"iii on behalf of those silenced and violated black girls and women, and the unnatural suppressed voices of their mothers, sisters, aunties, and grandmothers. These terrorized victims are so traumatized by visible acts of violence that they hush themselves and thereby silently and unwittingly acquiesce to the will of their victimizers. It is out of such a moment of self-silencing that a powerful movement to reclaim self evolves, compelled to join forces and be counted among that broader community of authentic Black women, models who continue the rich legacy of true Africana womanism. For example, there is that instance of one Africana woman's inability to utter comforting and necessary healing words to a young black girl who attempted to share her story of sexual abuse from her stepfather. Thus, a chasm was constructed where a bond between Africana woman and child should have been built. This is a spiritual disruption of sacred and secular proportion. This would be a catalyst to not only embrace the "least among us"iv but also for challenging and protecting our raised voices from being coopted by wealthy white women's agendas that have little to do with economically disadvantaged Africana women, the overarching class factor that interconnects with all aspects of Black life. Burke identifies the racism and sexism at the heart of criticisms of this global movement against injustice that targets Africana people.

Departing from what might be misread as a feminist or gender prioritized moment, she makes clear the interconnected collective contemporary struggles and movements for Black people respective of gender. In a 2020 BBC interview, Burke reminds listeners that "what we're seeing in Black Lives Matter . . . is *our* response to the response that *we* get. Black people aren't the only ones being killed by the police." But it is "the response when a *Black* person is killed by a police officer" which is most troubling. She first addresses state-sanctioned race-based responses to the violence and oppression against all Africana people, respective of gender. Burke then focuses on the response of Africana women's calls for justice: "White supremacy says, 'Black women you might have vision, you may have voice, you may have leadership, but I can't see that vision, voice, or leadership until you have a conduit that shows it to me through a white gaze'" (*BBC Newsbeat* July 9, 2020). v Burke requires no such conduit or instrument to fulfill her vision, raise her voice, and lead this movement as she is centered religiously, morally, and politically. Burke's faith, however, should not be read as an opiate that will magically relieve the pain that Africana women experience, far from it. Indeed, she reminds us of the spiritual force that empowers and enables her to go beyond a moment, or movement, toward what really matters: "You can't do this kind of work without being grounded in a faith that showed possibilities. Christianity is, really, when you take away all the pomp and circumstance, it's about hope and possibility."vi

Africana Womanism provides critical lenses that radically invite us to consider the depth and breadth of possibilities that the interwoven spiritual and political hold for Black women. Affirming, through their faith, the deep, profound spiritual understanding that in the final analysis,

> . . . the survival of our entire race [men, women and children] as a primary concern for Africana women will have to come from Africana men and women working together. If Africana men and women are fighting within

the community, they are ultimately defeating themselves on all fronts (Hudson-Weems 19).

Assuredly, Africana women here highlight the critical and necessary links between spiritual and felt needs of Black women, in perpetuity. Africana Melanated women leave no stone unturned in their quest for social justice and human rights. Cross-culturally, Black women, whether claiming Christianity, Islam, Judaism, Buddhism, Rastafarianism, African or other indigenous spirituality, agnosticism, atheistic, freethinking, vii or any diverse variety of practices and belief systems, find ways to integrate spirituality as they resist, challenge, and overthrow structures of oppression and actions designed to dehumanize Africana people both spiritually and physically.

Thus, Africana women, historically and contemporarily, have named not only themselves, they have also called out those tyrants and persecutors who would use coercive tactics to enslave, disenfranchise, and victimize them on all levels. Most important, they have christened and identified the spiritual as a source of liberation and power which placed them on the moral, figurative, and literal high ground to defy and attack race, class, and gender subjugation and oppression. By naming and articulating their God (or gods) and the meaning that such figures of otherworldly divinity connote and denote for their earthly existence, they command a sovereign power through which they channel their autonomy and self-determination. Ironically, such a God was often characterized by others as "white" and "male" and by some as inaccessible and incomprehensible to the supposedly inferior souls of Black women. Indeed, Black women—especially Christian and protestant women during the antebellum era—articulated the meaning of a seemingly foreign faith on their own terms. Nonetheless, Black women would not be denied ownership of their souls, of their inner selves, even under conditions of chattel slavery. If man could claim ownership of the most precious aspects of her humanity and claim for her a place of sub-humanity, his earthly authority did not translate into a perpetual divine sanctioning and commission to terrorize and supplant the power of an omniscient and omnipotent God, who had implanted the breath of life into her—that supernatural being who had created in her a perfect image of humanity.

Operating under the African principle of *nommo,* Africana women engaged in the prescient act of naming that extended beyond mortal words, ways, or wonders. Theirs was an act of invoking a life force that was bound to a supernatural source, which they in turn named based on their earthly calls to a spiritual presence. Whether it was the Divine Mother, Orisha, Allah, Christ, Buddha, Krishna, Yahweh, Supreme Being, Oshun, Ala, Jesus, God, Father, Father/Mother, or any other appellation, Africana women throughout time and memoriam have insisted on signifying a supremely spiritual authorizing and qualifying divine being that nourishes, heals, and embraces the fullness and duality of their sacred and secular experiences.viii Their works extend beyond simple, albeit well-articulated, understandings of religion as a tool of oppression, to instructive remedies with precedent setting paradigms for empowerment and social justice.ix In this they exemplify the necessary spiritual characteristics of Africana Womanism. Importantly, the historical, social, and political contexts imbedded in their lyrics and words testify to the significance of Africana women's spirituality that prays, works, and imagines the power of a people, thriving through the remembrance and respect of their past, and acknowledgment of the present, and future.

Their voices are the "evidence of things not seen"x but imagined in their artivistic works that fully embrace the power of faith to inspire change and chart the future and conditions under which Africana Melanated women, from Phillis Wheatley and Frances Harper to Audre Lorde and Maya Angelou, Lauryn Hill, Beyoncé, and beyond, exist as fully liberated humans. They speak, write, sing, dance, pray, and advocate for social justice and in ways that "#saytheirnames" and speak those truths, reclaiming their time for our time, as absolutely necessary for "a time such as this."xi Significantly, they push back against a government and a religion that conspired to monetize the black woman in perpetuity, using their words as liberatory weapons—expressed on behalf of those who remained in bondage.xii

As I began this peace (not piece) of writing, it was during perhaps one of the most challenging times for Africana women in our recent history. We are certainly no strangers to both the extreme pleasures and tremendous sorrows that accompany our way of being in this world. We are also no strangers to the many coping mechanisms that have attended our attempts to balance and navigate the dehumanizing instability of being Black, Woman, and disproportionately economically and socially underserved and marginalized. Yes, race, class, and gender biases and systemic institutional "isms" are the frames that attempt to hold Africana women hostage in order to hold us in bondage. So, what has kept us? What has enabled us to recover our physical and metaphysical selves? We can find a representative response to these and other questions in the words of an African American Christian hymn "I Know It Was the Blood" which invokes the torture, blood, and hanging of a redeemer who suffered for his people, who loved them enough to leave a legacy of personal, political, and spiritual struggle which not only survived but thrived. It is through "the blood," understood as a physical and ethereal manifestation of a life giving and sustaining force, that Africana women accept, protect, and bring forth life in the flesh and in the spirit. It's how they protect those most vulnerable and motivate those with privilege and power to join them to honor life and the blood without which there can be no redemption, no progress, and, as we have witnessed presently and historically, no justice for Africana people.

The enslaved poetic genius of the devout Christian, Phillis Wheatley, asserts that a God given "Love of Freedom . . . impatient of Oppression [yearning] for Deliverance" is a "principle' [that] lives in [all of] us" ("Letter to Rev. Sampson Occom Feb 11, 1774"). Importantly, it is not solely ideological or political freedom that is cause for which Wheatley must "pray" that "others may never feel" the tyranny of oppression ("Dartmouth" lines 30-31). Significantly, it is the enslaved adolescent's remembrance of the family she lost (because of slavery) that invokes such "wishes for the common good" (line 22). Namely, the "father" from whom she was "seiz'd," when still a "babe" (line 29), the image of her Mother pouring out water in morning ritualsxiii and those "excruciating" "sorrows [that] labour in [her] parent's breast" (lines 26-27). As "a victim of the largest involuntary human migration in history . . . kidnapped from her family in Africa and forced to spend up to two months crossing the Atlantic" (Carretta 1), Wheatley extends her sufferings beyond a singular view from the perspective of a victim, but rather that of one who has persevered through a human tragedy in the traumatic conditions of a system of human holocaust, who has held on to her very life as a young girl through the Middle Passage.

Wheatley renames herself a survivor, with a testimony of empowerment for other enslaved and freed Africana people. As Catherine Clay Bassard argues, "connotations of survivorship—black bodies, African cultures, and black texts—converge in the figure and poetics of Phillis Wheatley" (36).    What is also quite clear is that family-centeredness appears at the center of the works of one, who for all intents and purposes might be termed an orphan.  That is, while the enslaved poet was able to establish a much-needed familial relationship with her master and especially her mistress (Susannah Wheatley), it would hardly replace the great loss that she refers to in her "Dartmouth" poem, and one to which she referred frequently in her elegies, which not coincidentally permitted yet another way of connecting to families and centering their importance in her life from spiritual and political perspectives. Curtis Anthony Woods observes that "[s]he aligns her soul with oppressed blacks, regardless of the sanitized and sentimentalized 'family' offered by many New England slave-owners" (78).

Her letters to friends, Rev. Sam Occom and fellow Africana woman Obour Tanner, reveal a tone of familiarity that can be recognized by those who appreciate how extended family operates for Black people. In both blood and communal sharing of the best and worst of times, through thick and thin, they support, encourage, validate, chastise, and memorialize—and those are the folks who become one's family. Of course, Wheatley's faith served as at least one significant means of establishing an extended kinship lost in chattel slavery through her embracing and acceptance of the understanding of the Christian doctrine of family. "Wheatley adopted and later adapted evangelical theology as an instrument of remonstration that exposed the political and sociological tyranny wrought against African peoples in early America" (Woods 2).

Not unlike Wheatley, Frances Harper's poetry, too, allowed for the "poet's construction of self" through religious and political contexts. Harper's work, which ushers in an early call that is responded to by her twenty-first-century Africana melanated women descendants. In the preface to her 1854 *Poems on Miscellaneous Subjects*, abolitionist William Lloyd Garrison describes and decries the position of Black people under United States chattel slavery: "in one word, they are property to be owned, not persons to be protected" (3). Such is echoed and responded to in the refrain "Black Lives Matter." That is, Black people are not property; we are human beings deserving of the same rights and protections as every other citizen of this nation and the world—persons to be protected and valued. Garrison's claim that Harper is "identified in complexion and destiny with a depressed and outcast race" (4) asserts the primacy of race, a most debilitating and denigrating obstacle, not only for "the entire colored race" in general but also for the art and beauty that Black people contribute to the world (4). Indeed, as Hudson-Weems insists, which is strongly articulated in these assertions above by both Garrison during slavery ("Black people . . . are property . . . not people") and Black Lives Matter today, race remains first and, moreover, "racism, indeed, should be designated as a 'crime' . . . [ mandating] accountability," which is critical for Africana Womanism in its prioritization of race, class and gender (June 20, 2020 Hudson-Weems. https://www.columbiatribune.com/story/opinion/columns/2020/06/21/civil-rights-movement-then-and-now-anti-racism-to-stop-emmett-till-continuum-in-5-step-solution/113750502/ ).

Importantly, Carla Peterson further highlights Harper's call for the value of Black life:   She observes that Harper's attention to "the Syrophoenician woman as the weak and oppressed subject" and the "theme of the fallen woman" that is "common in  . . . Harper's poetry . . . universalizes the themes of hunger and poverty" and at the same time particularizes and politicizes the plight of Black women and their families in such a way that "allows those readers who so choose to apply these

circumstances to the specific historical experience of African Americans"
(Kindle Location 2024). Melba Joyce Boyd characterizes Harper's words
as evincing "the heart of an artist who could contextualize a world that had
too often been ignored and personalize voices that had too long been
silenced" (26). Similarly, Melissa Harris-Perry notes that "Harper's text
ultimately reveals the truth and the lie of freedom, autonomy and beauty of
African American womanhood" (794). Moreover, Peterson reads Harper's
"[p]oetry-in both its recited and printed forms" as "serving as a structural
frame through which she could fashion herself in the public role of poet-
preacher in order to articulate her vision of nineteenth-century America"
(Kindle Locations 1994-1995). "Harper conceived of poetry as moral and
didactic preaching in which originality was less important than the ability
to create character in the reader. . . in order to encourage her audience's
social activism" (Kindle 1996- 1999).

Similarly, Angelou's "Still I Rise" is created within a context that
celebrates not only the strength of Black people who endure through and
build upon adversity to create foundations for success in the worst of times.
What is most important is the connectedness to the Africana family through
centuries and the realization that overcoming oppression is rooted in the
legacy of intergenerational communal and familial "hopes and dreams" that
enable us to stand one shoulder upon the next. This is the center that reaches
through and across continents, centuries and other worlds. Angelou's
reminder of where we've been, where we are, and most important, who we
are: "past that's rooted in pain /. . . / Into a daybreak that's wondrously clear
/. . . / Bringing the gifts that my ancestors gave" ("Still I Rise" 31-39).
Connecting her faith as an extension of family and the sociopolitical reach
of churches such as that she experienced in Glide Memorial, Angelou
observed the eclectic congregants of "elected officials, lawyers, judges,
criminals, housewives and house-husbands and many elements of the
underworld." Pointing out that "[t]here is no place greater than the home of
God, except in our individual selves, than the places where women and men
set aside to go and worship, to just come together, and praise of the spirit
of God." Not unlike many Africana women, she explored a variety of faiths
including "Zen Buddhism . . .Judaism and . . . Islam." Following her
"spirit," Angelou ultimately concluded that she "really want[ed] to be a
Christian" and that she found its "teachings accessible."xiv

Such is seen in Lorde's apotheotic rendering of Yoruba deities
Yemoja, Oshun, and Shango in her familial circle of life: embracing and
celebrating the protection of children from womb to birth, strength, beauty,
sexuality, marriage in the familial lifegiving and sustaining forces.
Namely, the West African inspired spiritual reawakening in which she
announces "I will become myself/ . . . / and Mother Yemonja raises her

breasts to begin my labour/ near water/ the beautiful Oshun and I lie down together/ . . . / Shango will be my brother roaring out of the sea" ("Winds of Orisha," lines 21-29).

At the same time Lauryn Hill's admonition "You can get the money! You can get the power! But keep your eyes on the Final Hour" with her advice to "Observe how a queen do And . . . remain calm reading the 73rd Psalm" ("Final Hour") attempts to reach a higher spiritual ground. Her words recognize and privilege love, people, and family over the kind of power that secular and fleeting fame can bring by capturing the significance of religion beyond mere allusion to the Word. It is in her personal life as well as in her lyrics that we see an Africana woman grounded in spirituality and connected to family in songs like "The Final Hour" when Hill reverses a widely held myth about the evils of money, which was often recited prayer-like in economically disenfranchised communities, as a way to "comfort" those less fortunate, by focusing on the seemingly more valuable currency—their otherworldly salvation. In other words, such myths that relied on scriptures about the "meek" who "shall inherit the earth" or "it is easier for a camel to get through the eye of a needle, than for a rich man to enter heaven" often pacified and served to valorize poverty—and this was especially true for many black communities. Hill, however, reminds in her refrain, that it is not a question of acquiring either "money" or "power," but rather both are possible when one has a balanced focus on the overall goal. She considers what such "wealth" and "power" might bring, especially if you can "Let God redeem you" and "Watch out what you cling to." She posits herself, an Africana woman who came from humble means and who offers a vision of life that is rich on all terms. Redemption does not, in the lyricist's prayer about the final hour, depend on a life of poverty and denial, but rather a caution about not making a "god" out of one's earthy possessions. She concludes by pointing directly to a biblical verse that she intends to be read in a different way: "And I remain calm reading the 73rd Psalm." This verse is sampled for its multiple connotations and for its complex rendering of concepts such as the interconnectedness, like interwoven fabric, and the balancing of the spiritual with the material.

Hill's concluding citation of this scripture punctuates her refrain about "money," "power," and "the Final Hour." Travis Harris observes that "Hill do[es] not have a problem with getting money." Rather, her lyrics are a "cautioning to Hip Hop . . . that pursuit of money and prominence may signify an empty and envious heart." According to Harris, Hill's reference to "the 73rd Psalm which is a Psalm by Asaph pondering the prosperity of the wicked while the righteous suffer . . . [is her] realiz[ation] [that] despite the prosperity of the wicked, they will fall" (21). Celnisha L. Dangerfield points to the importance of songs like "Final Hour," among many songs in which Hill makes use of biblical "references [and] characters [and stories]" (216) as they point to the significance of "mythical references" and African American "cultural beliefs" represented in figures and narratives of "Moses and Aaron" for example (217).

Thus, contemporary Africana activists like Hill articulate their complex responses to the social inequality they observe as prevalent aspects of their experiences as marginalized and disenfranchised Black Americans. They do so by charting the retrieval of symbolic and literal humanity through religious and political compasses that operate on multivalent axes of race, class, and gender. For example, Hill's shifting of the "focus from the richest to the brokest" and her suggestion to "amend . . . every law that ever prevented" the "survival" of African American people is directly connected to her promise to "document" the history of two very different biblical brothers (Moses and Aaron), who worked together as allies and family for the mutual uplifting their people in crisis, as she issues a "Final Call" to oppressor and oppressed.

Interweaving and simultaneously veiling secular with sacred performances that engage the political with the spiritual, through which she invokes a god that can provide both physical and moral certainties, even as she cautions that the focus on the "success" that fame and fortune bring to the exclusion of all else, is a destructive obsession, a "hypnosis" that her "opus" means to "reverse." Hill's lyrical invocations are not as transparent as they appear, nor are they simply biblical analogy or paraphrase. For example, less "transparent" in this history Hill promises to document, but I would argue nonetheless present, is a key figure in biblical herstory. Importantly, the figure of Miriam, Moses and Aaron's older sister, to whom Moses owed his "survival since [his] arrival ... seen through" is the legacy of "Lauryn Hill from New-Ark to Israel." Hip-Hop scholars and related intellectual and cultural artisans and genres, in the works and words of Joan Morgan, Jessica Care Moore, Brittney Cooper, Missy Elliot, McLite, Queen Latifah, Nicki Minaj and Cardi B, as well as countless others claim "The Miseducation of Lauryn Hill" as an inaugural work that ushered in a contemporary era of black women's use of art as necessary propaganda in the movements for social justice. In this she joins her foremothers Wheatley, Harper, Lorde, Angelou and others. In an era of widening health disparities for Africana women across class, and rapidly growing concerns about infant mortality and fertility, as well as the anti-black violence perpetrated against black children, it is particularly relevant that Hill's "Zion" celebrates maternity and her black baby boy in particular. In fact, she frames her soon to be born son within a spiritual symbolism that evokes the imagery of the birth of Jesus and of the Rastafari African homeland.

She refers to the birth of Zion, her first born, as that for which she "had been chosen," despite being "overwhelmed." Hill then narrates the visit from "an angel" who spoke words of prophecy from Isaiah 9:6-7 about the coming of the Messiah: "For unto me a man child would be born." Her "crazy circumstance" is not unlike that of the biblical Mary, an unmarried woman of faith, whose future is uncertain. As in "The Final Hour," Hill reminds us of what matters most, as she refuses the advice of those focused solely on career and worldly possessions, and she "cho[o]se[s] her heart." This is a choice to embrace a heavenly calling to Zion with all its "perils" and it's "joy." Hill's religion is political and powerful as it bears witness to the significance of Africana women's power and her ability to bridge the tripartite oppression: "Race, class and gender, and the prioritization therein, . . . key issues for comprehending Africana Womanism" (Christian 131). She thus lyrically testifies of attempts to contain and lay claim to her physical and spiritual self, and spiritually venerates life and "Black" lives that matter through generations—all the while embracing an Africana womanist family-centeredness that evolves through her faith and is manifested in her activism. The same is true for the similarly grounded but iconic Beyonce's *Black is King,* which arguably deifies Africana people, declaring: "Not just some words in a Bible verse/ You are the living word/ . . . part of something way bigger" ("Bigger"), Africana melanated womanity is rehearsed, rewritten, restated in religiopolitical and family-centric terms.

From Wheatley, who wrote herself into humanity and birthed a subtle but powerful response to slavery, poverty, and sexism in her literary works during her very short life, to contemporary Africana social justice movements, we see the evidence of an historical legacy of foremothers for whom the religious was political, and for whom their socio-religious-politics are reflected in nearly every walk of life. Notably, Cori Bush, a candidate in St. Louis for the Democratic primary/1st congressional district, is an ordained minister; Alicia Garza, Patrisse Cullors, and Opal Tometia, co-founders of BLM, credited as having reinaugurated a global Africana movement for social justice and reform; and, GirlTrek, the health movement that has inspired Africana women to take back their health and their neighborhoods by walking and connecting more than 900,000 Black Women with a goal to reach one million—Africana Melanated women continue to demonstrate the power of the blood that flows in and through them. It is one, I argue, that sustains through their interconnectedness with a spirituality, religion, and faith in a higher power. Beyond physical conditions, limitations, and tripartite oppressions, Africana women remain spiritually centered and guided—naming God as the source of their strength and as an authorizing figure who enables and grants them moral authority.

Therefore, "when one looks at her in making everyday decisions, one senses her reliance upon the inner spirit or mind, the voice of God, the Father" (Hudson-Weems, *Africana Womanism*, Fifth Edition 46). Evidenced here is "the presence and power of God" as ultimate sustaining power personified!

Indeed, the religio-political work and words of Africana women are, as ever, critical to the survival and thriving of our people, especially in the current era of post-civil rights reconstruction, when our nation has returned to regressive politics. It is a work of remembrance, perhaps now even more relevant with the passing of our beloved Toni Morrison that we cherish our black women's words and the power they ignite in as many ways possible—as a subtle reminder they remain, as they have been throughout history, "fearfully and wonderfully" insurgent.xv

# Bibliography

Bassard, Catherine Clay. *Spiritual Interrogations: Culture, Gender and Community in Early African American Women's Writing*. Princeton: Princeton UP, 1999.

Beyoncé. "Bigger." The Lion King: The Gift, Parkwood Entertainment, 2019,https://www.beyonce.com/album/thegift/songs/

Boyd, Melba Joyce. *Discarded Legacy: Politics and Poetics in the Life of Frances E. W. Harper, 1825-1911*. Wayne State UP, 1994. Print.

Burke, Tarana. *BBC Newsbeat* July 9, 2020
https://www.bbc.com/news/av/newsbeat-53345945

Carretta, Vincent. *Phillis Wheatley: Biography of A Genius in Bondage*. University of Georgia Press. Kindle Edition.

Harper, Frances Ellen Watkins, and Daniel Murray Pamphlet Collection. *Poems on Miscellaneous Subjects*. Boston: J. B. Yerrinton & Son, Printers, 1854. Pdf. Retrieved from the Library of Congress, www.loc.gov/item/26020585/

Hill, Lauryn. "The Final Hour. *The Miseducation of Lauryn Hill*. Sony Music. 1998. CD.

Hudson-Weems, Clenora. *Africana Womanism: Reclaiming Ourselves*, Fifth Edition London and New York: Routledge Press, 2019.

Hudson-Weems, Clenora. *Columbia Daily Tribune*. Opinion June 20, 2020https://www.columbiatribune.com/story/opinion/columns/2020/0 6/21/civil-rights-movement-then-and-now-anti-racism-to-stop-emmett-till-continuum-in-5-step-solution/113750502/

Lorde, Audre. *The Collected Poems of Audre Lorde*. W. W. Norton & Company. Kindle Edition.

Peterson, Carla L. *"Doers of the Word": African-American Women Speakers and Writers in the North (1830-1880)*. Kindle Edition

Woods, Curtis Anthony. "The Literary Reception of The Spirituality Of Wheatley, Phillis. (1753-1784): An Afrosensitive Reading" Dissertation May 2018 (Southern Baptist Theological Seminary)

# Notes

i.      Matthew 6:10 (Bible KJV) part of the Lord's Prayer.

ii.     Matthew z25:40-45 (Bible KJV) "Verily I say unto you, Inasmuch as ye have done it unto one of the least of these my brethren, ye have done it unto me."

iii.    My reference here is based on several biblical references and what they have come to mean for Africana people, especially (but not only) Christians who intercede for those who are not able or unwilling at the present to do so for themselves. It is a demonstration of transformative empathy that enables positive change, as it fills broken or weakening spaces, and sometimes performs reparative actions necessary to correct what is negative and harmful. In the biblical text from Ezekiel 22:30, the prophet Ezekiel shares a vision of a corrupt society that has broken sacred and secular laws, had devolved into idol worship, and has most emphatically oppressed and victimized the poor and lowly people. In the vision God speaks to the prophet, and tries to provide a way out for these people—all of whom are implicated in the most horrendous of crimes—it is not only the collective sins but more importantly, it is the refusal of people to repent, pray, and the lack of anyone willing to intercede that will lead to doom and destruction of the land and its people: "And I sought for a man among them, that should make up the hedge, and stand in the gap before me for the land, that I should not destroy it: but I found none." In Psalm 106:23 it is Moses who stands in the gap for the people of Israel against an angry God: "Therefore he said that he would destroy them, had not Moses his chosen *stood before him in the breach*, to turn away his wrath, lest he should destroy them" (my emphases). Thus, standing in the gap can simultaneously make room for other more positive openings (windows and doors) through which those most oppressed can be empowered, liberated (sometimes) and seek other options. Standing in the gap for many people of faith also represents a reconciliation and reconnection with the Divine—their God—that enables and opens hearts.

iv.     Ibid (see note above) Matthew 25:40-45 (Bible KJV)

v.      https://www.bbc.com/news/av/newsbeat-53345945

vi.     Olga M. Segura "Founder Tarana Burk: 'Jesus Was the First Activist I Knew'" (*Sojourners Magazine* September 24, 2018). "Catholicism was a place, a way for me to gauge how to exist in the world. Inside of this trauma, there was hope." While Burke explains that she is no longer Catholic, she remains a Christian, and is clear in this article and other that faith figures prominently in the work she does—from her 1997 non-profit organization Just B to her 2007 founding of the Me Too movement to her current advocacy which extends beyond Me Too.

vii.    In her critique of Womanist theology, ("Must I be a Womanist?") which is not the same as Africana Womanism, Monica A. Coleman, lists some of the many possibilities in what she terms an already existing "third wave" of "this theological movement" known as Womanist theology: "We can identify ourselves as male and female, Christian, Muslim, pagan, new-thought, Buddhist, and Ifa. We can call ourselves academics and activists and ministers, priests, nuns, and iyalorishas [referring to Yoruba Ifa priestesses] . . . We will be straight, lesbian, and bisexual, faithful and humanist. . . Some of us may be southerners, Christians, and members of the NAACP. Others of us may be northerners, Dutch, South Africans, Black Nationalists, or Greens." Those who may confront such issues as "bisexuality, colorism and standards of beauty, eating disorders and obesity, class realities . . . mental health, progressive Christianity, paganism, indigenous spirituality, and participation in other world religions—like Baha'i and Buddhism" (95). While an analysis of Womanist theology, Alice Walker's term womanist, and concepts of Black feminism are all outside the scope of this essay, and have been handled more fully by Hudson-Weems' decades of scholarship, I point to Coleman's catalogue of possibilities as those which are representative of some of the possibilities for Africana Melanated women in their naming of their spirituality on their own terms.

viii.      Katherine Clay Bassard, Cedrick May, Joycelyn Moody, and Jennifer Rycenga (among others) have analyzed the intertextual fluidity of spirituality within the politicized voices of black women like Wheatley. Indeed, these scholars have gone beyond merely suggesting the simultaneously spiritual, political, and personal dimensions of these author's productions. They have shifted our lenses toward a more critical understanding of early black women's deployment of faith-based knowledge as vital elements in their spiritual mission truths. In short, these scholars have provided us with the necessary tools and lenses through their theories and methodologies to give proper justice to more rigorous and in-depth probing of their words for meaning that matters to and for (from my perspective) black women. They permit us to derive meaning such that early black Christian women's writing may direct us to where and when they enter discourses of gender, class, race, sexuality and social justice.

ix.       In particular, attending to their manipulation of the genre of African American written prayers, Bassard articulates the significance of understanding the diversity within black spiritual writing. Black people were "never a monolithic group of Bible readers, but have, from their first encounters with the text, evidenced a range of Bible-reading practices" (*Transforming Scriptures* 2). It is important to read black women's religious works as both spiritual and political, and particularly the earliest texts, because of what they reveal about the "biblical intertextuality" imbedded in authors' use of signifying scriptures (e.g. "the trope of the talking mule") to advance anti-slavery, women's rights, and social equality among free Black and White America.

x.        Hebrews 11:1 (KJV Bible): "Now faith is the substance of things hoped for, the evidence of things not seen."

xi.       These words are meant to signify on several fronts: First, there is the biblical reference from the book of Esther: Esther 4:14 King James Version (KJV) 14 For if thou altogether holdest thy peace at this time, then shall there enlargement and deliverance arise to the Jews from another place; but thou and thy father's house shall be destroyed: and who knoweth whether thou art come to the kingdom for such a time as this? Second, there is the reference to each woman's positioning herself as the one speaks truth to power precisely at the most crucial time and with regard to the most critical issues imposing her people: Wheatley's instructive reminder in "To The University of Cambridge in England" when she emphasizes her position as black instructor to white privileged men "An *Ethiop* tells you 'tis your greatest foe" (line 28); Lee's questioning of patriarchal authority: "why not the woman? seeing he died for her also"; and Stewart's ""Who shall go forward and take off the reproach that is cast upon the people of color? Shall it be a woman?." Third, and finally, the title of the short autobiographical sketch by Rev. Debora K. Blanks, AME minister and Chaplain, whose sermon "Tell God Where it Hurts" connects words that absolutely matter and reframe political contexts from nineteenth- to twentieth-century oppressive injustices. See: *This Is My Story: Testimonies and Sermons of Black Women in Ministr*y (ed. Cleophus G. Larue) Westminster John Knox Press (April 5, 2004).

xii.          As such, Africana women can be interpreted as those instruments of the divine who enrich and replenish lands contaminated by race, class, and gender inequity, by turning the soil and planting seeds for equality, social justice, and, most important, freedom for their sisters and brothers in bondage. Significantly, Bassard notes that "black women's consistent turn to scripture for literary material is an attempt to position themselves as inheritors of the prophetic mantle" (12 *Transforming Scriptures: African American Women Writers and The Bible*, Athens: U of Georgia P, 2011).

xiii.         From Margaret Odell's biography which observes that Wheatley "does not seem to have preserved any remembrance of the place of her nativity, or of her parents, excepting the simple circumstance that her mother poured out water before the sun at his rising—in reference, no doubt, to an ancient African custom."
              https://docsouth.unc.edu/neh/wheatley/wheatley.html#wheat9

xiv.          "Maya Angelou: Of Religion and Rainbows" *Los Angeles Times* (May 17, 1992)
              https://www.latimes.com/archives/la-xpm-1992-05-17-tv-76-story. html#:~:text=I%20spent%20some%20time%20with,want%20to%20be%2 0a%20Christian.

xv.           Here I meant to signify the power of religion in black women's history of "radical reckon[ing] with systems of oppression. This tradition of reckoning informs how Black women continue to mobilize and organize in the 21st century" (Treva B. Lindsey, 2017. Negro Women May Be Dangerous: Black Women's Insurgent Activism in the Movement for Black Lives, Souls, 19:3, 315-327, DOI: 10.1080/10999949.2017.1389596).

# 7

## NOBEL LAUREATE TONI MORRISON: MODEL AFRICANA WOMANIST LITERARY CRUSADER FOR SOCIAL JUSTICE

### *CLENORA HUDSON (WEEMS), PHD*

> True scholarship and activism, "social responsibility," together corroborate a fight to end the long-existing battle against [unjust] racial dominance. Here we witness a demonstration of how Africana Womanism advances itself and fits into ideals expressed in the lives of major iconic historical figures. (Hudson-Weems, *Africana Womanism*, Fifth Edition, Routledge 121)

The above quotation, appearing in Chapter 13 of the Fifth Edition of *Africana Womanism*, titled "Africana-Melanated Womanism and the King-Parks-Till Connection," comments on the common thread between the writer and the activist in continuing activities leading toward correcting centuries of societal ills, particularly the harsh brutalization of Africana people at the hands and minds of the dominant culture, which must be dismantled for total equity for all humankind. This chapter will highlight the role that Nobel Laureate Toni Morrison played for about a half century during her creative career as a novelist. As one explores her profound, massive literary contributions, constituting what later evolved into the Morrison Literary Canon, one readily sees the commonalities among this author's novels, vivid reflections of true Black life, and the political activities of the brave and awesome anti-lynching crusader herself, Ida B. Wells-Barnett. Indeed, both had a common bond, a common mission, both keeping it real and sticking to telling it like it was/is as a means of initiating positive change for a better world.

Focusing on Morrison offers an excellent opportunity to say what critically needs to be said in Black literary texts today, given our racist-ridden society, via utilizing the works of this author, who has mastered the art of doing just that:

Many feel that Africana women fiction writers have a critical mission to accomplish, which is to "tell it like it is." And since literature in general should reflect life, it is important that the literature of Africana womanist writers speak the truth—the whole truth (Hudson-Weems, *Africana Womanism* 51).

Indeed, Morrison does an outstanding job in making sure that her images and characters accurately reflect society, particularly highlighting the life-sustaining needs of Africana people. Thus, we, as serious readers and appreciators of authentic writings, find ourselves satisfied, having read her works, and moreover, leaving with a better sense of ourselves and how we, as men and women together, might advance our acts in order to further aid in improving not only our individual lives, but the world at large. This notion is spelled out in Chapter 8 of *Africana Womanism: Reclaiming Ourselves* Fifth Edition, Morrison's Beloved: All Parts Equal."

Of significant importance is how her female characters demonstrate awareness of the significance of their interaction with their family and their community. This becomes obvious as Morrison concentrates not only on the reality of Africana life and culture-its richness, its strengths, and its weaknesses--but, more important, on that community's strategies for survival in the concerted struggle of the men and women in the long-existing battle against racism. (Hudson-Weems, *Africana Womanism* 77)

Morrison starts with the true nature of her characters, who must act, represent and, moreover, be viewed, recognized and interpreted as authentic personalities going about their everyday lives as viable entities of life itself:

An astute scholar as well as a uniquely creative writer, Morrison has won the deepest respect and admiration of both her fellow writers and the populace at large. . . . Morrison's ultimate message is that each person should and must respect the reality of the human landscape of the world, with its unlimited possibilities and interpretations, if humankind is to achieve wholeness, if the global community is to once again be whole. Pass it on. (Samuels and Hudson-Weems, *Toni Morrison* 142)

To be sure, seeing and valuing each other is highly significant, however, it is equally critical that we truly understand the natural interconnected nature of things relative to the implied results of this mandate. Compelling respect as a pre-requisite for debunking negative stereotypes of Africana people, at the same time, will invariably ensure the elimination of the repeated portrayal of white characters as winning "heroes."

"I am really happy when I read something, particularly about black people, when it is not so simple minded . . . when it is not set up in some sociological equation where all the villains do this and all the whites are heroes, because it just makes black people boring; and they are not. I have never met yet a boring black person. All you have to do is scratch the surface and you will see. And that is because of the way they look at life." (Samuels and Hudson-Weems, *Toni Morrison* 1)

Here, in her own words, Morrison makes a profound commentary on the focus that she gives in her writings to Black life, particularly that of probing her characters' "relationship to . . . society" and concluding that they are not "bigger than life, . . . but [rather] as big as life." (Samuels and Hudson-Weems, 1).

Connecting the dots between Morrison, the intellectual Literary Crusader for Social Justice, and Wells-Barnett, the definitive Anti-Lynching Crusader for Social Justice, is not a difficult task for obvious reasons, as both symbolizing the ultimate Africana womanist in action, both in life and in literature reflecting life. Model Crusaders in their own distinct way during their lifelong battle for Social Justice, the latter, a brave journalist, exposed the brutal victimization of African Americans through the media, fearlessly waging a never-ending battle against unimaginable injustices suffered by her people. Indeed, she laid bare the ugliest and most horrific form of racial injustices—lynching. The former, Morrison, depicted various forms of such horrific Black life experiences, such as the actual lynching of Sixo in *Beloved*, as well as the symbolic lynching of Cee in *Home*, wherein this main character experiences eternal "lynchings" of her children who never were, forever denied conception by the cruel act of eugenics at the whelms of a selfish, racist physician/scientist. To be sure, there is a multitude of abominable infringements forced upon Morrison's characters, who are strong and resolute in their endless struggles against racial oppression. Men, women, and children alike suffered, and continue to do so today in a world that continues to practice global racial dominance. Appropriately, the celebrated author became the 1st African American female recipient of the Nobel Prize for Literature in 1993, her characters being the embodiment of the resolute activist, insisting upon our rights as human beings. And for her creative initiative, preserving such abominations, vividly depicting heroic figures in the on-going struggle for our God-given birthright, she was awarded with the Presidential Medal of Freedom in 2012 by President Barack Obama, the 1st Black U. S. president.

Clearly a legacy continuum exists between these two icons and thus, it was quite appropriate for Rust College, where Ida B. Wells spent time as a student, to host a special event in Morrison's honor-- "Remembering Toni Morrison: A Tribute" --shortly after her death on

August 5, 2019. As co-author of *Toni Morrison* (1990), with Dr. Wilfred D. Samuels, the very first full-length critical study of the works of this international icon, I was invited, as Distinguished Lecturer, to share my thoughts on the Nobel Laureate, having been earlier asked by the editor of *The Columbia Daily Tribune* to write a special tribute to the indisputable global giant of the literary world, shortly after her death. However, for the special occasion at the Ida B. Wells-Barnett Institute, I took another direction--assessing and analyzing Morrison's novels from an Africana Womanist perspective. Africana Womanism, which is a family-centered paradigm that prioritizes race, class and gender, offers an authentic Africana position relative to the everyday lives of Africana people world-wide on all levels. It insists upon the utilizations of an authentic tool of analysis for interpreting and embracing our beliefs, our values, and our God-given talents, as well as our primary commitment to our own for ultimate survival:

> Africanans have critical and complex problems in their community, most of which stem from racial oppression. The Africana woman acknowledges the problem of classism, a reproachable element in America's capitalistic system. However, even there the plight of the middle-class Africana woman becomes intertwined with racism. Given that both the Africana womanist and the Black feminist address these critical issues and more, there must be something that makes the issues of the Africana womanist different, and that something is prioritizing on the part of the Africana woman. In the final analysis, *Africana Womanism* is connected to the tradition of self-reliance and autonomy, working toward participation in Africana liberation. (Hudson-Weems, *Africana Womanism* 25)

My sense is that in tailoring our movement to accommodate our needs, we can conceivably achieve this goal via utilizing and practicing the eighteen (18) attributes of Africana Womanism. This concept offers a strategy whereby we start with Self-Naming and Self-Defining, the first two of the 18 characteristics for this Family-Centered construct. Both Whole and Authentic, we must also have a Respect of Elders, as well as embrace a "Concerted Struggle of the men and the women in the long-existing battle against racism" (Hudson-Weems 27). Male-Female Compatible, the Africana Womanists must also demonstrate Flexible Role Player, while allowing a sense of Spirituality to inform their direction. In addition, she is Adaptable and Ambitious, and has a sense of Genuine Sisterhood, supportive of each other as we share in protecting our children. The Africana Womanist is Respected and Recognized, with psychological and physical Strength needed for mastering Mothering and Nurturing without apology. To be sure, each of Morrison's main characters have "all of these qualities to a varying degree encompassing all aspects of her life" (*Africana Womanism* 35).

With that, allow me to offer a brief litany of Morrison's Award-Winning novels, demonstrating her activity as a Literary Crusader for Social Justice, since she is the writer whose characters play out their commitments to society as symbols, beginning with her first one, *The Bluest Eye* (1970). Herein, the author challenges the acceptance of an inauthentic, alien standard of "beauty," represented by the protagonist, Pecola Breedlove who endlessly pines for not only blue eyes, the epitome of white beauty, but the "bluest eyes." Morrison dismantles mainstream standards, a practice that debuted during the Civil Rights and the Black Arts Movements of the searing 60s and the 70s. It was during this time that James Brown, in "Say It Loud: I'm Black and I'm Proud," publicly topsy-turveyed the Eurocentric standard of beauty, while at the same time re-indoctrinated us into changing our learned position and attitude about what constitutes beauty in our community. Indeed, this was the inception of Morrison as Literary Social Justice Warrior, challenging the absurdity of succumbing to outside, inauthentic standards and definitions. Heretofore, she had edited manuscripts of other Black writers for a subsidiary publisher of a major press, before finally launching her own career as writer/author. At last, she was able to make her own attack on ideals contrary to the inclusion of the black body, mind and identity via first self-naming and self-defining, the first cornerstone characteristics of Africana Womanism. As we live in a diverse world, like it or not, wherein all should be respected as one among the broader body of the human race, this stands for what Dr. W. E. B. Dubois calls true diversity, not assimilation.

Morrison's three (3) subsequent novels, *Sula* (1973), *Song of Solomon* (1977), and *Tar Baby* (1981), prove to all be masterpieces in which the author narrates the sagas of protagonists of major issues relative to race, class and gender. For example, we witness the discovery of the authentic self via the title character in *Sula*, whose death also enables her best friend, Nel, to come to understand and appreciate the legitimacy of individuality. We also see Milk Man, the protagonist in *Song of Solomon,* who leaves his home in search of his African roots/history. Next is *Tar Baby* wherein one of the main characters, Jadine, is presented as one who must authentically cope with the dynamics of what she and others around her, including the white main character, Valerian Street, must deal with relative to race and racism. Then there is Morrison's ultimate masterpiece, her fifth novel, *Beloved* (1987), which graphically addresses "the unspeakable fate to which most female slaves [and Black males] were heiresses" (Samuels and Hudson-Weems, *Toni Morrison* 94). This is, indeed, Morrison's signature novel wherein she outlines a narrative of extreme racial oppression, dedicating it to "sixty million and more," which dates this homage back to the "unspeakable" experiences of countless Africans on their fateful voyage, the Middle Passage, to its continuum, American slavery. It is here on these shores, officially marked as the landing of the 1st Slave Ship in America in Jamestown, Virginia, 1619, although it has been more recently documented that Blacks had secretly landed here as early as 1526, that the slave narrator in *Beloved* situates the peculiar predicament of Blacks then. She muses, "Definitions belonged to the definer, not the defined." (Morrison, *Beloved* 190). In "The Legacy Lives On: Toni Morrison (1931-2019), Nobel Laureate," Hudson-Weems concludes, "Now Emancipated for over a century and a half, it is past time for us to seize total freedom – psychologically, politically and economically. And, of course, Pass it on!" (Hudson-Weems, *The Columbia Daily Tribune*, p. 3, August 10, 2019).

It should be noted here that it was, indeed, with *Beloved* (1987), for which Morrison was awarded the Pulitzer Prize, that she "out did" herself, a novel wherein one finds most all of the salient Africana womanist features prominently residing in the powerful unforgettable characters. Admittedly, *Beloved* remains the *it* novel of all times, crossing all boundaries, which is why I chose to do an in-depth reading in a whole chapter, "Morrison's *Beloved*: All Things Equal." In a similar fashion, I did an Africana womanist interpretation of other Africana womanist novels, including Zora Neale Hurston's *Their Eyes Were Watching God*, Mariama Bâ's *So Long A Letter*, Paule Marshall's *Praisesong for the Widow*, and Terry McMillan's *Disappearing Acts*, for the 1993 classic text, *Africana Womanism: Reclaiming Ourselves*, later reprinted in a 5th Edition (Routledge Press, 2019), with a five-chapter new section, Part III--"From Africana Womanism to Africana-Melanated Womanism." However, the *Beloved* chapter is seminal, as it specifically identifies most of the key Africana Womanist tenets in its protagonist, Sethe, the mother of the title character and model Africana Womanist.

In *Beloved*, the narrator makes a profound commentary on the power of the dominant culture to define not only its people as superior, but to define the other as well, but in an unfavorably manner via relegating Blacks to the level of low self-esteem:

> "That anybody white could take your whole self for anything that came to mind. Not just work, kill or maim you, but dirty you. Dirty you so bad you couldn't like yourself anymore." (*Beloved* 251).

And there were so many in the Africana community who were "dirtied" to the point that they had a zero image of themselves. Fortunately, however, Morrison's stellar work demonstrates her success in revealing the magic and the beauty of Black male-female relationships, complimenting each other, while insisting that they stick together for the survival and advancement of the family/race for ultimate freedom. Her memorable character, Sixo, expresses the powerful eternal love and bond between the Africana male and female via his relationship with his significant other:

> "She is a friend of my mind. She gather me, man. The pieces I am, she gather them and give them back to me in all the right order. It's good, you know, when you got a woman who is a friend of your mind." (*Beloved* 272-3)

Such a connection between this model couple, Sixo and his 30-Mile-Woman, makes it clear that we, Africana men and women, must remain "In It Together," as we have a critical mission before us—to protect and support our families in the on-going liberation struggle for our human rights, wherein the race factor is our first priority. Hence, according to Dr. Adele Newson-Horst's Africana Womanist reading of Gloria Naylor's *Mama Day*, "the key to Africana Womanism in her relation to her man . . . predisposes characters to being in concert in a common struggle" (Newson-Horst in *Contemporary Africana Theory, Thought and Action*," 368). This sentiment is continued in sister Souljah"s *No Disrespect*. According to Hudson-Weems in *Africana Womanist Literary Theory*, Sister Souljah's autobiographical novel is an authentic Africana womanist work in that this author also keeps the whole family in mind via the protagonist, representing her as she

> carefully delivers the full story of [her] life, . . . in quest for both her soul mate and ways of improving life for young Blacks, particularly those in the urban areas (Hudson-Weems, *Africana Womanist Literary Theory* 100).

Clearly her commitment goes beyond her preoccupation with finding her own Mr. Right; she is committed to the entire Africana community:

> Sister Souljah, through her odyssey culminating in her becoming an evolved model Africana womanist, ultimately emerges as one who truly counts in the Africana community, one who must offer assistance and possible solutions to the plight of Africana people and the relentless fight for not just mere existence but rather real survival on every level. (100).

The family, too, is the center! The Africana womanist is unquestionably the family-centered persona.

That said, continuing with a one novel representation per decade for Morrison, we witness her 6th novel, *Jazz*, the novel of the 90s; *A Mercy*, the novel of the 1st decade of the new millennium; and finally *Home,* representing the 2$^{nd}$ decade of this century, wherein Morrison's protagonist, 24-year-old, Frank Money, the 1950s Korean War Veteran, returns to his racist home in Lotus, Georgia to save his sister, Cee, from death at the hands of her racist employer, Dr. Beauregard Scott, a Confederate and practitioner of eugenics. He used her as the subject of his female sterilization experiments, an area of interest motivated by his wife's infertile status. In this novel, we witness the continuation of Morrison unmasking the culprits, while arming her people with knowledge of the boundless nuances of racism and its devastating impact on Black lives. Indeed, this is sometimes needed in order to stimulate an individual, as well as a communal commitment to rising up against toxicant racial oppression.

In conclusion, we witness that in all of Morrison's works, both her fiction and non-fiction, she comes across as an exemplar of a literary warrior, one who upholds the authentic agenda of the theory of Africana Womanism via slaying destroyers of Black life with powerful language, artistically bearing truth as a corrective for painful historical and current wrongs. Much like Ida B. Wells, Morrison, too, is a herald for Social Justice, as Blacks have no other choice than to place the race factor 1$^{st}$. For example, Harriet Tubman, the Underground Railroad Conductor, did so when she went down South nineteen (19) recorded times to rescue her people from slavery. Did she go down, with her rifle in her hand, for just her sisters? The question is rhetorical, for, as history reveals, she went to rescue not only her sisters, but men, too, as well as children, callously and selfishly held in captivity as slaves. Indeed, her agenda was clearly not gender-specific, which characterizes most female-based theories, although some critics factor other elements as secondary to the female factor. To be sure, Ida B. Wells-Barnett places the race factor first when she stood up for a male friend, who, along with his two male partners, was lynched because they opened a grocery store in a Black neighborhood on the corner of Mississippi Blvd. and Walker Avenue in Memphis, Tennessee. The three (3) lynch victims were deemed competitors of the white grocery store owner, and because of the economic factor, they were quickly eliminated. Finally, there were Dr. Martin Luther King, Jr., the father of the Civil Rights Movement, and Rosa Parks, the mother of the Movement, who fought against racial discrimination up until their deaths, and so did Malcolm X, a Human Rights advocate. Of course, the list continues, as Morrison, too, wages a continuous war on the violent crime of racial discrimination, fighting that battle to her end as a fierce word warrior for Africana people.

And the Legacy Lives On! "Immortality of a kind, via a constant evolving extension of the life and works of a thinker." (Hudson-Weems, *The Columbia Daily Tribune*, p. 3). Toni Morrison has left an empowering legacy from which Africana people and the world in general can truly benefit. Thus, the Morrison Canon is rich beyond imagination with myriad novels and endless layers of interpretations for generations of readers for centuries to come. And so the ideals of the powerful creator of memorable characters, graphically representing heroic figures in the on-going struggle for our God-given birthright., lives on, permanently crafted and etched to serve as a powerful legacy put forth in print by a powerful Crusader for Justice. We love you, Toni Morrison! And likewise, we love the indisputable Crusader for Social Justice, Ida B. Wells-Barnett, the anti-lynching Crusader, whom we can never forget for her commitment to her people, demonstrated in the risks she took in exposing the most horrid form of racist domination--lynching. Today, we are reminded of the battles she fought, as we witness the on-going continuum, represented in the Emmett Till Continuums wherein the abominable lynching of countless Blacks world-wide reigns high. These victims are crystalized in the global cry against it, ignited by the Anti-Racism demonstrations following the senseless murder of George Floyd and countless others, referenced by Rev. Deborah Jackson in the Forward to this book as being "2020, a year of racial reckoning."

It, then, becomes evident that we, as a people, must come and stick together for the ultimate survival of our world. Like Ida B. Wells-Barnett and Toni Morrison, I, too, must commit myself, as a faithful Africana womanist activist, to making this world a better one, indeed, a beautiful world in which all can co-exist with love and respect for one another. This was the underline premise upon which Africana Womanism was conceptualized and created, a paradigm designed to offer solutions via understanding and, thereby, addressing the very source of our dilemma of disharmony, which is mass confusion and callous lovelessness. But the model was set for us a long time ago. In The 10$^{th}$ Commandment, the Golden Rule, it is stated that we must "Do unto others as you would have them do unto you." Once that is secured, the beauty of co-existing will ensue. Hence, in the final analysis, in reviewing the history of the experiences of humankind, we will witness, with a clearer vision, the dynamics of a restless shift, and with that knowledge, execute the correction(s):

From Religiosity to New Age Philosophy, from Patriarchy to Feminism, from Socialism to Democracy; and through it all, racism, and religion, too, ranking high in the scheme of things, remains unchanged. Beneath the surface, the abominable racism, a seemingly insurmountable phenomenon, still lurks at the base or the very foundation upon which many institutional systems rest. The trillion-dollar rhetorical question, then, remains the same: Did it work? Of all of the possible resolutions relative to racism in our everyday lives and how we fit into its structure, the resounding question yet remains.   The rhetorical trillion-dollar answer, of course, is apparent— Absolutely not!  And it will remain unresolved until all these possibilities are factored into an historical and cultural matrix in which an all-inclusive paradigm for ultimate human survival can securely reside.   To be sure, addressing critical underline issues within the established political, social and economic structures is a sound approach, one which merits serious consideration.  Africana-Melanated Womanism meets that demand as an appropriate global construct designed with that in mind.  A family-centered paradigm that prioritizes race, class and gender, it offers truly an egalitarian solution to satisfying unbiased humankind in pursuit of a just human existence.   And we will be successful, but only if Our Heavenly Father is in front, guiding His children, all of them—men, women and children, collectively executing the order of God's plan that He has so omnisciently put forth. (Hudson-Weems, *Africana Womanism* 116-117)

# Bibliography

Hudson-Weems, Clenora. *Africana Womanism: Reclaiming Ourselves*, Fifth Edition. London and New York: Routledge Press, 2019.

Hudson-Weems, Clenora. *Africana Womanism Literary Theory*. Trenton, New Jersey: Africa World Press, 2004.

Hudson-Weems, Clenora. "And the Legacy Lives On: Toni Morrison (1931-2019), Nobel Laureate." *The Columbia Daily Tribune*, August 10, 2019.

Morrison, Toni. *Beloved*. New York: Alfred A. Knopf, 1987

Morrison, Toni. *The Bluest Eye*. New York: Holt, Rinehart, & Winston, 1070.

Newson-Horst, Adele S. "Mama Day: An Africana Womanist Reading" in *Contemporary Africana Theory, Thought and Action: A Guide to Africana Studies*, Clenora Hudson-Weems, Editor. Trenton: Africa World Press, 2007, 359-372.

Samuels, Wilfred D. and Clenora Hudson-Weems. *Toni Morrison*. Boston: Twayne/Prentice Hall, 1990.

# PART III:

# MORAL RESPONSIBILITY & GENERATIONAL WEALTH— AN AFRICANA WOMANISM PERSPECTIVE

Clearly something vile & deadly roamed the earth during the spring & summer of 2020—something proponents of anti-blackness could not dismiss, something without prejudice, something "seeking whom it shall devour" (1 *Peter* 5:8 KJV). Anti-blackness as a vile & deadly force was not newly born that year. In fact, its xenophobic assaults, aimed at extinguishing Black lives without fear of retribution or retaliation, have existed in America since slavery. So, it is no surprise that long before Daryl Curry & *The Dad Gang* marched in support of the Black family, Black men were stereotyped as an absent presence seen only as sub-human foils in the narrative of a dangerous, unruly & pathological Black family matriarchy. [Today issued] a call to not only denied & maligned Black fatherhood, but to all who hear it. It is a call to listen & understand, says one of the victim's mother]: "If America does not shake up after all these incidents, the tears we all shed as mothers will be the tears that will break America."
**(Debra Walker King, PhD)**

# 8

# Pre-Africana Womanist, Ida B. Wells-Barnett" The Embodiment of the Principles of Africana Womanism

## Hilda Booker Williams, EdD and Charles Williams, PhD

Stimuluses such as race, class and gender have existed long before the enslavement of African people in the New World, and they have been significant in defining one's identity. Scholars such as W.E.B. Dubois and activists such as Ida B. Wells-Barnett recognized early the interconnectedness of race, class and gender and the quality of life in society, in particular, as it related to Black people. However, none of these factors stand alone. There are other impetuses contributing to interconnectedness in relation to how we survive the throws of life, via prioritizing the daily, and oftentimes even life-threatening, obstacles in determining whether or not a Black person will experience a long and healthy life. The interest in the destiny of Africana people is a major cornerstone for the theory. For, according to Dr. James Stewart and Dr. Ama Mazama in the Foreword to *Africana Womanism*, 5th Edition (2019), "Africana Womanism prioritizes racial oppression as the central focus of liberation efforts and emphasizes the importance of organic partnerships between Africana women and men" (xiv). Moreover, Dr. Mark Christian aptly observes in the Afterword to that same edition, "Race, class, and gender, and the prioritization therein, have always been key issues for comprehending Africana Womanism" (131).

An individual can possess many identities, some of which are given by their cultural group or, in some cases, by the person himself or herself. Each identity contributes to one's interconnectedness imposed by the society in which they live. Therefore, one's many identities—as man or woman, prescribed or non-prescribed gender, ethnicity, culture, prescribed ability or disability, among others--are inextricably linked to each other.

Recognizing that we all carry many identities that come with varying levels of power and privilege has been called intersectionality. In *Africana Womanism*, Fifth Edition, Hudson-Weems contends that this is "a sort of expansion of an existing, established practice of inclusivity, . . . an evolution from gender exclusivity to intersectionality" (Hudson-Weems 109). Intersectionality was outlined by Kimberle Crenshaw in 1989, about five years after Africana Womanism hit the scene, and which suggested a crossing and departure of various impulses and/or experiences related to different reflections of a moment in time. However, interconnectedness as advanced by Hudson-Weems, suggests an eternal interweaving nature of concerns in everyday Black lives.

In relation to Wells-Barnett's many identities, she, as a Black woman of the late 19th century, was the embodiment of Hudson- Weems' "Africana Womanism" because she refused to be defined by the dominant society in which she lived. A noted, serious activist, she was among the few black women of her time to live-out the interconnectedness of social identities, and how those defined identities, relative to the prioritization of race, class and gender, work in relation to systems of domination and oppression.

Some of the salient "pillars" of Africana Womanist theory and ideology, developed in the mid-1980s, were mirrored in Wells-Barnett, including Self-Naming, Self-Definition, Spirituality, Family-Centrality, In Concert with the Male in the Liberation Struggle, Adaptability, and Mothering. These pillars will be discussed here in relation to some of the life experiences and works of Ida B. Wells-Barnett.

The first of seven children, born to James and Elizabeth Wells, Ida was born during the summer of 1862 in Holly Springs, Mississippi, just six months before Abraham Lincoln issued the Emancipation Proclamation. Even though she was born into slavery, she never let that inhuman and unjust societal disadvantages stop her from achieving national and international prominence on the world stage in the fields of journalism, civil rights, education, and community organizing. (Willis 1) Wells-Barnett refused to be limited by race and gender factors and other circumstances of life.

However, according to *Crusade for Justice: The Autobiography of Ida B. Wells* (1970), edited by her daughter, Alfreda M. Duster, and others (Thompson, 1990; DeCosta-Willis, 1995; and Giddings, 2008), Wells-Barnett's childhood had been a happy time because she was reared by parents who thought and lived as "freepersons" (Giddings 10). Her parents were avid Republicans and Methodists and were firmly established in the black middle class of Holly Springs and Marshall County Mississippi. As the oldest child, Wells-Barnett's early life was centered on church life, going to school at Rust College, formerly Shaw University, and on race politics as a result of her father's involvement.

According to the autobiography of Ida B. Wells-Barnett, *Crusade for Justice* (1970), it was not until 1878, that Wells-Barnett's life changed tragically when the yellow fever epidemic brought death to her parents and youngest sibling. Almost immediately, she was introduced to a life not of her own choosing and filled with perils and hardships. Having to drop out of school at the age of 16, Wells-Barnett immediately took on the role of caretaker of her younger siblings. She stubbornly refused to allow well-meaning close friends and relatives to separate her siblings and was adamant in her persistence that she would provide for them. This was the first time that Wells-Barnett assumed by choice, a new identity. She no longer saw herself as the older sister, but now the surrogate, provider, caretaker, protector, and sociological parent for her siblings. Ever resourceful, Wells-Barnett changed from being a "light-hearted school-girl" to a public-school teacher. She took and passed the teacher's examination and began teaching in a rural school in Marshall County, Mississippi to provide for herself and her siblings.

In relation to the Africana Womanism "pillar" identified as "mothering" by Hudson–Weems, Ida B. Wells-Barnett, at the age of 16, was thrust into the "mother" role following the deaths of her father, mother and baby brother. Similar to the Covid-19 outbreak of 2020 in the United States, which has taken the lives disproportionally of many "essential workers of color," the Yellow Fever outbreak in 1878 took the life of James Wells, Ida's father, an "essential worker of color." He was a skilled carpenter who contracted yellow fever while building coffins for those who had died of the disease. Elizabeth, James' wife, and their infant son Stanley contracted the disease; both Elizabeth and Stanley quickly followed James in death. As a result of the yellow fever epidemic and the subsequent deaths of her parents and youngest sibling, Ida B. Wells and her five younger siblings were orphaned, leaving Ida to assume the "other mother" role for her five remaining siblings.

Professor Stanlie M. James, a sociologist, in her article entitled "Mothering: A Possible Black Feminist Link to Social Transformation," identifies Wells-Barnett as an "other mother" (48):

> Other mothers can be defined as those who assist blood mothers in the responsibilities of child care for short or long-term periods, in informal or formal arrangements. They can be, but not confined to, such blood relatives as grandmothers, sisters, aunts, cousins or supportive fictive kin (45).

Wells-Barnett at the age of sixteen became the "other mother" for her five younger siblings. She told well-meaning friends of her father and mother who wanted to separate the children, and in effect become the children's foster parents, that she could not allow them to separate her siblings. She informed them that "it would make her father and mother turn over in their graves to know their children had been scattered like that" (*Crusade For Justice* 16). She informed the well-meaning friends that she would take care of her siblings herself. Young Ida, seemingly without hesitation, modeled "adaptability," to the "other mother" role, another of Hudson-Weems' eighteen characteristics of Africana Womanism.

Later in 1882, Ida moved to Memphis, Tennessee to live with an aunt. Wells-Barnett soon learned that beyond the vicissitudes of her personal life, the town and country of her birth had a long and shameful history of building institutions intentionally to limit and oppress newly freed Black people. These institutions, namely, Jim Crow Laws, were rooted in racism, classism and sexism and limited the opportunities of Black people relative to citizenship and equal rights. Influenced by her father, Wells-Barnett would write about issues of race and politics in the South, particularly, a number of articles she had published in black newspapers and periodicals under the moniker "Iola" (*Ida, A Sword Among Lions* 78). Wells eventually became an owner of *The Memphis Free Speech and Headlight Newspaper*.

Wells-Barnett had come face-to-face with the cruel and immoral realities of newly entrenched system of Jim Crowism in the South. First, In 1884 (71 years before Rosa Parks refused to give up her seat on a bus during the Montgomery Bus Boycott in 1955), Wells-Barnett was confronted by a train conductor with the Chesapeake & Ohio Railroad. He ordered her to give up her seat in the first-class lady's car because she was Black, and to move to the segregated smoking car already crowded with other passengers. Secondly, in 1891, Wells-Barnett was dismissed from her teaching post by the Memphis Board of Education because of an article she wrote criticizing conditions in the Black schools of Memphis and Shelby County Tennessee. Well-Barnett was probably devastated by the dismissal, but definitely undaunted. By way of her newspaper, Well-Barnett had become a force to reckon with for both the white and black community of Memphis and Shelby County Tennessee.

Beyond a shadow of a doubt, Wells-Barnett was a thorn in the side of Jim Crowism and the white community that created it to maintain an underclass of black people in the Deep South. Under the pen name, "Iola," she wrote article after article, attacking racism in the South that was upheld by Jim Crow policies. Decrying the lynching of her friend, Tom Moss, and two other upstanding Black men, she willingly and often without support, put her own life at risk, traveling throughout the South, gathering information on other lynching incidents. Therefore, practically all of Wells-

Barnett's early newspaper work targeted lynching, and she may have been among the first, male or female, to keep before the public, nationally and internationally, the horrors of lynching which had become a national crisis in America during the late 19th century, following the emancipation of enslaved black people. The Anti-lynching crusader was tenacious in her agitation against the horrors of  lynching and was rightfully recognized by Fredrick Douglass in a letter he wrote which stated:

> *Dear Miss Wells:*
> *Let me give you thanks for your faithful paper on the lynch abomination now generally practiced against colored people in the South. There has been no word equal to it in convincing power. I have spoken, but my word is feeble in comparison. Brave woman!*
> —Frederick Douglass (1895)

In Wells-Barnett's mind, lynching and inequality were two of the main tools in the toolbox of Jim Crowism and used under the guise of protecting the honor of white women. In her early writings and newspaper work, she was known nationally and internationally for primarily targeted lynching. In her provocative Southern Horrors, *Lynch Law in All Its Phases*, published in 1892, Wells-Barnett revealed the undisclosed principle of lynching: "an excuse to get rid of Negroes who were acquiring wealth and property and thus keep the race terrorized." (*The Memphis Diary of Ida B. Wells* 191)

She also wrote an article for the front page of *The Memphis Free Speech and Headlight*, suggesting that African Americans should leave the town of murderers and move west for their own safety, after Thomas Moss, Calvin McDowell, and Henry Stewart were lynched (murdered) by a White mob because they opened a grocery store that competed with a White owned grocery store in the area. She informed the Black community that there was no justice for Blacks in Memphis. As a result, thousands of Black people fled Memphis, Tennessee (*Crusade for Justice*, p.57).

Wells-Barnett also wrote and published a searing article in her Memphis newspaper which disputed Whites' justifications for lynching Black people. The article also suggested that in some cases, White females secretly initiated liaisons with Black men. This article so infuriated leading White male citizens of Memphis, Tennessee that they stormed her newspaper office and destroyed the office and her printing press equipment. They sent word to Wells-Barnett, who was out of the city at the time, that if she ever returned to Memphis, she would be killed. Wells-Barnett took this threat to heart and never returned to Memphis, Tennessee (*Crusade for Justice*, p. 62).

Regarding "family centeredness" as a pillar of Africana Womanism,

Hudson-Weems views "family" in "family centeredness" as not only referring to the individual Black nuclear family and extended family unit's needs, desires, and aspirations, but also to those needs, desires, and aspirations of the total Black community.   Given Hudson-Weems' conceptualization, we find Wells-Barnett also operating as a modeler and promoter of collective "family centeredness" activism.

Wells-Barnett's "family centeredness" as it related to her caring about the needs, desires, and aspirations of the total Black community, and her "mothering" capabilities, converge as she becomes what Professor Stanley James (1993) describes in her article as "community other mother:"

> A community other mother is …in a position to provide analyses and/or critiques of conditions or situations that may affect the well-being of her community. Whenever necessary, she serves as a catalyst in the development and implementation of strategies designed to remedy these harmful conditions (48).

Keeping this definition in mind, Wells-Barnett served in many, many instances as a "community other mother" when situations and conditions negatively affected the Black community in the United States. The examples are numerous.  For example, Wells-Barnett as a teacher in Memphis, Tennessee, was appalled at the poor conditions of the facilities and educational system for Black children, and as a result, she publicly criticized the school board for its failure to make corrections (*Crusade For Justice*, p. xviii). Other well-known accomplishments of Wells-Barnett include her involvement in the founding of the National Association for the Advancement of Colored People (NAACP) and her organizing of the Alpha Suffrage Club (*Crusade for Justice, 345*).

Additionally, in 1922 after having settled in Chicago, Illinois and after becoming owner of the *Chicago Conservator* newspaper, Wells-Barnett did again act as a "community other mother" as she fearlessly returned to the South.  She travelled to Arkansas to investigate the case of - twelve (12) Black farmers, who had been jailed and sentenced to death for conspiring to murder Whites. Wells-Barnett discovered that these men had been entrapped in a scheme devised by Whites to confiscate the properties of these Black farmers. That was the reason these Black men had been falsely accused, jailed and sentenced to death (*Crusade for Justice*, 403). After learning the facts of this case, Wells-Barnett returned to Chicago and wrote and published the facts of the case in her newspaper, *The Chicago Conservator*.  She shined the light of truth on the situation, and eventually all twelve of the Black farmers were freed (*Crusade for Justice*, 404).

Also, Wells-Barnett played the "community other mother" role when in 1910 she helped establish the Negro Fellowship League in

Chicago, Illinois (*Crusade for Justice*, 404). She saw how many young Black men coming to Chicago from the South easily got into trouble, and then they would find themselves locked in jail. To remedy this situation, Wells-Barnett helped to establish the Negro Fellowship League. The League provided a safe haven for young Black men coming to Chicago to find work. The League provided sleeping quarters, a reading room, employment opportunities and Sunday worship services (*Crusade For Justice*, 306).

Wells-Barnett is most widely known for her "family centeredness" activism in relation to the Black community and her serving as a "community other mother" as she launched an international anti-lynching campaign. She investigated numerous cases of lynchings of Black men, women and children throughout the U.S., and she exposed the wrongs and injustices suffered by Blacks to many audiences in the United States and in Great Britain. To stop the lynching of Blacks, it was Wells-Barnett's plan to especially enlist the aid of the British "to exert moral force against the lynching evil" (*Crusade for Justice*, p. 189).

For years in the late 19th century and early 20th century, Wells-Barnett advocated for the establishment of anti-lynching law in the United States. It is sad commentary to have to point out that in the United States today, year of 2020, a bill to establish a national anti-lynching law, advocated by Wells-Barnett almost 100 years ago, has been blocked from passing in the United States Senate.

Many, questions have been asked such as why did Wells-Barnett risk her life in the struggle for social justice and civil rights for Black people? What propelled her forward to pursue this dangerous, life threatening and many times thankless work? Was it something in her DNA? Was it the influence of her father who was known as a "race man," an early social justice/civil rights activist for the Black community? It was said that he had an "independent spirit even during slavery and sought and attained his full independence in the period following emancipation" (*Crusade for Justice*, xiv). Or was it the beliefs of Ida's mother who "was a deeply religious woman" (*Crusade for Justice*, xiv)? Perhaps Wells-Barnett's activism was influenced by the actions and beliefs of both of her parents. In the article, "Ida B. Wells-Barnett: Answering the Call to Serve," Hilda Williams (2018) asserts that Wells-Barnett was highly motivated by her own spirituality, her deep abiding faith in God, as revealed in the illuminating volume, *The Memphis Diary of Ida B. Wells*, edited by Mirian DeCosta–Willis.

As evidence of her Christian spirituality, we find Wells-Barnett, a young, single, Black female schoolteacher in Memphis, Tennessee, penning this prayer in her diary:

God help me to be a Christian! To so conduct myself in my intercourse with the unconverted. Let it be an ever-present theme with me, & O help me to better control my temper! Bless me for the ensuing year. Let me feel that Thou art with me in all my struggles. May I be a better Christian with more of the strength to overcome the wisdom to avoid & have the meekness & humility that becometh a follower of Thee. (p. 261)

Wells-Barnett's prayer in this case reveals her spiritual belief in God and her seeking God's help for her Christian walk in life. In another instance, we find Wells-Barnett pouring out her anguish and devastation to God in her prayer. Williams further explains that Wells-Barnett had been forcibly removed from the lady's car of a train because of her race. As a result, she filed a discrimination suit against the Chesapeake and Ohio Railroad Company. She won the suit in the lower court; however, the Tennessee Supreme Court reversed the ruling" (p. 6). Angry and dismayed by the reversal, Wells-Barnett again cried out in her diary:

O God, is there no redress, no peace, no justice in this land for us? Thou has always fought the battles of the weak and oppressed. Come to my aid at this moment and teach me what to do, for I am sorely bitterly, disappointed. Show us the way, even as Thou led the children out of bondage into the Promised land. (141)

Not only did she express her dismay in this prayer, but more important, she implored God to "teach [her] what to do" in her social justice/civil rights struggle.

Fearless, and in the face of danger to her personal well-being, Wells-Barnett would not be deterred, and spoke directly to the matter saying, "One had better die fighting against injustice than to die like a dog or a rat in a trap." (Wells-Barnett, Crusade For Justice, p. 62) Again, Wells-Barnett's attitude and demeanor toward equality and social justice were quite evident throughout her life.

In the trajectory of her career as a journalist and investigative reporter, Wells-Barnett's life, reflected key tenants of Africana womanism, including self-naming, self-defining. Being an accomplished, successful woman, well-respected and a member of the black middle class, Wells-Barnett was obviously quite concerned about her personal persona and her identity, as a journalist. As a journalist in particular, she was aware of how easily her statements could be recorded, tracked, searched, and made accessible to the entire world.

After reading Sarah Igo's new book, entitled *The Known Citizen: A History of Privacy in Modern America* (2018), wherein she skillfully exams our fraught relationship with both confidentiality and exposure, some reconsideration surrounding Wells-Barnett's personal and private life, specifically her self-naming, self-definition, and working in concert with males, has come to the forefront. Several source materials, including the autobiography of Wells-Barnett herself, have provided key and relevant information about this iconic figure.

The act of naming has always carried implication of power and authority. To name is to master. Anthropology, through comparative ethnography, indicates that it is human to name one's self, others, and things. All people and cultures, in particular Europeans during the Age of Discovery, have always used this process to show mastery or, in most cases, dominance over others, possessions, and things in the natural world. According to VomBruck and Bodenhorn (2009), since names can in many cultures indicate such valuable information as gender, marital status, birthplace, nationality, ethnicity, religion, and position within a family, naming in itself becomes a linguistic practice through which the underlying ideological processes behind names can be accessed.

Anthropologists have argued that naming agency is unavoidably constrained because naming is a social and reflexive act in which name-givers consider how they want the named person to be identified, regarded and treated by others (Vom Bruck and Bodenhorn, 2006; Pina- Cabral, 2012). Bestowing names is part of the process of socialization by which individuals are inducted into society and begin to acquire a social identity. For example, Wells-Barnett categorized herself as a journalist and used the pen name, "Iola." The chances are that she adopted the identity of a journalist and began to act in the ways she believed journalists act (and conform to the norms of the group).

## *Acting in Concert with Men & the Struggle*

"Acting in concert" is a phrase connoting when parties undertake identical investment actions to achieve the same goal. Acting in concert requires the cooperation of individual or groups to make the same transactions based on a prior arrangement, or mutual agreement. Therefore, in the case of Wells-Barnett, her work as an educator, journalist, suffragist, writer, speaker, and organizer for civil rights and African American women's rights, inevitably crossed racial, ethnic, and gender boundaries. Many of these encounters, whether favorable or unfavorable for Well-Barnett, are well documented such as her professional relationship with the iconic Frederick Douglass and with W. E. B. DuBois in relation to the founding of the NAACP. However, there are several cases in which Well-Barnett acted in concert with males that have gone under the radar screen.

In particular, soon after Wells-Barnett relocated to Memphis, she became editor and co-owner with J. L. Fleming of *The Free Speech and Headlight*, a black-owned newspaper established by the Reverend Taylor Nightingale and based at the Beale Street Baptist Church in Memphis. In collaboration with Reverend Taylor Nightingale and J. L. Fleming as journalists, this new found partnership successfully and in the face of overwhelming odds covered local, and horrendous incidents of racial segregation and inequality (*The Memphis Diary of Ida B. Wells*, p. 143).

Prior to marriage to Attorney Ferdinand L. Barnett of Chicago, Illinois in 1895, Wells had worked with Frederick Douglass, Ferdinand L. Barnett, and I. Garland Penn to produce in 1893 the famous booklet entitled: The Reason Why the Colored American Is Not in the World's Columbian Expositions –The Afro-American's Contribution to Columbian Literature. Again, this is another example of Wells-Barnett acting in concert with her male counterparts as co-equal to make the same transaction, in this case, shining the light of truth on exclusion of African Americans from the World's Columbian Exposition because of racism (*Crusade for Justice,* p. xx).

For the purpose of placing Wells-Barnett's life in historical context in terms of Africana womanism, there are several notable examples to refer to for this writing. First and foremost, Wells-Barnett was such a towering public figure nationally and internationally that it defied societal conventions of that time, whether due to race or gender. The scrutiny and scholarly appraisal of her public life far outweighed that of her private life. Even though several scholarly works, DeCosta-Willis (1995), McMurry (1998), Schechter (2001), and Giddings (2008), were major contributions that captured the life and legacy of Wells-Barnett, virtually none fully addressed her private life or the relationships she had with her male counterparts as defined by the concept of "In Concert With Men."[1] Even as a young, single, intelligent, vibrant and vivacious Southern Black woman during the 19[th]century, Wells-Barnett's professional and nonprofessional lives were prototypical of Africana  womanism. According to Miriam Decosta Willis, editor of Wells-Barnett's diary, "she portrayed herself as a fiery, ambivalent, and fiercely independent woman, at war constantly with contrary instincts; an incipient feminist, countered by a straitlaced Victorian femininity: a desire for companionship, but no wish for marriage; and a longing for personal freedom, checked by a sense of duty to her family". (Duster 1970, 251) Nevertheless, in the quest for racial freedom and self-liberation, Well-Barnett was not unique in this regard. Whether born slaves, free, or freed in later life, many Black women during that time, such as Fannie Barrier Williams, Josephine Silone-Yates, Mary Church Terrell, and Josephine St. Pierre Ruffin, represented the ideal of black womanhood on a national level as portrayed by Elizabeth L. Davis in *Lifting as They Climb* (1933). Even though the aforementioned women were married, highly educated and considered in the high Black social class, they were active participants and advocates in public activities on behalf of racial uplifting. In reference to Mary Church Terrell, the daughter of Robert R. Church, whom Wells-Barnett describes in her dairy as "Mollie," is perhaps one of the few Black women of her age that she truly admired (*Ida: A Sword Among Lions*, p. 139).

Wells-Barnett had defined early in life, especially after the death of her parents, that "respectability" was a principal virtue that she would maintain at all costs. For example, Wells- Barnett's reputation was maliciously compromised during an innocent relationship with Dr. D. H. Gray. After the death of Well-Barnett's father, James, the white physician, Dr. Gray, came in possession of the monetary remains of the Wells family, and setup a meeting to return the money to Wells-Barnett at the train station. Following the encounter between Wells-Barnett and the white Dr. Gray, rumors were circulated locally that implied that young, orphaned Ida was selling herself to a white man. Unfortunately, Wells-Barnett could never get beyond this false rumor. In concert with men is the African woman's push to develop strong relationships with like-minded men in the struggle for overarching Black liberation and the eventually Black women's liberation. And it helped to shape her personality and relationship with men until marriage. Wells-Barnett explained in her autobiography that even friendly northerners could draw hasty conclusions about the honor of black women (Wells, 1970 43).

In regard to Wells-Barnett's self-identification, Schechter (2001) may have said it best, and argues that Wells-Barnett constructed an identity that simultaneously revealed a young black woman coming into adulthood during the Victorian Era with a defiant personality. She was critical, outspoken, rebellious and a critic that railed against black accommodation and white racism, whether the advocators were male or female. Ambivalent about marriage, yet desirous of intimacy, Well-Barnett struggled to reconcile her "feminine" role as a woman and her "masculine" desires in the public arena. Against the backdrop of Victorian womanhood, Wells-Barnett's activism often crossed the defining lines between male and female public space, which often threatened the social and political domain and authority of men. Refusing to adopt the traditional restrictive role assigned to black women, she often stepped outside those boundaries, creating conflict between, black and white men, and black and white women. (Schechter, 2001).

Historically, women's main route to status and influence involved attracting high-status romantic partners. But while the movement for gender equality today has changed things, during the Victorian era, cultural scripts about romance involving women's social roles were status quo. Heterosexual romantic relationships during Wells-Barnett's time, and when she would have been in her prime as a young woman, men courted and "kept" women. And there was a powerful tradition of men being suitors and women being girlfriends and mistresses. Surely, Wells-Barnett was well aware of societal dictates of the day for men and women; however, she chose for herself a different path to deal with suitors. One of Wells-Barnett's biographer (Paula Giddings, 2009) wrote that she was very popular among her male suitors and received a half-dozen Valentine's Day cards from men vying for her interest (*Ida: A Sword Among Lions*, p. 99). Clearly, Wells-Barnett had several prominent suitors such as Dr. Sidney Burchett, a young physician; Isaiah J. Graham[1], a fellow teacher; Louis M. Brown, a newspaper man, and Charles S. Morris, a student at Howard University. This might lead one to ask, "Was she flirtatious?" Was Wells-Barnett, according to DeCosta-Willis (1995), one who played "the feminine game [that] exposes her to the charge that she is a silly flirt and a heartless coquette who toys with men's affections?" She writes of her "pity and contempt" for B. F. Poole, a journalist and former suitor. Looking back on that period of her life, she explained, "[M]y good name was all that I had in the world, [because] I had [no means]. Wells-Barnett's diary, which she started in 1885 through 1887, gives a rare glimpse of the 'private self' at a particularly difficult time. In particular, one key passage in the diary states, according to DeCosta-Willis, that "Wells's discomfort with the societal roles that she was supposed to play is most clearly reflected in her rebellion against the courtship rituals of her day. Very few of the men in Wells-Barnett's world were a match for her intelligence, independence, tough mindedness, and she was both derisive of their failure to live up to her expectations and unwilling, to play romantic games in order to "earn" their company: "I will not begin at this late day by doing that that my soul abhors; sugaring men, weak, deceitful creatures, with flattery to retain them as escorts or to gratify a revenge" (JAN, 30, 1886).

Concurring with Washington (ix), "the diary became a place for Wells-Barnett to record those intimate thoughts she could not share with others, a place to "talk-out" those issues she could not seem to resolve and a way of clarifying and affirming her own growth." In one very painful encounter with a former lover who married someone else, she concluded, somewhat arrogantly, that, since she herself did not have the necessary qualities of submission, and meekness to be a good wife, he had made the right choice. Further, Washington (xvii) contended that the diary also "exposes a private side of Wells –her vulnerabilities and hesitancy—it also reveals the tenacity, intellectual power, and self-determination that are the hallmark of her public persona.

In summary, Ida B. Wells-Barnett had a strong commitment to both her family and her people. One is reminded of today's BLACK LIVES MATTER MOVEMENT, with the national and international chanting of "BLACK LIVES MATTER!! BLACK LIVES MATTER!!" This is the same sentiment trumpeted by Ida B. Wells-Barnett, a Black female social justice/civil rights activist of the late 1800s thru the early 1900s in America. She is best known for expressing this sentiment in the press, as she reported the criminal and horrible acts by White mobs who lynched (murdered) thousands of innocent Black men, women and children.

Ida B. Wells- Barnett's actions were similar, in some respects, to the young woman who shined the light literally thru her cell phone camera to film the public murder of George Floyd by Minnesota police officers. Ida B. Wells-Barnett figuratively shined the powerful light of truth thru her investigative journalism efforts on many injustices suffered by Blacks at the hands of Whites in America during the late 19th and early 20th centuries. To be sure, her strong sense of "spirituality," "family centeredness," and "mothering" in her social justice/civil rights activism can serve as an exemplar of these pillars in Africana Womanism. She is the embodiment, the personification, the supreme paradigm of the true Africana Womanist in action, although too often, she "has been erroneously referred to by many as a pre-feminist, much like many other Black women writers/activists" (Hudson-Weems, "Africana Womanism: Authenticity and Collectivism" in *Africana Paradigms* 14). This position was upheld in an article on Anna Julia Cooper (1858-1964), one of Wells-Barnett's contemporaries, written by Dr. Larese Hubbard and titled "Anna Julia Cooper and Africana Womanism: Some Early Conceptual Contributions." Both these perceptive writers were powerful Africana Womanists, with a powerful Africana womanist mission. In fact, one might surmise that in writing her autobiography, *Crusade for Justice*, Ida B. Wells Barnett did not complete her last sentence. Instead, she stopped in mid- sentence, writing the word "Go." Perhaps this word "Go" ends her autobiography with a powerful challenge to all who read her autobiography. Thus, she is challenging all of her readers, especially Black people, to continue the struggle for Social Justice and Civil Rights because, indeed, **Black Lives Do Matter!**

# Bibliography

Bodenhorn, B., and Bruck, G., editors. "Entangled in Histories: An Introduction to the Anthropology of Names and Naming" in *An Anthropology of Names and Naming*. Cambridge: Cambridge University Press, 2006, 1-30.

Christian, Mark. Afterword in *Africana Womanism: Reclaiming Ourselves,* Fifth Edition. London and New York: Routledge, 2019, 131-133.

Davis, Elizabeth Lindsay. *Lifting as They Climb*. New York: Macmillan Publishing Company, 1996.

Dubois, W. E. B. *The Souls of Black Folk*. Cambridge, MA: A.C. McClurg & Co.; University Press John Wilson and Son, 1903.

Gabbidon, Shaun L., Greene, Helen Taylor, Young, Vernetta D. *African American Classics in Criminology and Criminal Justice*. Newbury Park, CA: Sage Publications, Inc., 2001.

Giddings, Paula. *Ida: A Sword Among Lions*. New York: Harper. Collins Publishers, 2008.

Hudson-Weems, Clenora. "Africana Womanism: Authenticity and Collectivity in Securing Social Justice" in *Africana Paradigms, Practices and Literary Texts: Evoking Social Justice*. Dubuque, Iowa: Kendall Hunt Publishing Company, 2021, 1-22.

Hudson-Weems, Clenora. *Africana Womanism: Reclaiming Ourselves*, Fifth Edition. London and New York: Routledge, 2019.

Hudson-Weems, Clenora. A*fricana Womanist Literary Theory*. Trenton: Africa World Press, 2004.

Igo, Sarah. *The Known Citizen: A History of Privacy in Modern America*. Cambridge, MA: Harvard University Press, 2018.

James, Stanlie M. "Mothering: A Possible Black Feminist Link to Social Transformation?" in *Theorizing Black Feminism*. Stanlie M. James and Abena P.A. Busia, editors. London and New York: Routledge, 1993.

Stewart, James B. and Ama Mazama. Foreword in *Africana Womanism: Reclaiming Ourselves*, Fifth Edition. London and New York: Routledge, 2019, xiii-xv.

Thompson, Mildred. *Ida B. Wells-Barnett: An Exploratory Study of an American Black Woman, 1893–1930*. Malone, New York: Carlson Publishers, 1990.

Wells, Ida B. *Crusade for Justice: The Autobiography of Ida B. Wells.* Alfreda Duster, editor. Chicago and London: The University of Chicago Press, 1972.

Wells, Ida B. *The Red Record: Tabulated Statistics and Alleged Causes of Lynching in the United States, 1895*. Moscow, Russia: Dodo Press, 2009.

Williams, Hilda B. *Ida B. Wells-Barnett-Answering the Call to Serve.* Memphis, TN: GrantHouse Publishers, 2018.

Willis, Miriam DeCosta, editor. *The Memphis Diary of Ida B. Wells.* Boston: Beacon Press, 1995.

# Note

[1] J. Graham, a native of Georgia, became the principal of Virginia Avenue School in Memphis, TN was highlighted in *The Bright Side of Memphis* (1908) by G. P. Hamilton as "a teacher of long and successful experience and has been connected with the city schools of Memphis since 1884.

# 9

## FROM PUBLIC/PRIVATE SCHOOLS TO THE ACADEMY: *AFRICANA WOMANISM*—INTERCONNECTIVITY AND THE AFRICANA FAMILY

### *TAMMY S. TAYLOR, DISSERTATOR*

Every now and then there emerges an idea that is so rich, so ripe and so very revolutionary that the theoretical arena is forever changed. At the same time, it is so simple—deceptively, so immediately identifiable, and so fully verifiable that one has to wonder why no one ever thought of it before. Such is the case of Africana Womanism was espoused by Clenora Hudson-Weems, who has shaken the very foundation of Women's studies in America and abroad with her highly sought after public addresses and numerous publications, including her seminal work, *Africana Womanism: Reclaiming Ourselves*. (Reed, Foreword in *Africana Womanist Literary Theory* xv)

### Introduction

Dr. Clenora Hudson-Weems, progenitor of the concept of Africana Womanism, identified the elevation and empowerment of the Africana race and community as the center of consciousness for the Africana Womanist. She postulates that Africana men, women, and children share a unique connection, allowing the triumvirate to garner strength from each other, realizing that they are far better together than either of the three could ever be apart from one another. As an Academician, Dr. Hudson-Weems has spent her life challenging the status quo. Her legendary work, identifying Emmett Till as the catalyst of the modern Civil Rights Movement, positioned her as an authority on the Black Community. However, her careful examination and presentation of Africana Womanism as a theoretical construct has confirmed her as an expert and authority not only in the Black Community, but also in the system that represents – Institutions of Higher Education (The Academy) across the globe. In the Afterword to *Contemporary Africana Theory, Thought and Action: A Guide to Africana Studies*, Africana European scholar, Dr. Mark Christian of Liverpool, England, insisted upon the following:

> As Africana Studies focuses on the totality of Africana life and the interrelatedness of all African people – men, women and children globally – so must the Africana woman place the needs of her greater Africana family, who have for centuries suffered racial domination and exploitation, at the top of her list of priorities for ultimate human survival. Admittedly, the destiny of the collective Africana community lies within a concerted collective world-view wherein African centered thought and practice must co-exist on equal terms. (Christian 464)

Unlike Dr. Hudson-Weems, an iconic theorist, I am a principal, and a practitioner in the PK-12 public school system. I personally find Dr. Hudson-Weems' work to be fascinating and timely, as the coronavirus pandemic has seemingly created an even greater gap in the trajectory of students' matriculation from the PK-12 education system into higher education. As an educator and practitioner, I understand the magnanimity of pedagogically communicating the 5 Ws to a listening or reading audience. As such, this introduction will explain the - **Who, What, When, Where**, and **Why** of this chapter:

## WHO and WHAT?

The who in this work has been clearly defined. Dr. Hudson-Weems' name has become synonymous with the words – Africana and Womanism. Her work has separated her from other theorists because her work is so inclusionary. She does not seek to exclude her Africana brothers or our children from her quest to empower Africana people. Instead, she has adopted the philosophy that we are all better together, which she states in the opening of her 4-stanza-poem, "Africana Womanism: 'I Got Your Back, Boo'" (2009):

> Don't you know by now, girl, we're all In It Together!
> Family-Centrality--that's it; we're going nowhere without the other.
> That means the men, the women, and children, too,
> Truly collectively working—"I got your back, Boo."

Of course, she does not minimize the subjugation of the Africana woman, for she contends that the Africana woman has, in fact, been marginalized on three dimensions: race, class, and gender. However, she is very clear, on her position, which is that marginalization for the Africana woman has occurred in that very order – race, class, and gender. To be sure, Africana Womanism does not focus on gender empowerment to the exclusion of all else. My mission, then, is to bridge yet another chasmic gap existing between PK-12 and The Academy, for as an educator, I see first-hand the need to connect PK-12 education to the Academy or Higher Education in order to better benefit Africana families and the entire Africana Community, as well.

To define the theory of Africana Womanism, it is important to first understand what Africana Womanism is not. Africana Womanism is not the black version of feminism, as some have purported. Why not? Hudson-Weems explains, "To begin with, the true history of feminism, its origins and its participants, reveals its blatant racist background, thereby establishing its incompatibility with African women." (*Africana Womanism* 12). During the Women's Suffrage Movement, it became very clear that the agenda of the White women leading that cause did not include their black counterparts. Although the original message of the Movement was said to have been the abolition of slavery and equal rights for all people, the white women in the Movement were very clear and vocal about their disappointment when the Fifteenth Amendment to the Constitution of the United States ratified the voting rights of Africana men, leaving women, particularly White women's rights, unaddressed (Painter).

Africana Womanism is intended to unite the Africana community. The characteristics of this framework are solidly the characteristics found in Africanans since antiquity. Those characteristics are Self-Namer, Self-Definer, Genuine in Sisterhood, Strong, In Concert with Males in Struggle, Authentic, Whole, Flexible Role Player, Respected, Male Compatible, Respectful of Elders, Ambitious, Adaptable, Mothering, Spiritual, Family Centered, and Nurturing, all natural embodiments of Africanans. These characteristics are demonstrated in all facets of life, including experiences of Africanans present in the PK-12 public and private school systems.

## WHEN?

Africanans have been involved in an age-old-struggle for centuries, and still struggle up to the present. Diasporic Africanans have had to fight enslavement and blatant disregard in search of their rightful positions in society. These experiences are critically important – as students must begin to be connected to their past and their purposes in order to move forward successfully.

# WHERE?

Dr. Hudson-Weems has experienced myriad cultures as represented around the world. These cultural experiences have helped her shape the Africana Womanism Theoretical construct as one that is inclusive of Africana people everywhere. Scholars from across the globe have affirmed the work of Hudson-Weems as both timely and relevant, as well as scholarly and impactful. For example, the late Dr. Zula Sofola, Professor and Head of Department of the Performing Arts University of Ilorin Kwara State, Nigeria, wrote the following:

Africana Womanism strongly makes the point that the Eurocentric definition of woman is alien and destructive to the woman of African heritage. Consequently, subscribers to the disparate Eurocentric and Afrocentric definitions cannot share in a common movement whose essential definition and course of action are anathema to the Afrocentric worldview (Sofola, Foreword in *Africana Womanism*, 5th Edition xii). As such, this is just one of many confirmations that the Africana Womanism theory is a world-wide, global phenomenon. A very important benefit of the theory is that it solidly presents a tool to unite Africana people and communities around the world.

# WHY?

In the Foreword to *Africana Womanist Literary Theory*, Dr. Delores P. Aldridge articulates that the most significant challenges for Africana/Black Studies and Women's Studies in American higher education for decades are the lack of inclusion of Africana women in particular, and respect for their experiences in the Academy. She said that

> While both movements addressed some very real inadequacies, such as paucity faculty, absence and distortion of curriculum content, and programmatic resources in the Academy, neither fully embraced the unique and authentic experiences of women of African descent in America or on the African continent and throughout the African diaspora. Thus, it became imperative to launch major efforts to recognize and include Africana women in the Academy, with a focus on their scholarship – scholarship being at the center of academe (Aldridge xi).

Many of the same perils befall the PK-12 public/private school systems, as well. Connecting the Academy to the PK-12 public and private education sector is a necessary task in determining the future of the Africana community world-wide. This conversation has begun under the powerful leadership of the Africana Womanism scholar and expert herself,

Dr. Clenora Hudson-Weems.  I am both humbled and honored to be able to add to this extremely important discussion by furthering the work and bridging some enormous gaps currently existing in the field.  The impact of such a strongly forged and committed partnership is sure to benefit Africanan people for years and years to come.  Despite the controversies associated within the field surrounding Africana Womanism when compared to Black or African Feminism, such a needed discussion can have a lasting impact on the Africanan community by continuing to expose the glaring disparities when the three ideologies are carefully compared.

The impact on education can be a lasting one.  The PK-12 curriculum does not provide a comprehensive view of Africana history.  There are huge gaps in the literature that must be closed.  These gaps are undermining of the true richness of Africana heritage and almost exclusively begin the Africana people's story with slavery.  This travesty only adds to the possibility of Africana children and staff feeling more subjugated and inferior to an age-old oppressive system.  This system, the one through which they matriculated, does not honor their true heritage and, therefore, creates an unnecessary gap for Africana children in particular when thinking about their futures.

Another very important connection Africana Womanism can make for Africanans – men, women, and children – is a firm affirmation that Africanans are not naturally/inherently less capable, less intelligent, or substandard to their White counterparts in any way.  Embracing their true heritage and developing a genuine understanding of who they are as Africanans can help them to realize that there is a level of genius in each of them and that it's up to them to dig deep and find it.  Teachers and administrators in PK-12 systems must come to this realization, as well.  They must be accountable by holding Africana children accountable at high levels by not allowing them to fall short of their God-given potential and propensities.  A respected scholar in the field of education, Dr. Chike Akua, once quoted Dr. Asa Hilliard as saying,

> There can be no question but that the achievement of African students is, in general, far below their potential.  This gap, however, should not be thought of as the gap between Black and white students.  It should be thought of as the gap between current performance of African students and levels of excellence.  When we choose performance as the goal, academically and socially, we change the teaching and learning paradigm in fundamental ways.  By setting the required performance level at excellent, we require excellent performance to be articulated (Hilliard 138).

This means that we must not settle for less than our Africana students' very best.  Excellence must become our standard for working with and committing to all our Africana students. We have to help them to find the power of unity and the impact it can have on their lives and futures. The long-term goal, of course, would be for more Africana students to graduate from high school and go on to earn advanced degrees at higher rates. As Fredrick Douglas so brilliantly assesses, "It is easier to build strong children than to repair broken men" (Douglass in Mapp & Gabel).

# Men

For centuries, Africana men have been the subject of much controversy and debate. In many ways, society has sought to emasculate them and diminish them in the eyes of Africana women and children. The attempt to whittle away at their position of authority must be seen for what it is – an effort to disintegrate the Africana family. It is quite startling and very appalling that Black males still on an average earn less money, are less likely to graduate from college, are more likely to be arrested and sent to prison, and die at young ages than other men in our society. As a society, we must demand – and work together for – dramatic, lasting change (*USA Today*, September 2020). Some startling statistics continue to reveal the reality of Africana men more than fifty years after the modern Civil Rights Movement, as we knew it.

In 2019, only 28% of Black men held a bachelor's degree or higher compared to over 40% of white men. Additionally, only half as many Black men hold advanced degrees when compared with their white counterparts. Black workers, regardless of gender, earn less than white workers. Black men earn $378.00 less per week than white men and $125.00 less than white women. According to the U.S. Bureau of Labor Statistics, it is estimated that participation rate for Black men aged 20 and over is 5.6 percentage points lower than for white men. Black men have the highest unemployment rate of civilian non-institutionalized Black and white men and women over age 20. The Bureau of Labor Statistics confirmed that there was a large race gap in unemployment, independent of gender, even before COVID-19 swept the United States. Prior to March 2020, Black men consistently had among the highest unemployment rates of Black and white workers. Black men are twice as likely to be unemployed as white men. Although women live longer than men, on an average, there is a big race gap. Life expectancy is lowest for Black men, among Black and white people, both at birth and at age 65. Black men die four years earlier than white men. During the global pandemic, Black men have been the most likely among Black and white Americans to die of COVID-19 at a rate of 2.4 times that of white men, according to CDC data through July 2020. In general, Black men are more likely to die from

COVID-19 period. Black men face a much higher chance of being incarcerated, according to the Bureau of Justice data. Black men are overrepresented among prisoners by a factor of five (32% v. 6%). These are hard facts but ones that have to be faced and dealt with in order to respond to the once-in-a-generation moment of racial reckoning taking place in our country right now. Policymakers must consider the experiences of Black men and facts such as these through a lens of interconnectivity through frameworks for dissecting these challenges to examine how Black men's identities can combine to create specific nodes of disadvantage (brookings.edu/blog, 2020). Dr. Hudson-Weems' Africana Womanism theory provides such a framework to emphasize the family centrality of Africana people. Men, women, and children in Africana Womanism thought work together for the advancement of the communities in which they live and serve. As such, Africana men and women are tasked with organizing our families for Black liberation. In our communities, working together is what is most important, not working in isolation or in absentia of one another. Therefore, we must prioritize race, class and gender, as the Africana Womanism framework is not gender exclusive. The Africana Womanism paradigm allows us the fortune of viewing the challenges Black men face through a scope of interconnectedness. According to Hudson-Weems, this interconnectivity respects that just like the Black woman, the Black man has many different levels. However, his primary focus, like hers, has been and always will be on the family and our community, even though that view can sometimes be obstructed by other things and the many challenges life can bring.

## Women

  For decades, Black Women have struggled to earn appropriate recognition as the incredible leaders they are. From the Antebellum South, through Jim Crow and on throughout the Civil Rights Movement, to the challenging and perplexing present, filled with social and political unrest, Black Women have demonstrated their intelligence, fortitude, superior leadership skills in sundry ways. These women, who served as agents of societal change, have paved the way for Black Women in education, politics, and other careers to blaze new trails. Many of these important women's names have not been recorded in history, while versions of others' stories have been allowed to be told to document an account of history that has been accepted as truth by many. However, those women's stories have often been modified and adjusted to create a textbook version of some very dark and demoralizing times in US history. Unquestionably, many very important women in the history of Blacks in America have been deliberately written out of history because they challenged white counterparts and what were considered to be the societal norms of the time (Painter).

One such example can be noted in the life of Frances Ellen Watkins Harper. During an interview with Leonard Lopate, historian Nell Painter describes Mrs. Harper, as a free born Black. Quite an anomaly of the time, Mrs. Harper was also an educated black person who held Underground Railroad Conductor, Harriet Tubman, in very high esteem. As an abolitionist, suffragist, poet, and author, Harper was bold and unafraid to challenge the norms of the time. During this interview, it was shared that she also connected with other abolitionists of her day, whether free born or enslaved. At one point in history (1865 - 1867), there was a mixed group, including both black and white women abolitionists who were working for reform as a unified group. When Elizabeth Cady Stanton and Susan B. Anthony became vocal about their opinions of black men gaining the right to vote, that movement soon began to fall apart. Harper challenged their belief that racism and classism had no place in the movement during an 1866 convention. It was at that May 1, 1866 Eleventh National Women's Rights Convention" in New York City that she delivered her powerful and illuminating speech, "We Are All Bound Up Together," creating a rift between her and the white women suffragists because Anthony and Stanton refused to understand that for Black Women, women's rights could not be separated from issues of race (Painter).

Harper was quoted in the abolitionist newspapers (Primary Source) where many other suffragists were introduced. However, unlike Sojourner Truth, she was not included in the women's history that came from those newspapers and made it to modern accounts of Women's History. Portions of Mrs. Harper's speech challenged the entire suffrage movement and created, no doubt, a level of discomfort for white suffragists. Frances Ellen Watkins Harper boldly declared:

"I do not believe that giving the woman the ballot is immediately going to cure all the ills of life. I do not believe that white women are dewdrops just exhaled from the skies. I think that like men they may be divided into three classes, the good, the bad, and the indifferent. The good would vote according to their convictions and principles; the bad, as dictated by prejudice or malice; and the indifferent will vote on the strongest side of the question, with the winning party.
You white women speak here of rights. I speak of wrongs. I, as a colored woman, have had in this country an education which has made me feel as if I were in the situation of Ishmael, my hand against every man, and every man's hand against me. Let me go tomorrow morning and take my seat in one of your street cars — I do not know that they will do it in New York,

but they will in Philadelphia — and the conductor will put up his hand and stop the car rather than let me ride."

She concluded this powerful declaration with a tribute to Arimenta Harriet Ross, also known as Minty to her family and friends. She said,

> "We have a woman in our country who has received the name of 'Moses,' not by lying about it, but by acting out - a woman who has gone down into the Egypt of slavery and brought out hundreds of our people into liberty. The last time I saw that woman, her hands were swollen. That woman who had led one of Montgomery's most successful expeditions, who was brave enough and secretive enough to act as a scout for the American army, had her hands all swollen from a conflict with a brutal conductor, who undertook to eject her from her place. That woman, whose courage and bravery won a recognition from our army and from every black man in the land, is excluded from every thoroughfare of travel. Talk of giving women the ballot-box? Go on. It is a normal school, and the white women of this country need it. While there exists this brutal element in society which tramples upon the feeble and treads down the weak, I tell you that if there is any class of people who need to be lifted out of their airy nothings and selfishness, it is the white women of America."
> (Proceedings of the Eleventh National Woman's Rights Convention).

Such an unexpected controversial speech, rendering Harper's assessment of the true nature of the Women's Suffragist Movement, delivered to an entire convention of women, is what most likely left Mrs. Harper on the outside of the suffrage movement, but certainly not on the outside of working for the rights of Blacks. She was co-founder of the National Association of Colored Women's Clubs. There are other documented accounts of Harper supporting white suffragists like Anthony and Stanton later in that movement; however, Frances Ellen Watkins Harper is not a household name associated with Women's History.

While Frances Ellen Watkins Harper's story has largely been omitted from the widely accepted accounts of history, stories of other significant Black Women have been altered or adjusted to reflect an acceptable version or account for our history books. Harriet Tubman, who was held in high esteem by fellow abolitionists like Frances Ellen Watkins Harper, represents one of those females. In a documentary of Harriet Tubman's life, it can be seen that although Harriet has been hailed as "Moses,' a heroine by many for her commitment to bringing southern slaves to the North to freedom by way of the Underground Railroad, the story of her heroism has been reduced to freeing over three hundred slaves. During the 19 documented trips back to the southern states to free slaves, Harriet encountered numerous challenges and unexpected detours that required quick thinking and courage. A very hefty reward had been placed on Harriet's life. The reward described Harriet as an illiterate woman with a scar; therefore, many of her trips were made as a man with a book. Harriet Tubman is a perfect example of how males and females are in concert in our liberation struggle. On her trips back to the south, Harriet Tubman did not commit to only freeing her enslaved sisters. Rather, her trips to freedom included both men, women, and children, too. Frederick Douglas, a Black Male who is regarded for his radical ways and courage, said this to Harriet Tubman,

> "Most of that I have done, and suffered in the service of our cause has been in public. I have had the applause of the crowd and the satisfaction that comes with being approved by the multitude. While the most you have done has been witnessed by the few trembling, scared, and foot-sore bondsmen and women whom you have led out of the house of bondage and whose heartfelt God Bless You has been your only reward!"

Frederick Douglas' words indicate his awareness that although Harriet Tubman was a noble and brave woman who fought the fight for freedom of southern Black slaves, she was basically invisible to the cause not simply because she was a woman, but mostly because, she was a Black Woman (Fernandez). This important acknowledgement by a respected abolitionist like Frederick Douglas is very significant, because it can serve as confirmation that as a black man, he recognized and respected the contributions Harriet Tubman made to the liberation struggle of their people. This, once again, relates to how, although unnamed before Dr. Hudson-Weems defined the theory of Africana Womanism, the concepts have been a part of the history of Africana people for centuries.

For almost two centuries women have had to posture for an equitable place in society. Since the death of George Floyd in May 2020, the discussion of such inequalities has gained more national and even international attention. The discussion has highlighted that white women, despite belonging to a widely marginalized group themselves, can often also be marginalizers in their continual reticence and apathy towards the fight for Black female equality (Barratt). Black females are more likely to experience occupational segregation, as well as earn less than their white counterparts. On an average, women earn 19% less than white men in the United States. Black women specifically earn 39% less than white men. These less than surprising statistics suggest Black female professionals are facing discrimination for both their race and gender. With such a widespread problem, women are often guilty of discriminatory practices against each other, as well. For example, these facts include Black women in administrative roles in the school system. Although the number of Black female principals has increased over the past the number still is less than representative of the number of females who serve in the role of teacher. In an article that appeared on *UConn Today*, an official news website for the University of Connecticut, it was reported, beyond being underrepresented in the role of school leader, that black female principals face additional challenges in these positions in the form of microaggressions (Barrat). Women in leadership is not a new phenomenon. Black Women have been faced with the woes of the interconnectivity of their race, gender, and in many instances, their class for centuries. Dr. Hudson-Weems examines the organic nature and authenticity of Africana Womanism as the nucleus of the Africana family and the goal of always applying such ideals to the betterment of the entire Africana community.

Transformative leadership is creative and adapts non-traditional approaches to lead in their particular contexts. These transformative women eschewed top-down leadership and encouraged others to develop their own approaches to leadership and then supported them to achieve their goals. Transformative leadership develops an atmosphere of trust, which is a major component of transformative leadership (Bell). Some of the main characteristics that develop an atmosphere of trust are commitment, consistency, reliability, and diligence. Another very important aspect of transformational leadership is respect. Respect manifests itself in reliability, transparency (disclosing intentions and actions), and inclusiveness. Transformational leadership among these women, just like in women today, encouraged maximum participation and the taking on of leadership roles to effect positive change. This type of leadership is motivational and inspirational to others (Bell).

Servant leadership reflected leaders who were rooted in their desire to first serve their communities and others, as opposed to gaining power or fame for themselves. Black women have embraced work without recognition for centuries. Although they didn't seek recognition, they realized strategic recognition would help their causes and foster them while furthering their work. It's important to note, Servant does not mean servile. The ultimate servant leader was considered to be Jesus Christ (Bell). Harriet Tubman is a powerful example of servant leadership. She led hundreds of slaves to freedom, never seeking notoriety for herself or personal gain. She continued to sacrifice to help others throughout the remainder of her life. She served as both a Union Army scout and spy. After the Civil War, she established a home for the aged in New York (Fernandez). Servant leaders are gentle, humble, and generous. Those characteristics are also true of Social Justice leaders today (Bell).

Adaptive leadership ensures that leaders thrive in challenging environments and receive the support and sustenance necessary to continue their work over a lifetime. Black Women Leaders developed a sense of confidence and self-worth through the Civil Rights movement and the contributions they made. This allowed them to have life-long development in their personal and professional lives. Having a firm grasp on Black culture and recognition of their cultural heritage helped them to develop effective coping mechanisms, allowing them to lead without being paralyzed by fear of the unknown. Their individual growth and dedication to improving the lots of Black people were natural consequences of their personal circumstances and philosophies. This type of leadership forced Black women to be courageous in the face of fear. Myrlie Evers, widow of Medgar Evers, lived with the fear of their home being bombed and the threat of assignation looming over them at all times (Bell). However, she continued to work alongside her husband for the betterment of Blacks in America. Black women's leadership is compassionate and loving, focusing on the values of redemption, forgiveness, and peace. Black Women understood that being forgiving was not an act of weakness, but one of assertiveness and power. Being able to forgive allowed women to exhibit a moral authority and grace. Examples of this powerful phenomenon are Mamie Till Bradley, the mother of the murdered Chicago teen, Emmett Till, and Coretta Scott King (Bell). Just as Black Women faced challenges and trials in leadership over time, Black women leaders today face similar woes and obstacles in all aspects and arenas of leadership, especially education. Black Women leaders are tasked with improving schools, creating successful schools, and moving the academic needle, all while creating a strong, positive school culture and climate that can be sustained through all situations that may arise. Additionally, Black Women principals are often forced to find the style of leading that supports their philosophies of education, while allowing them to be true to their beliefs and convictions about students and learning. The Africana Womanism paradigm has identified both nurturing and mothering as important characteristics. Black Women are naturally nurturers and possess a mothering nature. These characteristics make an educator's service respectable and honorable. Moreover, Black women and black men are committed to creating a culture of learning for Black children that is inclusive and personalized to ensure students' success.

Leadership has an impact on every aspect of a school from environment to academics. If Black Women principals are not supported in efforts to become effective leaders, they often struggle with making decisions that can move the school forward. Often times, Black Women principals are not supported in their efforts to move school because their styles of leadership are non-conventional and don't align with what is traditionally or widely accepted in the field of education today. This can create a real disconnect and present principals with unnecessary struggles. Black Women principals must also learn to adapt to the situations facing them in their respective schools and apply the leadership necessary to navigate their trials. This natural leadership in Africana women, just as in Africana men, speaks to the Africana Womanism ideology that we are an interconnected fabric, woven together by all of the individual parts that make us who we are. The Africana womanist is by nature a unifier; therefore, we must utilize her strengths to bring about needed changes in the family and school structures to create lasting changes.

## Children

In Whitney Houston's legendary song, "Greatest Love of All," she emphasizes the importance of teaching children to look inside and understand; they have everything they need inside:

> I believe the children are our future
> Teach them well and let them lead the way
> Show them all the beauty they possess inside
> Give them a sense of pride to make it easier
> Let the children's laughter remind us how we used to be
> Everybody searching for a hero
> People need someone to look up to
> I never found anyone who fulfill my needs
> A lonely place to be
> And so I learned to depend on me
> I decided long ago
> Never to walk in anyone's shadows
> If I fail, if I succeed
> At least I'll live as I believe
> No matter what they take from me
> They can't take away my dignity
> Because the greatest love of all
> Is happening to me
> I found the greatest love of all
> Inside of me
> The greatest love of all
> Is easy to achieve
> Learning to love yourself
> It is the greatest love of all
> I believe the children are our future
> Teach them well and let them lead the way
> Show them all the beauty they possess inside

Give them a sense of pride to make it easier
Let the children's laughter remind us how we used to be
I decided long ago
Never to walk in anyone's shadows
If I fail, if I succeed
At least I'll live as I believe
No matter what they take from me
They can't take away my dignity
Because the greatest love of all
Is happening to me
I found the greatest love of all
Inside of me
The greatest love of all
Is easy to achieve
Learning to love yourself
Is the greatest love of all
And if, by chance, that special place
That you've been dreaming of
Leads you to a lonely place
Find your strength in love

Africana Womanism, just like the lyrics to the song, is designed to help Africana children to know their value and to see their worth. When introduced as an affirmative perspective, Africana Womanism can have a positive impact on every member of the Africana community.

One characteristic of Africana Womanism that we must take our children back to is the concept of Respect. We must begin to not only teach our children that respect is important, but we must also begin to require that respect to be given to all, especially our elders. Far greater than any other level of respect, we also must teach our youth to have a sense of self-worth and a respect for themselves that motivates them to strive for more in order to attain a level of EXCELLENCE that only comes from putting forth one's very best. Our responsibility is to lead them in the right direction so that they will grow up to become responsible leaders themselves, who in turn will pass the lessons on to the future leaders and generations.

Two additional very important characteristics of Africana Womanism we must ensure Africana children are immersed in each day are being ambitious and being adaptable. These characteristics are so crucially rudimentary to our children's healthy growth and development, because in a society filled with hidden rules that are designed to force children away from their natural inclinations towards a societal acclimation to the accepted norms of the dominant culture, children have to be able to adapt to different situations, different expectations, and different conditions in order to survive. We have to teach our children how to become more ambitious and determined to be successful in school with future goals in mind. We have to teach our children to understand, appreciate, and embrace their cultural heritage as a means for matriculating through the PK – 12 school system, with a smooth transition to the Academy, the workforce, and/or the military upon high school graduation. Preparing our children will benefit the entire Africana community world-wide.

# The Academy

While Black students are catching up to their white counterparts in terms of college enrollment, there has been less progress in closing the degree attainment gap. In 2019, 29% of the Black population aged 25 to 29 held a bachelor's degree or higher, compared to 45% of the white population in the same age range.

## *Enrollment/Degree Attainment*

• The college enrollment rate for Black students who enter immediately after completing high school (GED recipients included) was 57% in 2019, lower than in 2000 (66%).
   -Between 2000 and 2010, Black undergraduate enrollment increased by 73% (from 1.5 million students to 2.7 million).
   -However, between 2009 and 2019, Black undergraduate enrollment decreased from 2.5 million students to 2.1 million students.

• Of the 16.6 million undergraduate students enrolled in the Fall of 2019, Black students made up 2.1 million students of the undergraduate population but they were not equally represented at different institution types.
   - Black students made up 12% of the student population at 4-year public institutions, 13% of the student population at 4-year private nonprofit institutions, and 29% of the student population at 4-year private for-profit institutions.
   - Only 15% of Black students attended a highly selective institution, and only 8% of Black students attended an elite research institution.
   - Black students earned 14% of all Bachelor's degrees, 7% of all Master's degrees, and 5% of all Doctoral degrees conferred in science, technology, engineering, and mathematics (STEM) fields in the 2018-19 academic year.

• Bachelor's degree attainment for Black people aged 25 to 29 has increased more slowly than among white people:
- 29% of Black people aged 25 to 29 held a bachelor's degree or higher in 2019, up 11 percentage points from 18% in 2000.
- By comparison, degree attainment for white 25- to 29-year-olds increased from 34% to 45% during the same time period.

• In 2019, approximately 40% of Black adults aged 25 to 29 had at least a two-year college degree, an increase from 26% in 2000. Among white adults, this level of degree attainment grew from 44% in 2000 to 56% in 2019. (Facts from: Postsecondary National Policy Institute, 2021.)

Statistics like those reported by the Postsecondary National Policy Institute, 2021, makes the need to study Africana history imperative. Such programs in the Academy in history, politics, and culture provides students with a deeper understanding of the world and the history of an entire Africana people. Such opportunities to study help to give students perspective. They can also help students to become better informed and more respectful of the cultural differences of themselves and others. That level of self-actualization and awareness could have lasting and positive impacts on the admission and completion rates of Black students enrolling in colleges and universities. In our current society, the challenges with connecting our current PK -12 education system to the Academy comes in sundry trials. One major opposition to a strong connection is the push to extricate Critical Race Theory (CRT) and other factual presentations of American History from state curriculums. These unreasonable demands from legislators and others must be met with a refusal to do anything other than provide our children with a factual account of the history of Africana life–no matter how barbaric it may sound or feel to others.

We need more courageous leaders in the educational system, unafraid to challenge the Academy, such as Dr. Hudson-Weems, with her single voice during the 1980s, willing to declare Emmett Till as the real catalyst for the modern Civil Rights Movement. Her pioneering factual 1988 Ford Doctoral Dissertation, "Emmett Louis Till: The Impetus of the Modern Civil Rights Movement" (U of Iowa), was, in fact, the 1st to establish the brutal lynching of the 14-year-old Black Chicago youth as the true catalyst of the Movement. We need those declarations over the creation of new curriculum PK-12, up to the Academy that adequately defines the history and heritage of the Africana culture and the people who make up that culture. We need people who are willing to dig deep down to the substratum and root causes of why in 2021; we are still plagued with many of the same struggles of our ancestors and forefathers. We need to continue this discussion with PK-12 educators and representatives from higher education to truly change the trajectory of education and to write a new narrative for true Social Justice.

## Conclusion

As Sojourner Truth demonstrates in her legendary *Ain't I a Woman* speech (US Department of Interior 2017), Black women have long since faced more marginalization and oppression than their white counterparts (Barratt). This marginalization and unfair treatment in what is considered to be a civilized and progressive society has led to much controversy and debate when dealing with the harsh realities of Black women from all aspects of life. One aspect of life impacted by these marginalizations is occupation. Public school education is no exception. In public education, women constitute the bulk of the work force while men are most likely to hold positions in school administration (The Condition of Education 2020). Being a woman in the workplace presents its own set of unique challenges; however, there is no denying that being a Black woman in the workplace has even more significant challenges. Black women are often subjected to both gender driven microaggressions, as well as being subjected to racial ones (Barratt). The interconnectivity of race, class, and gender can be referenced in Truth's moving speech, which Hudson-Weems declares as a supreme representation of self- actualization. She noted that in "Cultural and Agenda Conflicts in Academia," originally published in *The Western Journal of Black Studies* (1989), later published as Chapter 2 in *Africana Womanism* (Hudson-Weems 23). Sojourner Truth's speech references the race factor first – the "Negroes" of the South's debate with the women of the North (mainly white women) over who should have the right to vote. Then she looks at class (and to a degree gender) when she exclaims, "Nobody ever helps me into carriages, or over mud-puddles, or gives me the best place!" She went on to conclude her thought with a question that is refrained throughout the legendary speech, "Ain't I a woman?" Finally, she looks at gender when she challenges a position of one of the men present:

> "Then that little man in black there, he says women can't have as much rights as men, 'cause Christ wasn't a woman! Where did your Christ come from? Where did your Christ come from? From God and a woman! Man had nothing to do with Him." (US Department of Interior 2017)

Her speech ended with a powerful statement on gender, but that comes last, after the opening remarks on the race factor:

"If the first woman God ever made was strong enough to turn the world upside down all alone, these women together ought to be able to turn it back, and get it right side up again! And now they is asking to do it. The men better let them." (US Department of Interior 2017)."

Although slightly altered over time, replacing the Black dialect with standard language, Sojourner Truth's speech is a very strong indicator of the way race, class, and gender interconnect in the lives of Black Women, Black men, and Black children. Black women, Black men, and Black children have strong leadership skills and have demonstrated them for centuries. Their leadership has been shown in all aspects of Black History and Black culture. As is still the reality today, many of these heroines are without a prominent place in history because of their commitment to their cause more so than their commitment to exalting themselves (Bell). Black Women, Black men, and Black children have long since had a triple consciousness that includes race, class, and gender. Many of these visionary pragmatists faced their fears by demonstrating remarkable courage in accepting the uncertain and sometimes dangerous consequences of their leadership. Janet Dewart discusses in her well-known work, Lighting the Fires of Freedom, these Black Women, generally embodied the three modes of leadership previously discussed: transformational leadership, servant leadership, and adaptive leadership (Bell).

In *Africana Womanist Literary Theory*, Hudson-Weems outlines a summation list of 15 Positive/Negative Elements of Male/Female Relationships. These elements are essential in solidifying the notion that in a paradigm as progressive and inclusive as Africana Womanism, with men and women together, oftentimes finding them collectively working in the liberation struggle, is welcomed.

| Positive | Negative |
|---|---|
| 1. Love | 1. Contempt |
| 2. Friendship | 2. Rivalry |
| 3. Trust | 3. Distrust |
| 4. Fidelity | 4. Infidelity |
| 5. Truth | 5. Deceit |
| 6. Mutual Respect | 6. Disrespect |
| 7. Support | 7. Neglect |
| 8. Humility | 8. Arrogance |
| 9. Enjoyable | 9. Mean-Spirited |
| 10. Compassionate | 10. Callous |
| 11. Sharing/Caring | 11. |
| Selfish/Egocentric | |

| 12. Complimentary | 12. Critical |
|---|---|
| 13. Secure | 13. Insecure |
| 14. Interdependence | 14. Dependence |
| 15. Spiritual | 15. Non-Spiritual |

(Hudson-Weems, *Africana Womanist Literary Theory* 97).

Attention to these elements will provide the Africana community with a foundation from which the community can begin to heal and move forward towards that struggle for liberation that has always been a part of the Africana reality.

In the Afterword of the highly hailed work by the author, Dr. Molefi Kete Asante, Founding Chair and Professor of African American Studies at Temple University, explained the following:

> The fact of the matter is that Africana Womanism is a response to the need for collective definition and the re-creation of the authentic agenda that is the birthright of every living person. In order to make this shift to authenticity, Hudson-Weems has called us back to the earliest days of African cultural history. (138).

The urgency found in Dr. Hudson-Weems' work will lead us to the changes we need to see in Africana communities, as well as, in the world today.

There is hope, for if there is no hope, then the work that I have dedicated my life to, as well as many of my colleagues having committed their lives to – changing the future of Africana children across the world - would be in vain. Therefore, we must consider this the beginning of the bridge that must be built to close the opportunity and attitude gaps for Africana students worldwide.

In his latest Best-Selling book, *The Equity & Social Justice Education 50*, the legendary Principal Baruti Kafele explains that

> Any and all aspects of social and racial justice have historical implications. He says that in order to understand contemporary social and racial justice issues, we have to understand what got us to this point. Therefore, we must be willing to research the Black experience and our Black existence in America for the past four centuries.

In order to do such a work, we must utilize the myriad of resources available to us. Let's embrace the concept of Africana Womanism – and include the study of those characteristics in both the PK-12 school systems, and colleges and universities throughout. Let's accept new authentic workable paradigms, grounded in our cultural past, realizing that with the knowledge of our history, made possible with our educators who are committed to truth, we can change our current realities. We must commit to this cause – and refuse to settle for less than the testimony of Africana people identified in a familiar spiritual among Africana people for centuries – "IT IS WELL with OUR SOULS."

# Bibliography

Aldridge, Delores, P. Foreword in *Africana Womanist Literary Theory*. Trenton: Africa World Press, 2004, xi – xiii.

Allen, Kenneth. *Black Males Face Appalling Inequities in America: Why There's a New Reason for Hope*. USA Today Online, USA Today, September 12, 2020. https://www.forbes.com/sites/biancabarratt/2020/06/19/the-micro aggressions-towards-black-women-you-might-be-complicit-in-at-work/?sh=6c6e06b92bda

Asante, Molefi Kete. Afterword in *Africana Womanist Literary Theory* by Clenora Hudson-Weems. Trenton: Africa World Press, 2004.

Barrett, Bianca. *The Microaggressions Towards Black Women You Might Be Complicit In At Work.* Forbes Online, Forbes, 19 June 2021. https://www.forbes.com/sites/biancabarratt/2020/06/19/the-microaggressions-towards-black-women-you-might-be-complicit-in-at-work/?sh=6c6e06b92bda.

Bell, Janet Dewart. *Lighting the Fires of Freedom: African American Women in the Civil Rights Movement.* New York: New Press, 2018.

Christian, Mark. Afterword in *Contemporary Africana Theory, Thought and Action: A Guide to Africana Studies.* Trenton: Africa World Press, 2007.

Fernandez, Robert, Director. Lewis, Eric & Westmoreland, Carl, Actors. *Harriet Tubman: They Called Her Moses*, 2018. *[Documentary: Special Interest].* https://www.amazon.com/Harriet-Tubman-They-Called-Moses/dp/B07JQWR4W7

Hilliard, Asa. *Young, Black, and Gifted: Promoting High Achievement Among African-American Students.* Boston: Beacon Press Books, 2003.

Hudson-Weems, Clenora. *"Africana Womanism and the Critical Need for African. Theory and Thought"* The Western Journal of Black Studies, 21:2 (Summer) 1997, 79 – 84.

Hudson-Weems, Clenora. *Africana Womanism: Reclaiming Ourselves Africana -Melanated Womanism.* London; New York: Routledge, 2020.

Hudson-Weems, Clenora. *Africana Womanist Literary Theory.* Trenton: Africa World Press, 2004.

Hudson-Weems, Clenora. *Emmett Till: The Sacrificial lamb of the Civil Rights Movement.* Troy: Bedford Publishers, 1994.

Kafele, Baruti. *The Equity & Social Justice Education 50: Critical Questions for Improving Opportunities and Outcomes for Black Students.* Alexandria: ASCD, 2021.

Mapp, Susan.& Gabel, Shirley Gatenio. *"It Is Easier to Build Strong Children than to Repair Broken Men"*. *J. Hum. Rights Social Work* 4, 145–146 (2019).  https://doi.org/10.1007/s41134-019-00106-z

"National Postsecondary Student Aid Study: 2016 Undergraduates." National Center for Education Statistics, U.S. Department of Education. Accessed July 2021.

Painter, Nell Irwin. *"American History XX:   Frances Ellen Watkins Harper" Interview by Leonard Lopate.* The Leonard Lopate Show.  4 July 2012.  https://www.wnyc.org/story/220029-american-history-xx-frances-ellen-watkins-harper/.

Reeves, Richard, Nzau, Sarah, and Smith, Ellen.  "The Challenges Facing Black Men – and the Case for Action." Brookings, November 19, 2020. Accessed 08 October 2021.  https://www.brookings.edu/blog/up-front/2020/11/19/the-challenges-facing-black-men-and-the-case-for-action/.

Sofola, 'Zulu. Foreword in *Africana Womanism:  Reclaiming Ourselves*. London and New York: Routledge, 2019, xi – xii.

# 10

## TODAY'S CIVIL/HUMAN RIGHTS: GENERATIONAL WEALTH & AFRICANA MEN & WOMEN AGAINST RACISM & EMMETT TILL CONTINUUMS—A 5-STEP SOLUTION

### *CLENORA HUDSON (WEEMS), PhD*

Before there can be any substantive, corrective dialogue on racism, it is critical to first understand the basis, the *raison d'être* for the creation and existence of this discriminatory doctrine and practice, which has created despair and damnation for Africana people worldwide. The focus for this chapter is the racist practices heaped upon African Americans for centuries, culminating in the Civil Rights Movement of the fifties and the sixties. Racism is a strategic practice, resulting in economic exploitation, a reality that has been systematically used in marginalizing Africana people and used as a primary means of monopolizing generational wealth. This passing down of wealth to future generations of a "privileged" class has proven to be a toxic, immoral, and destructive phenomenon. Hence, racism must be totally eradicated, not simply placated via assimilation, tokenism and/or surface acts of benevolence. Indeed, true justice and equity must be established for the benefit of all for a peaceful co-existence. The Africana-Melanated Womanist, in a collective effort with the male counterpart, aspires to ultimate human survival, including her own.

The supreme embodiment of racist victimization is Emmett Louis "Bobo" Till, the 14-year-old Black Chicago youth, brutally murdered in 1955 for whistling at a 21-year-old white woman, Carolyn Bryant in Money, Mississippi. 33 years later, my 1988 Ford Doctoral Dissertation (U of Iowa), "Emmett Louis Till: The Impetus of the Modern Civil Rights Movement," published in 1994 as *Emmett Till: The Sacrificial Lamb of the Civil Rights Movement*, became the 1st to established Till as the true catalyst of the Civil Rights Movement of the 50s and the 60s. According to renowned Duke University Professor emeritus, Dr. C. Eric Lincoln,

> In *Africana Womanism*, Hudson-Weems sent unaccustomed shock waves
> through the domain of popular thinking about feminism and established
> herself as an independent thinker, unafraid to unsettle settled opinions. In
> *Emmett Till*, she drops   the other shoe and challenges the most sacred
> shibboleths of the origins of the CivilRights Movement. Not everyone will
> want to agree with what she has to say. But few will lay the book down
> before she has had her say. And she says a lot America needs to hear again
> right now. (Lincoln, *Emmett Till* Jacket Blurb)

An international *cause celébrè*, the brutal lynching created global
voices that unanimously echoed opposition to the abominable crime against
nature.  Today, that cry has advanced to action in a collective cry for justice
in global demonstrations against the callous murdering of African
American men, women, and youths, too.  According to Hudson-Weems in
"Africana-Melanated Womanism and the King-Parks-till Connection,"
Chapter 13 of the new section in her 1993 classic, *Africana Womanism*,

> the proper parameters, wherein resides true scholarship and activism, . . .
> together [corroborating] a fight to end the long-existing battle against racial
> dominance . . . [demonstrates] how Africana Womanism advances itself
> and fits into ideals expressed in the lives of major iconic historical figures,
> such as Dr. Martin Luther King, Jr. and Rosa Parks, as well as Emmett Till,
> particularly as they represent those in defining incidents of great socio-
> political significance.  Thus, we have Africana Womanism and the King,
> Parks and Till connection, which specifically addresses the subject of the
> civil rights of Blacks. (121)

Despite the raging demonstrations during the searing 1960s and the 1970s,
the Civil Rights Movement is not over yet. Instead, we find ourselves
witnessing a new Civil Rights Movement, which must be recognized, rather
than ignored. It is my conjecture that were racism properly designated as a
"crime," it could alter the minds and acts of the dominant culture: "Once
this is established, people will be more inclined to refrain from committing
such acts, which would force them into accountability." (Hudson-Weems,
"Civil Rights Then and Now," *Columbia Daily Tribune*, 20, June 2020).

Granted, the history of racial dominance is deep, but it is now past
time for this absurdity to end.  For over 400 years, indigenous African
Americans have suffered tremendously at the cruel hands of the monster
itself--RACISM:

> Dating back to the horrific beginnings of American slavery, the landing of
> the first Slave Ship in Jamestown, Virginia, 1619, marked the defining
> moment for indigenous African Americans some 400 years ago. Indeed,
> African Americans have suffered immeasurably from crimes on these

shores, which Nobel Laureate Toni Morrison refers to as "the unspeakable!" (Hudson-Weems, "Civil Rights," 2020)

Racism has been meticulously perfected via the continuing creation and establishment, whenever necessary, of unfair statues, such as Jim Crow laws, to support and enforce the ultimate goals and objectives of the dominant culture. Interestingly, classism, has become the covert parent to racism, an unnatural order of things in the universe, and thus, the eradication of this abominable monster makes it all the more urgent today in order that both the victim and the culprit can come together for the benefit of all humanity.

A preliminary revisitation of the legal establishment of racial dominance is important at this critical time in history. Just six years prior to the January 1, 1863, signing of the Emancipation Proclamation by President Abraham Lincoln, which rendered the much-contested freeing of Blacks from American slavery, the 1857 Dred Scott Decision was entered in the St. Louis, Missouri system, which held that "Blacks had no rights that the white man was bound to respect." Seven years after the Emancipation Proclamation, 1970, the 15th Amendment to the Constitution was ratified, giving Black men the right to vote. That was a victory for the entire family, as Black women, too, celebrated this, knowing that Black men would naturally discuss the pros and cons of political candidates with their spouses so that they could together chose the best candidate for Blacks. The pendulum shifted again some 26 years later with the 1896 United States Supreme Court Plessy versus Ferguson Decision. That infamous Jim Crow law was set in order to continue the legalization of racial dominance via enacting the constitutionality of the "separate but equal" segregation laws. And the reign of racial dominance continued, strengthened by forced submission of Blacks via horrific consequences of their resistance, such as countless lynching, etc., which continue even today, graphically symbolized in what I initiated as "Emmett Till Continuums."

Needless to say, however, neither the 1863 signing of the Emancipation Proclamation by President Abraham Lincoln, nor the 1964 signing of the Civil Rights Bill by President Lyndon B. Johnson, a little over a century later, stopped the definitive racist crime against nature. The rhetorical question is simple: Have not the Blacks dispelled the myth of inherent Black inferiority time and again? The concocted myth, used by pro-slavery advocates in justifying their humble benevolent efforts to save those "biological inferiors" from their own inadequacies, rendering them unable to even care for themselves, let alone care for their children, was preposterous and only self-serving. In fact, Aubrey Bruce, Senior Sports' columnist for *The New Pittsburgh Courier,* contends that "achievements by Black Americans are monolithic and confirm that we have achieved greatness in whatever vocation that we choose" (Hudson-Weems, *Debunking Racism,* unpublished). Consider the following tiny samplings of Black legendary figures of many talents, their contributions, and their attributes throughout the centuries, affirming truth, which must be established before we can truly successfully move forward:

1. **Muhammad Ali** (1942-2016)—"The Greatest" boxer of the 20th century, Olympic Gold Medalist, world heavyweight champion won 56 out of 61 fights. His daughter, **Laila Amaria** (1977)—Undefeated Super middleweight, Light heavyweight boxer won all 24 fights, with 21 Knockouts (KO)
2. **Angela Bassett** (1958)—Actress, Producer, Director & activist, she has won Golden Globe Award for *What's Love Got to Do With It,* *Black Movie Award* for *Akeelah & the Bee,* NAACP Image Award for *Malcolm* and the Screen Actors Guild Award for *Black Panther.*
3. **Atty. Alvin O. Chambliss, Jr.** (1944)—Lead Counsel--Ayers vs Fordice Supreme Court Case; Last Civil Rights Attorney in America
4. **Dr. Charles Drew** (1904-1950) --developer of techniques for the storage of Blood Plasma, thus, revolutionizing Blood Plasma
5. **Medgar Evers** (1925-1963)—Civil Rights Activist; NAACP Field Secretary; Organizer for the Voter Registration Drive in MS
6. **Aretha Louis Franklin** (1942-2018)—Queen of Soul; winner of many awards, including the Grammy Award
7. **Dick Gregory** (1932-2017)—Comedian, Author, Civil Rights Activist, known for his satirist style in addressing racism
8. **Cathy Hughes** (1947)—1st African American woman to head a publicly traded corporation, Radio/Urban One, TV One.
9. **Ice Cube** (1969)—Rapper, Actor, Filmmaker and Activist. In his films, he highlights Black life in the Black community, ranging from devastation to ultimate hope.
10. **Mae Jemison** (1956)—Engineer and Physician, she was the 1st African American female astronaut & the 1st African American woman to travel into space.
11. **Dr. Martin Luther King, Jr.** (1929- 1964)—Father of the Civil Rights Movement, he was the youngest person ever to receive the Nobel Peace Prize.
12. **Lewis Howard Latimer** (1848-1928)—invested a method for an improved the light bulb with carbon filament

13. **Toni Morrison** (1931-2019)—the 1$^{st}$ African American female to win Nobel Prize for Literature, she received the Presidential Medal of Freedom in 2012.

14. **Nas-Nasir** bin Olu Dara (1973)—Rapper, Songwriter, Entrepreneur, he has released 12 studio albums since 1994, 7 certified platinum & multi-platinum.

15. **Barack Hussein Obama** (1961)—The 1$^{st}$ African American U.S. President. 9 months after his inauguration, he received the Nobel Peace Prize. His wife, **Atty. Michelle Obama**—the 1$^{st}$ African American 1$^{st}$ Lady, a role model, highlighting issues relative to everyday life & an overall good health regiment--food, exercise, etc.

16. **Rosa Parks** (1913-2005)—Mother of the Civil Rights Movement, Parks was a revered Civil Rights Activist/leader.

17. **Quavo**—Quavious Keyate Marshall (1991)—Rapper, Singer, Song Writer & Music Producer; a member of the 3 Migos hip hop & trap rappers

18. **Condoleezza Rice, PhD** (1954)—The 1$^{st}$ African American woman to hold the position of Secretary of State, the highest-ranking African American woman in U. S. history

19. **Robert F. Smith** (1962)—Billionaire & benevolent philanthropist who pledged $40 million to the 2019 Morehouse College graduating class of 400 to clear all their student loans, an estimated pay-off of $1 million per student. He demonstrates Giving back to the community.

20. **Emmett Louis "Bobo" Till** (1941-1955)—Son of **Mamie Till-Mobley**; Black youth (14), lynched in MS for whistling at a white woman (21); became the true catalyst of the Civil Rights Movement, established 1$^{st}$ in the 1988 Ford Doctoral Dissertation (U of Iowa)

21. **Usher**—Usher Raymond (1978)—Singer Songwriter, Music Producer, Dancer & Businessman, he won Grammy & Billboard Music Awards.

22. **Cordy Tindell Vivian** (1924-2020)—A Minister, Author, Civil Rights activist, he was awarded the Presidential Medal of Freedom.

23. **Ida B. Wells-Barnett** (1862-1931)—Anti-Lynching Crusader for Social Justice, she spent her life fighting for Human Rights of Blacks.

24. **Malcolm X** (Little)**--El-Hajj Malik El-Shabazz** (1925-1965)—A strong Human Rights Activist during the Civil Rights Movement, he received the Presidential Medal of Freedom posthumously.

25. **Andrew Young** (1932)—Executive Director of the Southern Christian Leadership Conference (SCLC) & United States Ambassador to the United Nations

26. **Tukufu Zuberi, PhD**--Antonio McDaniel (1959)—Social Critic, Documentary Filmmaker, Professor & Author; host of *History Detectives* & Director for award-winning *Africa Independence*.

Given the above refutations of inherent Black inferiority, the standing question remains: Why is racism and myths of Black inferiority still in existence, and how can this be corrected? Moreover, when will America be forced to hold true to its foundational principals of American Democracy? Will the dominant culture ever reject "white privilege," with the realization that accolades simply on the basis of color alone says little about the possibility that they may very well have much more to offer society? In the final analysis, racism is ludicrous and groundless, causing many to question the abilities of the dominant culture, wondering "Are you really that smart, or are you just white?" The rhetorical question yet rings.

Today, many of the dominant culture are questioning "What can we do now?" My response, echoing the title of Spike Lee's film, is simple- - *Do the Right Thing*. Of course, this

does not mean mere perfunctory apologies and donations to the cause. . . . for the dominant culture has benefitted greatly for centuries as heirs of "white privilege" in a horrible abuse of the humanity of others, clearly demonstrating their unwillingness to hold true to the rules of democracy. They proclaim that justice and equality for all is the basis of our democracy, yet that reality has never existed for Blacks. If we are serious about making it right, then the dominant culture must [first] challenge their practice of "white privilege"--in the private place, in the workplace, art, religion, politics, and in education, where we learn and begin to appreciate a greater sense of morality (Hudson-Weems, *Columbia Daily Tribune* 2020).

Referencing Nobel Laureate Toni Morrison, in her opening Nobel Prize Acceptance Speech, in recounting the words of an elderly blind clairvoyant Black woman being challenged by the youths, she advises them that "It's in your hands." I find myself pondering the rhetorical question-- "Will you do it?" Of course, in the end, all can, in fact, benefit: Blacks, will finally be granted the God-given "birthright of every living person" (Asante, in the Afterword of Hudson-Weems' *AWLT*, 138), proclaimed in Paragraph 2 of The *United States Declaration of Independence*, the foundation of American Democracy:

"We hold these truths to be self-evident, that **all men are created equal**, that they are **endowed** by their Creator with certain **unalienable Rights**, that among these are **Life**, **Liberty** and the **Pursuit of Happiness**."

With all being said, my position on racial dominance encompasses Five Steps to Ending Racism: ACKNOWLEDGEMENT, REMORSE, ATONEMENT, REDEMPTION, and FORGIVENESS. In executing these steps, one will see how workable, indeed, they are. Both historical and current wrongs will be held up and accounted for, thereby, enabling Africana people, members of the human race, too, to at last experience a coming together, ". . . that ye be like-minded, having the same love, being of one accord, of one mind" as fellow human being (*Philippians* 4:16).

Beginning with the first step, *Acknowledgement* of the crime, is crucially important, as this step allows for a focus on the crime that almost invariably results from toxic racist misconceptions about who Blacks really are and what they have contributed to society. The select list of Legendary Africana People from A to Z, listed earlier, debunks those false notions of inherent Black inferiority, with proof of the many things connected directly to the talents and contributions of Africana people. What naturally follows is *Remorse* on the part of the dominant culture for having committed and continuing to commit brutal crimes against not only our bodies, but crimes of deception and misinformation as well. thereby, enabling a genuine sense of responsibility as a means of finally initiating correctives for the so-called "race problem."

Once those two initial steps have been taken, there is the pivotal element, *Atonement* for the crime(s), wherein one renders both personal and civic accountability, dating back to practices of centuries of enslavement, free labor, and unfair wage discrimination even up to now. This step calls for the immediate addressing of those systemic racist assumptions, the basis and justification of the crime (racism), resulting from a mentality ultimately manifested into toxic external racism. This crime, commonly marked by racial discrimination on all fronts, critically limits the success of Africana people, victimized by the problem, sadly undergirded by an internal racist mentality on the part of whites toward Blacks. Indeed, Atonement is in order, with *reparations* being one of its many forms. As suggested by many, an excellent example of this could be in the form of the exemption from paying taxes, for African Americans have paid enormously with 400 years of free labor. Moreover, we should also be exempted from paying tuition for any college chosen, particularly since for centuries we were denied an education, as it was illegal for Blacks to acquire. The recipients for these exemptions should be specifically for the American descendants of Africa, referred to as American Descendants of Slavery (ADOS) by co-founders of the Movement, Yvette Carnell and Atty. Antonio Moore. At an ADOS conference in Louisville, Kentucky, Dr. Cornell West stated that the concerns of this current Movement resume the concerns of Dr. Martin Luther King, Jr. and Malcolm X during the Civil Rights Movement. According to Malcolm X, the year before his assassination, in his 1964 Reparations Address in Paris, France,

"If you are the son of a man who had a wealthy estate and you inherit your father's estate, you have to pay off the debts that your father incurred before he died. The only reason that the present generation of white Americans are in a position of economic strength...is because their fathers worked our fathers for over 400 years with no pay...We were sold from plantation to plantation like you sell a horse, or a cow, or a chicken, or a bushel of wheat...All that money...is what gives the present generation of American whites the ability to walk around the earth with their chest out...like they have some kind of economic ingenuity. Your father isn't here to pay. My father isn't here to collect. But I'm here to collect and you're here to pay." *(*Malcolm X, November 23, 1964)

Hence, accountability, compensation awarded to the victims for their unimaginable suffering, would be a true way of righting the historical wrongs. The results for righting the wrongs would be the ultimate, **Redemption**, which is God's gift to humankind for doing good.

A classic example or symbol of the interconnected giant steps above is the course of action taken by the attorney for the murderers of Emmett Till, Atty. John Whitten, Jr., who was then 34 years of age. His blessings came only after he experienced remorse for his role in the 1955 infamous Emmett Till Murder Trial. Subsequently, he spent the rest of his life atoning, ultimately awarding him Redemption from God. During the trial, he delivered the defining closing remarks, dramatically proclaiming: "Every last one of you has the courage to free these men." Of course, in reality, we know too well that the white murderers would never have been found guilty of the crime at that time, which occurred before the 1964 signing of the Civil Rights Bill. The infamous 1857 Supreme Court Dred Scott Decision of nearly a century before was still the rule of the land then, as it set the stage for young Emmett, whose race denied him any legal protection. Whitten's subsequent act of *atonement*, evolving years later, could be considered a redeeming one, as he offered *pro bono* legal representation for Blacks in the Mississippi Delta, reputed as the most racist of all areas in the state of Mississippi, the metaphor for racism. Haunted by his earlier legal role in the murder case, he repeatedly expressed profound remorse for having represented 24-year-old Roy Bryant, the husband of Carolyn Bryant, and his 36-year-old stepbrother, J. W. Milam. From redemption came his pleas for **Forgiveness,** though realizing that this was a huge request. (Hudson-Weems, *Emmett*, 2014). Nonetheless, if, indeed, granted, this could be a major step that could possibly bring about racial healing, which is an ultimate mission and goal for the true Africana-

Melanated womanist, having been granted their just and God-given inalienable human rights!

That being said, it becomes crystal clear that racism, an unfair and unlawful crime that yet lives, should be put to rest forever so that all humankind can exist freely, without racial limitations, for true humanity for all human beings. Now that the basis for this crime has been proven yet again to be false, the notion of inherent biological Black inferiority, it should be call to a halting order for a new premise, based upon truth and true equity, can be permanently placed for ultimate "Life, Liberty and the Pursuit of Happiness!" This could be **American Democracy** at its best, bringing forth **The American Dream,** as aspired to and as it should be, proudly realized by all, Blacks included.!

If you really think that America is great now, just think of what it would be now had it not been predicated upon cruel and blatant racism, violently heaped upon Africana people for centuries, and still reigning even today! But, of course, there is the silver lining, and the subtle move today toward rectifying the unlawful acts that perpetuate the race divide is evidenced in the recent case of return of property by Southern California officials to the heirs of an ambitious African American couple, Willa and Charles Bruce, who purchased a beachfront property in Manhattan Beach in 1912. A kindred spirit of Ida Bl Wells-Barnette, she, too, was born in 1862, less than a year before legalized slavery ended, and was quite out-spoken as well, unafraid to voice her desires. In fact, Willa initiated the idea of buying this property, though heretofore, she and her husband had been denied such an opportunity in their pursuit of the American Dream. They had been turned down repeatedly, whenever they attempted to use their savings to purchase land, with the intentions of building a haven for African Americans to experience all the comforts and joys of life. Like the Africana Womanist, Willa was right there beside her man/husband, and together they supported each other in their decisions and efforts to move upward. He had once proudly stated that he "owned" that proper and that he intended to keep it, no matter what demands stood against him/them. However, that commitment was destroyed, for in less than a decade and a half after the purchase, and the creation of this prestigious, joyous Black Beachfront Resort, it all collapsed with the collaboration of legal cohorts, and unethical, cruel and unlawful conspirators, such as the KKK in action.

Nearly a century later, their two great-grandsons, Marcus and Derrick Bruce, became recipients of what is considered Generation Wealth, via property initially valued at over 20 million dollars today, but later changed, within a week, to $75 million. It was the first African American Beach Resort in Southern California, during which time, the Bruces experienced much racial strife, culminating in the seizing of their land in

1924, via feigned eminent domain, executed by manipulative local authorities. A New York Journalist, Hannah Frishberg, reveals the obvious folly in their reasoning for taking the Bruces' property:

> The area, the council claimed at the time, was urgently needed for a park, the LA Times reported. [However,] It subsequently sat empty for decades before being transferred to the state and then LA County before eventually becoming a parking lot and lifeguard training headquarters. The seizure ruined the Bruces, who spent the rest of their lives working as diner cooks. (*New York Post*, 7/1/2022)

And what a tragic ending for these two prominent landowner-entrepreneurs – Willa and Charles Bruce (1862-1934 and 1860-1931 respectively)! They were both in the early 70s when they died, relegated to poverty, which escalated to poor health – kidney failure for Charles and a mental breakdown for Willa.

In a June 28, 2022 article, "Land taken from Black couple returned to heirs – Racial Injustice California Beach," presented details of the Bruce's Beach saga:

> The Los Angeles County Board of Supervisors voted Tuesday to return ownership of prime California beachfront property to descendants of a Black couple who built a resort for African Americans but were stripped of the land in the 1920s.
>
> The board voted 5-0 on a motion to complete the transfer of parcels in an area once known as Bruce's Beach in the fashionable city of Manhattan Beach.
>
> ... The transfer includes an agreement for the property to be leased back to the county for 24 months, with an annual rent of $413,000 plus all operation and maintenance costs, and the county's right to purchase the land for up to $20 million.
>
> "This may be the first land return of its kind, but it cannot be the last," Hahn said. (Antezak, 2022)

Although ostensibly it appears to be a fair and perfect case, regarding the resolution of a critical historical wrong, one must question a curious stipulations – granting LA county the "right:" to buy the land, with a ceiling price of no more than $20 millions, after their two-year leasing. Given the enormous price escalations regarding any and everything conceivable, who is to say what that Beachfront property will be worth two years from now?  In fact, the last figure given for the current value of the land is $75 million. Moreover, since, in fact, the property owners are now the heirs, they should be the ones with the "right" to determine if they will sell the property or not, and for whatever price they chose to sell it.

Be that as it may, on a very positive note during the hearing, it was also revealed that

> Supervisor Janice Hahn launched the complex process of returning the property to heirs of the Bruces in April 2021. A key hurdle was overcome when the state Legislature passed a bill removing the restriction on transfer of the property.

> "We can't change the past and we will never be able to make up for the injustice that was done to Willa and Charles Bruce a century ago, but this is a start," an emotional Hahn said before the vote.

> Hahn said returning the property will allow the heirs "the opportunity to start rebuilding the generational wealth that was denied them for decades."

> Anthony Bruce, a family spokesman, said in a statement that the return means the world to them but it is also bittersweet. (Antezak, July 2022)

Of course, one could look at this case as a starting point for addressing the denial of Generational Wealth for Blacks, and what course of action should be taken to correct such historical wrongs suffered by African Americans that continue even today. In a form of reparations, the remorse for the immeasurable losses suffered by the African American here on this continent alone, represented in the unanimous vote in favor of reversing the long-existing injustices suffered by the Bruce family, could conceivably represent the 1$^{st}$ of 3 steps needed to properly address this reality. The other 2 steps may begin with a feasible freeing of Blacks of income and property taxes in perpetuity, as our financial losses of 4 centuries, and still counting, can never be truly repaid. This brings us to the 3$^{rd}$ and final step here in correcting historical wrongs, which is to exempt Blacks from paying tuition for any school of their choice, a privilege which we are due, given that Blacks were denied education during slavery, and still suffer educational holdbacks due to racism today, let alone the fact of how much we have contributed to this land, some of which are identified earlier in the listing of only one example of the attributions and/or contributions of Legendary Africana People from A to Z.

In conclusion, we now have a glimpse at the enjoyment of a promised fulfillment for a life of abundance for us, despite the historical wrongs that can be righted! Perceiving the victory of the Bruce family at last as the beginning of victories for all African Americans, and by extension Africana people globally, our mission and responsibility to each other, characterizing Authenticity and Collectivity, need to be emphasized. As our legacy of "In It Together" strongly exemplifies our centuries of persistence, of never giving up on the boundless possibilities underlying our past, present and future lives, Generational Wealth for us is, indeed, inevitable, and moreover, a mandate for true social justice, forevermore! The closing words in the Opening Chapter, "Africana Womanism: Authenticity and Collectivity for Social Justice," of *Africana Paradigms, Practices and Literary Texts: Evoking Social Justice*, sums it up, commanding Truth as a basis for all good:

> We must, therefore, call a halt once and for all to anything that prohibits us from achieving what is ours, including the right to secure and celebrate who we really are [the whole truth], and moreover, what course of action we should be taking. And we can do this as a strong Africana people, working together – Men, Women, Children – In Concert in a global stride toward Victory for our own. This is the ultimate goal of true Africana Womanism! Moreover, by extension, isn't this precisely what the quest for human/civil rights is all about in the first place – the humanity of all humankind? (Hudson-Weems, 19)

# Bibliography

Antczak, John. *Yahoo!news.com.* June 28, 2022.

Asante, Molefi Kete. Afterword in *Africana Womanist Literary Theory.* Trenton: Africa World Press, 2004.

Carnel, Yvette and Atty. Antonio Moore. Co-founders of the Movement: American Descendants Of Slavery (ADOS) for reparations for African Americans.

Christian, Mark. Afterword in *Contemporary Africana Theory, Thought and Action: A Guide to Africana Studies.* Clenora Hudson-Weems, editor. Trenton, NJ: Africa World Press, 2007.

Frishberg, Hannah. "Bruce's Beach, seized by LA in 1924, returned to Black family's descendants." *New York Post*, July 1, 2022.

Hudson-Weems, Clenora. "Africana-Melanated Womanism and the King-Parks-Till Connection" in *Africana Womanism: Reclaiming Ourselves,* Fifth Edition. London and New York: Routledge, 2019, 121-128.

Hudson-Weems, Clenora, Editor. *Africana Paradigms, Practices and Literary Texts: Evoking Social Justice.* Dubuque, Iowa: Kendall Hunt Publishing Company, 2021.

Hudson-Weems, Clenora. "Civil Rights Then and Now: Anti-Racism to Stop Emmet Till Continuum in a 5 Step Solution" in the *Columbia Daily Tribune*, June 20, 2020. https://www.columbiatribune.com/story/opinion/columns/2020/06/21/civil-rights-movement-then-and-now-anti-racism-to-stop-emmett-till-continuum-in-5-step-solution/113750502/

Hudson-Weems, Clenora. *Debunking Racism: Legendary Africana People from A to Z* (Under Review).

Hudson-Weems, Clenora. *Emmett: Legacy, Redemption and Forgiveness.* Bloomington: AuthorHouse, 2014.

Hudson-Weems, Clenora. *Emmett Till: The Sacrificial Lamb of the Civil Rights Movement.* Troy, MI: Bedford Publishers, 1994.

Morrison, Toni. "Nobel Prize Acceptance Speech." Stockholm, Sweden, December 1993.*The United States Declaration of Independence.*

# SOCIAL AND RACIAL JUSTICE
# IN TEACHER EDUCATION:
# AN AFRICANA WOMANIST MANDATE

## LASANA D. KAZEMBE, PHD
## AND TAMBRA O. JACKSON, PHD

### Africana Womanism as *Rootwork*:
### Opening of the Way

From its beginnings, Africana Womanism has always been conceptualized as a framework of reclamation and reinscription. As espoused by Hudson-Weems (2004), Africana Womanism functions as an ideological composite of theory and praxis, a site of struggle, and a cultural repository of thought/speech/action rooted in the rich, complex histories and life praxes of Africana women. Hudson-Weems (2003, 2004), Dove (1998), and Phillips (2006) conceptualize and articulate Africana Womanism as reflecting the collective cultural mindset of Africana women. Characteristics of Africana Womanism include Africana women in the role of 1) self-namer; 2) self-definer; 3) family-centered; 4) genuine in sisterhood; 5) strong; 6) in concert with the Africana man in struggle; 7) whole; 8) authentic; 9) flexible role player 10) respected; 11) recognized; 12) spiritual; 13) male-compatible; 14) respectful of elders; 15) adaptable; 16) ambitious; 17) mothering; and 18) nurturing. Akin to their struggles within/across other racialized and gendered contexts (e.g., labor market, academia, business), Africana women's roles in education have and continue to be shaped by centuries of struggle for dignity, personal and professional recognition, and self-actualization.

Within a context of racial and psychocultural oppression, the work of reclaiming and reinscribing is complicated by philosophical and existential challenges to Africana agency, memory, identity, and epistemology. For Africana people collectively, their cultural ways of knowing, being, and interpreting evolve in tandem with centuries-long struggles against [racial and gender] imperialism, White supremacy/nationalism, colonialism, racial terrorism, and epistemic apartheid. Through the years, Africana people have simultaneously and strategically resisted and adopted non-Africana theories, materialist conceptions, and ideologies in the long struggle for a material and meaningful interpretation of life. Under the best circumstances, the dialectic of resistance/adoption of non-Africana theoretical models and ideological stances – while tending to Africana peoples' survival – have proven problematic to their development.

As Cabral (1966) avers, ideological deficiency on the part of Africana people is due, in part to lack of knowledge of their historical reality, indigenous cultural formations, and theoretical models. Thus, when Africana people resist or adopt European theories, such work tends to distract from the *rootwork* of interrogating, apprehending, and leveraging their own culturally autonomous theoretical models. Simultaneously, much of Africana peoples' diasporic experiences have involved the syncretization of select concepts, theories, and approaches in order to survive and thrive in a context of constant oppression and racial terrorism. Examples of this would include creolized versions of Christianity practiced by people of African ancestry in Brazil, Cuba, and the southern United States. Candomblé, Santeria, and Black Christian worship (respectively) emerged from centuries of blending, morphing, and cultural incubation within these various geographic zones. In their final expression, these forms represented an admixture of European-inspired Christianity (e.g., Roman Catholic, Methodist, Protestant) and Africana religious and cultural elements (e.g., symbology, mythology, aesthetics, linguistics, eschatology) drawn from Yoruba and other West African sources. Relatedly, as Dove (1998) iterates, the formation of the modern western world should be regarded as an inherited world owing to ancient cultural antecedents diffused from West and Central Africa and influencing such fields as technology, philosophy, writing, spirituality, health care, schooling, and education (p. 518).

Countless scholars have elucidated that Africans relocated across the ocean carried with(in) them a complex cultural architecture reflecting their centuries-old experiences with religion, spirituality, language, literature (spoken, written, sung), ancestral reverence, land/nature, male/female dynamics, communal living, institution-building, and other forms of cultural expression. Over time these constituent cultural elements (particularly religion and spirituality) formed the primary threads in the quilt of present-day African American identity. A central thesis shared by Gomez (1998), Manning (2010), and Hall (2005) that African captives, though newly enslaved in the United States, were (at the same time) still congregated and managed to sustain (and express) far more of their indigenous cultural elements than previously thought or realized. This compelling thesis and reasoning is not new but based on and supported by major voices in the field, including Lovejoy (1983), Curtin (1969), Thomas (1999), Rodney (1972), Blassingame (1973), G. M. Hall (2005), Herskovits (1941), van Sertima (1987), and Weiner (1971).

Gordon (1993) asserts that "acts of liberation and empowerment are manifested when African Americans recast their paradigms, theoretical and methodological frameworks, policies, and procedures as normative and not otherness" (456). As poet Lorenzo Thomas (2000) observes, in societies that devalue and destroy their citizens for profit, "what is considered normative may actually be toxic." Thomas' metaphor gains expanded significance alongside Hilliard's (2000) critique of American public education as a structure of dominance that seeks to

> suppress the history of the victims; destroy the practice of their culture; prevent the victims from coming to understand themselves as part of a cultural family; teach systematically the ideology of white supremacy; control the socialization process; control the accumulation of wealth; and perform segregation or apartheid (24-25).

For Africana people, in general, and women, in particular, their epistemic cultivation has long taken place within the field of education. Within the U.S., the education of Black people has always been a politically contested site. In this sense, then, developing curricula and implementing pedagogical theories and methods that are culturally responsive (Gay, 2010) and affirming to the historical experiences and lived realities of Africana people represents a way of recognizing and resisting ideological domination and fostering openings that are more expansive, substantive, and worthwhile. It is a liberating praxis requiring educators, particularly teacher educators, to be attuned and orientated to the material and collective existential experiences of Africana people.

## Social and Racial Justice in Teacher Education

If our goal is to attend to and ensure the liberation of Black children, then we have to also consider the liberation of their teachers and the institutions that prepare teachers. In recent years, many teachers education programs and professional organizations have included references to social and or racial justice in their mission and vision statements. However, simply including or appropriating social justice language does not result in effective teachers of Black children. Critiques of the field's poor outcomes for producing highly effective and culturally responsive teachers have centered the demographic imperative between a predominantly white profession and a predominantly Black and Brown student population. However, we posit that focusing on the demographic imperative alone is a distraction, and more attention needs to be given to the frameworks from which teacher education programs and curriculum operate. Racial and social justice in teacher education has to be comprehensive and systemic for positive, viable and widespread outcomes for Black children.

Sears (1992) highlights the need to build *praxeological significance* into thinking and choices involving classroom practice, curriculum development, textbook selection, and educational policy decisions. Curricula that are culturally responsive, sustaining, and worthwhile take into account history, ecology, time, memory, genealogy, and the swirling confluence of social and political forces that shape human experience (Ladson-Billings, 2009; Paris & Alim, 2017). For Africana people, this takes on even deeper and more meaningful significance owing to the steady and ongoing current of oppression within education and society. Generally speaking, this destructive current has (in many cases) induced amputated memory and cultural dislocation among Africana people. It has likewise adversely affected the psychology and actions of the dominant group by embedding within its collective membership a hard-wired mythology that undergirds an incomplete and inaccurate rendering of reality.

## Spirituality

Ramose (2002) has observed the unfortunate pattern of discourses on/about Africa being dominated by non-Africans. For their part, Africans are usually rendered either silent at best, or invisible at worst, and regarded as outsiders to cultural systems and formations which were subjected to hostile scrutiny and outright assault by those opposed to African autonomy and agency. Within Black educational circles, the nature, nurturing shape and spiritual character of Africana women's unique pedagogy, is ever-present in their threefold roles as abolitionist teachers, liberatory educators, and/or culturally responsive practitioners.

The need to formulate an appropriate theoretical framework for analyzing and interpreting educational struggles is a key aspect of the work of those committed to the futurity and prosperity of Black children. Therefore, the struggle of committed Black educators to conceptualize and claim liberatory stances in education takes on a spiritual significance in that it aligns with historic and nascent sociopolitical struggles in other zones of

Black existence. Africana Womanism is among the critical discourses devoted to the analysis of the challenges, needs and strivings of Africana people. Among the various sites of struggle for Africana people, the field of education is one of the most vibrant in terms of its socializing impact, its cultural breadth, and its transformative potential. For educational practitioners and stakeholders committed to the academic success and holistic empowerment of Black children and youth, their work in this regard is inspired and shaped by a deeper, more sacred calling that regards education as a form of salvation (Darling-Hammond, et. al, 2007).

As a core characteristic of Africana Womanism, adherence to spirituality has long-shaped how Africana Women view and move in the world. Specifically, where education is concerned, the tasks of Black educators are often coterminous with the related tasks of decolonization and liberation from mental bondage. Africana people are the inheritors of centuries of organized, systemic racial attacks that range from subtle microaggressions to racialized psychic violence to state-sponsored discrimination and genocide. Moreover, the culture, languages, religious/belief systems, customs, stylings, learning styles and, indeed, the very humanity of Africana people are constant sites of scrutiny, hostility, and denial by individuals, institutions, and oppressive societal/cultural structures. For Africana people, the seriousness and significance of education/educating takes on a spiritual aspect in that it is often interpreted as the work of liberating the minds and the souls of Black folk.

An Africana Womanist analysis of contemporary Black U.S. education necessitates linking the experiences of Black people in the U.S. with those of Black people throughout the African Diaspora. For example, analyses of the educational struggles of Blacks in the U.S. can be favorably compared and contrasted to Africana peoples' (e.g., those in Panama, Colombia, Caribbean, Europe, Africa) global struggles to withstand the interconnected onslaught of racial, class, gender, and socioeconomic oppressions. With regard to spirituality and spiritual thrusts, Africana Womanism encourages culturally responsive actions, methodologies, and pedagogical impulses that inspire Africana teachers to interrogate, apprehend, and demonstrate practices that reflect the primacy and richness of Africana culture and intellectual inheritances.

As Gaines (2016) avers, the utility of Africana Womanism is "centrally concerned with Black male–female agendas of activism and oppression" (325) and can be espied and operationalized across and within its eighteen tenets. In addition to its nurturing properties, Africana people have quite often leveraged spirituality in tandem with and as a distinctive form of organized resistance to oppressive conditions touching Black lives. For Africana people, the spiritual epistemology and praxis dimension of their work and struggles within educational circles is accompanied by the hard reality articulated by Gaines (2016): "Black bodies in the cultural fabric of America exist in a perpetual state of terror" (331). Indeed, a major aspect of the educational struggles of Black folk in the U.S. has included efforts to render a radical ethos of compassion and fundamental care for Black children, families, and communities (Muhammad, Dunmeyer, Starks, and Sealey-Ruiz, 2020). This has been described as the activation of a culturally affirming *love praxis* that is deeply humanizing, nurturing, and necessary (Kazembe, 2020 in press).

The quest for social and racial justice in teacher education must encompass spirituality. Teaching is a spiritual act and spirituality involves consciousness (Dillard, 2006). Thus, "we can see being spiritual as a legitimate frame from and through which to participate in the social and political struggles of the world" (p. 41). Drawing upon Dillard's (2006) paradigm for the purpose of spirituality in academic teaching and research, we adapt her principles for teacher education. In so doing, then teaching: (a) *becomes a way and means to both serve humanity and become more fully human in the process* (p. 41); (b) *is creative and seeks to heal mind, body, and spirit* (p. 42); and (c) *is a political life, with peace and justice as its aim* (p. 43). Notably, spirituality has been part of the ethos and pedagogy of Black women teachers (Dillard & Neal, 2020).

## Respect for Elders

The notion and practice of venerating elders is a key aspect of Africana communal societies both on the continent and throughout overlapping African diasporas (Asante, 2003; Diop, 1959; Hilliard, 1997; Karenga, 2004, King, 2018, Obenga, 2000). The African cultural concept of Eldering (i.e., respect for elders) is operationalized as sentient cultural memory (*Sankofa*) through and by which Africana people transmit collective values, regulate their environment, and sustain families and communities. Thus, Eldering serves as a cohesive mechanism and culturally unique, translatable social practice that functions within and across multiple Africana social contexts (e.g., parent/child relationships, rites of passage programs) and institutions (e.g., family, church, community, and school).

The central tenets of Africana Womanism (such as Eldering) are clearly in concert with the educational and social activism of Africana women forerunners in education. As Hudson-Weems (2005) asserts, Africana Womanism emerges out of a broader context of Africana womanhood and exists as an authentic and adaptable paradigm that is fundamentally committed to the liberation and flourishing of the Black family and community. Small wonder, then, that the academic and cultural excellence flowing from Africana women in education has historically situated them as stewards of community and servant-leaders who exemplified what King (2016) refers to as "the emancipatory pedagogy called Eldering" (33). For Africana women education leaders, Eldering is reflected in personal practices between teacher-students, professional apprenticeships, and through broader communal practices and relationships between Africana women and communities.

Generally speaking, a key mission within the field of teacher education calls for teacher educators to prepare and train individuals to assume roles as professional, skilled educators, administrators, and policymakers. Ideal candidates are reflective, critical, culturally responsive, and demonstrate a deep commitment to education, life-long learning, and teaching every child. Building on and broadening this general call, Black teacher educators, as King (2005) iterates, operate within a rich pedagogical tradition that situates Black education as "a fundamental requirement of human freedom in a civilized world" (3). Robinson (1997) notes that time functions as a catchment for events. As such, the critical work of Black teacher educators is at once and always informed by the histories and life experiences of Africana Elders and Ancestors who functioned and continue to function as architects, informants, and exemplars of Black educational excellence. The sentient folk wisdom of these Africana women education pioneers activates the Africana Womanist tenet of Respect for Elders within the broad synthesis of African cultural continuity and Black educational struggle.

The field of teacher education continues to be informed, enriched, and challenged by the leadership and pedagogical vision of Africana women Ancestors, such as Anna Julia Cooper, Barbara Ann Sizemore, Marva Collins, and Septima Clark. Their living contemporaries (e.g., Jacqueline Jordan Irvine, Geneva Gay, and Clenora Hudson-Weems) continue to make enormous strides in the field by helping to articulate an astute pedagogical vision and a leadership stance informed by traditions of Black achievement and educational excellence. The cultural knowledge and praxis shared by cultural elders, such as Marimba Ani, Nah Dove, Joyce E. King, and Carol D. Lee, has shaped learning and understanding for successive generations of teachers and teacher educators. As Africana women, their theoretical and methodological contributions have expanded the field and funds of Africana heritage knowledge within teacher education, curriculum development, cultural theorizing, and education research.

Curriculum development and restoration is another critical area within teacher education. When interrogated through the shared lens of

Africana Womanism and the Black Intellectual Tradition, the efforts of Africana women, such as Madeline Stratton Morris (née Madeline R. Morgan) and Darlene Clark Hine, have contributed to the larger curriculum project of situating Africana history as a space to humanize the Black experience (King and Simmons, 2018). Morris, a Chicago public school teacher for more than three decades, created a K8 Black history curriculum (*Supplementary Units for the Course of Instruction in Social Studies*) in 1941. The text was adopted by Chicago Public Schools one year later and became the first-ever curriculum adopted by a major urban public school system. As a lifelong educator, historian, and activist, Morris' Black studies curriculum garnered national acclaim and helped to lay the early groundwork for the current focus on Culturally Relevant Pedagogy, Culturally Sustaining Pedagogy, and Culturally Responsive Teaching.

In addition to helping to institutionalize Black Studies and articulate its formal curricular structure, Darlene Clark Hine's extensive contributions to Africana historiography and curriculum development have influenced generations of teacher educators in social studies, language arts, history, geography, and other core fields. Similar to other human groups, Africana people exist and function as products of their personal and collective group history. Indeed, the history of any ethnic or cultural group serves as a foundation and springboard for the group's current functioning within the broader society. For example, the current status of First Nations groups was/is indexed by the history of genocide, cultural dislocation, land theft, and European/Euro American settler colonialism. The dialectic of the struggle against epistemicide (de Sousa Santos, 2014; Kazembe, 2020 in press) manifests as ongoing struggles for self-definition and articulation of I/indigenous pedagogies of culture, meaning, and being. As this example teaches, history continues to exert influence on our present-day social relations, as well as on inquiry, cognition, and learning within the context of education and Black struggles for educational equity.

As a core tenet of Africana Womanism, respect for Elders is operationalized culturally as a discourse, a disposition, and a disciplinary practice within education. Moreover, it functions as a thought mechanism, informed by a broader domain of subjectivity borne from centuries of struggle for dignity, agency, and self-actualization. The work of Black critical scholars within the field is made possible by the contributions of Africana women forerunners (Elders and Ancestors) who leveraged the sociocultural and sociohistorical experiences, thoughtforms, and theoretical traditions of Africana people as pedagogies of liberation.

## Family Centeredness

Spiraling inequity within U.S. K12 education calls for skilled culturally responsive Black educators to effectively leverage the cultural and heritage lives of Black children and families (Gonzalez, Moll, & Amanti, 2005; Milner, 2010, 2012, 2016). Yosso (2005) describes community cultural wealth as specific knowledges that people bring from their families and communities into educational spaces (70). This idea aligns with Africana Womanism's emphasis on family centeredness as a root within Africana culture that nurtures, protects, and sustains. At this critical time, what is needed now more than ever is a deeper interrogation and implementation of culturally responsive, family centered practices that have always informed and encouraged traditions of Africana educational excellence.

Africana Womanism reinforces the importance of building caring, family centered communities by emphasizing the cultural lives of Black students and families. For Africana teachers, researchers, and educational stakeholders, family solidarity functions as an ethical extension of their culturally responsive and sustaining practices. The formation of learning communities is another culturally affirming pedagogical practice of Africana teachers serving students and families. Whether school- or community-based, learning communities exist and operate as formal/informal educational spaces to bolster academic learning, cultural and historical exploration, political activism, civic engagement, and relationship-building among Black children and families. Researchers have long emphasized the benefits of literacy communities in that they serve as spaces for nurturing educator and student cultural identities (Minthorn and Shotton, 2018), promoting cultural and social capital (Gay, 2013, 2018), and expanding sociopolitical consciousness (Jackson and Knight-Manuel 2018).

Hudson-Weems insists that the mandate of Africana Womanism rightly and naturally includes the entire family (adults and children) in the ongoing struggle against racism and cultural hegemony. As a core tenet of Africana womanism, family centeredness is emphasized and sustained both through habits of mind and outward cultural practices. Within an educational context, developing long-lasting, reciprocal relationships with families is a key component of developing effective educational institutions and experiences for Black children. The centuries-long assault against Black families is especially evident within the field of education and continues to negatively impact the cultural, academic, and socioemotional lives of Black children. As Alexander-Floyd and Simien (2006) point out, respect, mothering, nurturing, and spirituality are vital to the ethos and mission of African Womanism. As inherent cultural practices, they support the prosocial cultural empowerment and sustainability of the Africana family.

## Mothering

Africana womanism recognizes the salience of mothering and positions mothering and nurturing as essential components of the liberation of Black people. Hudson-Weems (2019) shares that Africana womanists are "committed to the art of mothering and nurturing, her own children in particular and humankind in general. This collective role is supreme in Africana culture, for the Africana woman comes from a legacy of fulfilling the role of supreme Mother Nature- nurturer, provider, and protector" (48). For Africana womanists, mothering is positioned as a verb. Thus, the *act* of mothering and nurturing are powerful tools for resisting and dismantling racial oppression. Moreover, mothering and nurturing are not limited to biological mothers. As girls, Black women are socialized to mother and nurture as "othermothers" in their roles as sisters, cousins, aunts, and neighbors before they have children of their own. Networks of Black women othermothers have been crucial for the economic sustainability of Black families, and othermothering networks are also an important aspect of mental and emotional well-being for Black women. Mothering, nurturing and taking care of other people's children has been key to elevating and sustaining the Black community. A public example of this is Ida B. Wells' insistence, when both her parents died during the Yellow Fever outbreak, upon keeping her younger siblings together, getting a job and caring for them at the tender age of 16, rather than having them split up into different homes. Wells later became the formidable Anti-lynching Crusader for Social Justice.

The role of Black mothers and the act of mothering are also essential in successfully creating racially and socially just schooling spaces for Black children. Black mothers are our children's first teachers, and in many ways Black mothers are community educators who build networks in professional and social spaces to support the education and uplift of Black children. Black women scholars have documented the ways in which Black women teachers have mothered and nurtured Black children in schooling spaces (Beauboeuf-Lafontant, 2002; Dixson, 2008; Jackson & Flowers, in press; Jeffries, 2019). Jackson (in press) describes Black mother educators as the Dora Milaje for Black children in schools. Similar to the fictional guild of women warriors in the movie, *Black Panther* (Feige & Coogler, 2018), as well as the real-life women soldiers of Dahomey from which the inspiration for the Dora Milaje emerged, Black mother educators serve as protectors of Black children in schools. Thus, in the centering of mothering, the pedagogical practices of Black mother educators need to be studied and drawn upon in the quest for social and racial justice for Black children.

## Conclusion

This chapter has attempted to highlight the importance of implementing social and racial justice in education by employing a theoretical lens, philosophical stance, and praxis rooted in Africana perspectives and in the centrality of Africana culture in order to move toward liberation. Our analysis has focused on core tenets drawn from Hudson-Weems' theorizing on Africana Womanism: spirituality, respect for elders, mothering, and family centeredness. A key aspect of this work challenges us to critically interrogate (i.e., unlearn/relearn) non-Africana knowledge hierarchies while simultaneously re-orientating and re-rooting ourselves in liberating paradigms and practices drawn from Africana culture and traditions of educational excellence.

For Africana/Black people, a quintessential feature of their history and praxis is their propensity to conceptualize, engage, and evolve modes of struggle, organizing, and educational activism drawn from forebears. Indeed, the most creative, innovative, and effective expressions of survival priorities on the part of Africana/Black people are informed by individual and collective understanding of the mutualistic, generative nature of the living past and the present. As a site of cultural work, Africana Womanism is an encouraging call to leverage our work in education as a praxis for intellectual, cultural, and spiritual liberation. Deeper interrogation and application of Africana Womanism as a rooted pedagogy, a philosophical orientation, and a culturally affirming set of cultural practices will contribute to greater educational and social justice outcomes for Black children, families, and communities in particular, and for the benefit of people in general, no matter the ethnicity.

# Bibliography

Alexander-Floyd, N. G., & Simien, E. M. "Revisiting 'What's in a Name?' Exploring the Contours of Africana Womanist thought." *Frontiers: A Journal of Women's Studies, 27*(1) 2006, 67-132.

Asante, M. K. *Afrocentricity: The Theory of Social Change.* Chicago: African American Images, 2003.

Beauboeuf-Lafontant, T. "A Womanist Experience of Caring: Understanding the Pedagogy of Exemplary Black Women Teachers". *The Urban Review*, 34, 2002, 71-86.

Blassingame, J. W. *Black New Orleans: 1860-1880.* Chicago: University of Chicago Press, 1973.

Cabral, A. (1966). *The Weapon of Theory* (n.d.). Retrieved October 6, 2020, from
https://www.marxists.org/subject/africa/cabral/1966/weapon-theory.htm

Curtin, P. D. *The Atlantic Slave Trade: A Census.* Madison: The University of Wisconsin Press, 1969.

Darling-Hammond, L., Williamson, J., & M. Hyler. "Securing the Right to Learn: The Quest for an Empowering Curriculum for African American Citizens." *The Journal of Negro Education, 76*(3), 2007, 281-296. Retrieved October 10, 2020, from
http://www.jstor.org/stable/40034571

Dillard, C.B. *On Spiritual Strivings: Transforming an African American Woman's Academic Life.* Albany, NY: State University of New York Press., 2006.

Dillard, C.B., & A. Neal. "I Am because We Are: (Re)membering Ubuntu in the Pedagogy of Black Women Teachers from Africa to America and Back Again." *Theory Into Practice*, 2020. Advance online publication: https://doi.org/10.1080/00405841.2020.1773183

Diop, C. A. *The African Origin of Civilization: Myth or Reality.* Chicago, Ill: Lawrence Hill Books, 1997.

Dove, N. "African Womanism: An Afrocentric Theory." *Journal of Black Studies*, 28(5), 1998, 515–539.
https://doi.org/10.1177/002193479802800501

Dixson, A.D. In Search of Our Mothers' Gardens: Black Women Teachers and Professional Socialization. Teachers College Record, 110, 2008, 805-837.

Gaines, R. (2016). "Critical Negotiations and Black Lives: An Africana Womanist Analysis to Raise Consciousness." *Cultural Studies ↔ Critical Methodologies*, 16(3), 324–332.
https://doi.org/10.1177/1532708616634838

Gay, G. (2013). "Teaching to and through cultural diversity." *Curriculum Inquiry*, 43(1), 48-70.

Gay, G. (2018). *Culturally responsive teaching: Theory, research, and practice* (3rd ed.). New York, NY: Teachers College Press.

Gomez, M. A. (2001). *Exchanging our country marks: The transformation of African identities in the colonial and antebellum South*. Chapel Hill [u.a.: Univ. of North Carolina Press.

González, N., Moll, L. C., & C. Amanti (Eds.). (2005). *Funds of knowledge: Theorizing practices in households, communities, and classrooms*. Lawrence Erlbaum Associates Publishers.

Gordon, B. M. (1993). "African American cultural knowledge and liberatory education: dilemmas, problems, and potentials in a postmodern American society," *Urban Education*, 27(4), 448-470.

Hall, G. M. (2005). *Slavery and African ethnicities in the Americas: Restoring the links*. Chapel Hill: University of North Carolina Press.

Herskovits, M. J. (2017). *The myth of the Negro past*. United States: Andesite Press.

Hilliard, A. G., III. (1997). *SBA: The reawakening of the African mind*. Makare Publishing Company.

Hilliard, A. G. (2000). Race, identity, hegemony, and education: What do we need to know now? In *Race and education: The roles of history and society in educating African American students*, Watkins, W. H., Lewis, J. H. & Chou, V., Editors. Boston: Allyn and Bacon, 7-33.

Hudson-Weems, C. *Africana Womanism: Reclaiming Ourselves*, Fifth Edition. London and New York: Routledge, 2019.

Hudson-Weems, C. *Africana Womanist Literary Theory*. Trenton, NJ: Africa World Press, 2004.

Hudson-Weems, C. "Africana thought-action: An authenticating paradigm for Africana studies." *Contemporary Africana Theory, Thought and Action: A Guide to Africana Studies*. Trenton, NJ: Africa World Press, 2007, 17-27.

Jackson, I. Knight-Manuel, M. (2018) "Color does not equal consciousness": Educators of color learning to enact a sociopolitical consciousness. *Journal of Teacher Education*, 1-14.

Jackson, T.O. "Introduction: Black mother educators: The Dora Milaje of Black children in schools" in *Black Mother Educators: Advancing Praxis for Access, Equity, and Achievement,* T.O. Jackson and N.C. Flowers, Editors. Charlotte, NC: Information Age Publishing, in press.

Jackson, T.O. and N. C. Flowers. *Black Mother Educators: Advancing Praxis for Access, Equity, and Achievement*. Charlotte, NC: Information Age Publishing, in press.

Jeffries, R.B. (2019). Queen mothers: Articulating the spirit of Black women teacher-leaders. Charlotte, NC: Information Age Publishing.

Karenga, M. *Maat, the moral ideal in ancient Egypt: A study in classical African ethics*. New York: Routledge, 2004.

Kazembe, L. D. "Curriculum Studies and Indigenous Global Contexts of Culture, Power, and Equity" in *Curriculum Studies*. M. F. He & W. Schubert, Editors. New York: Oxford University Press, forthcoming. doi:10.1093/acrefore/9780190264093.013.1591

King, J. E., & American Educational Research Association. (2009). *Black education: A transformative research and action agenda for the new century*. New York: Routledge.

King, J. E. & Swartz, E. E. (2016). *The Afrocentric praxis of teaching for freedom*. New York, NY: Routledge.

King, J. E. & Swartz, E. E. (2018). *Heritage knowledge in the curriculum: Retrieving an African episteme*. New York, NY: Routledge.

King, L., & Simmons, C. (2018). "Narratives of Black History in Textbooks" in *The Wiley International Handbook of History Teaching and Learning* (93–116). https://doi.org/10.1002/9781119100812.ch4

Ladson-LaBillings, G. (2009). *The dreamkeepers: Successful teachers of African American children*. San Francisco: Jossey-Bass.

Lovejoy, P. E. (1983). *Transformations in slavery: A history of slavery in Africa*. Cambridge: Cambridge University Press.

Manning, P. (2010). *The African diaspora: A history through culture*. New York: Columbia University Press.

Milner, H. R. (2010). *Start where you are, but don't stay there: Understanding diversity, opportunity gaps, and teaching in today's classrooms*. Cambridge, MA: Harvard Education Press.

Milner, H. R. (2012). Beyond a test score: Explaining opportunity gaps in educational practice. *Journal of Black Studies*, 43(6), 693-718.

Milner, H. R. (2016). A Black male teacher's culturally responsive practices. *The Journal of Negro Education, 85*(4), 417-432.

Minthorn, R. S., & Shotton, H. J. (2018). *Reclaiming indigenous research in higher education.*

Muhammad G., Dunmeyer, A., Starks, F. D., & Sealey-Ruiz, Y. (2020): Historical voices for contemporary times: Learning from Black women educational theorists to redesign teaching and teacher Education, *Theory Into Practice*, DOI: 10.1080/00405841.2020.1773185

Obenga, T. (2000). *African philosophy during the period of the Pharaohs, 2800-330 B.C.* London: Karnak House. In Paris, D., & In Alim, H. S. (2017). *Culturally sustaining pedagogies: Teaching and learning for justice in a changing world*. New York: Teachers College Press.

Phillips, L. (2006*). The Womanist reader*. New York: Routledge.

Ramose, M. B. (2002). The philosophy of ubuntu as a philosophy. In P. H. Coetzee & A. P. J. Roux (Eds.). *Philosophy from Africa: A text with readings*. Oxford University Press.

Robinson, C. J. (1997). *Black movements in America*. London: Routledge.

Rodney, W. (1972). *How Europe underdeveloped Africa*. London: Bogle-L'Ouverture Publications.

Santos, B. S. (2014). *Epistemologies of the South: Justice against epistemicide*. Boulder, Colorado: Paradigm Publishers.

Sears, J. (1992). The Second Wave of Curriculum Theorizing: Labyrinths, Orthodoxies, and Other Legacies of the Glass Bead Game. *Theory Into Practice*, 31(3), 210-218. Retrieved November 1, 2020, from http://www.jstor.org/stable/1477106

Thomas, H. (1999), *The slave trade: The story of the Atlantic slave trade: 1440-1870*. New York: Simon & Schuster.

Thomas, L. *Extraordinary Measures: Afrocentric Modernism and 20th-Century American Poetry*. Tuscaloosa: University of Alabama Press, 2000.

Van, S. I. *African Presence in Early America*. New Brunswick, N.J: Transaction Books, 1987.

Wiener, L. *Africa and the Discovery of America*. New York: Kraus Reprint Co., 1971.

Yosso, Tara & Ltd, Francis. "Whose Culture Has Capital? A Critical Race Theory Discussion of Community Cultural Wealth." *Race Ethnicity and Education*, 2005. 8. 69-911470. 10.1080/1361332052000341006.

# CALL "MAMA": GOD, FAMILY AND THE UN-MASKED AUTHORITY OF BLACK MOTHERHOOD

## DEBRA WALKER KING, PHD

### Part One: Sunday Morning

"A lot of black fathers don't have this opportunity, to be a father, because they die at the hands of police," [Daryl] Curry said. "The opportunity is taken from them, and it's damaged the community. Negative stereotypes of absent and uncaring [Black] fathers need to be challenged," he said. "We're here because we want to lead our children." (Boorstein & Anderson, "On Father's Day," *The Washington Post*, June 21, 2020.)

On Sunday morning, June 21, 2020, Brookland video educator, Daryl Curry (quoted above), joined more than two hundred others in support of the Black family. It was Father's Day and an organization calling itself *The Dad Gang* made it a top priority to celebrate Black fathers in our nation's capital. Beginning at the National Museum of African American History and Culture, the powerful march ended at the National Mall. Christened the "March of Dads," the event subverted American blindness as celebrants doused the flames of imposed stigma and lies with visual streams of truth. In respectful recognition of past and present struggles, many protestors and celebrants challenged myths labeling Black men as willfully absent and uncaring members of pathologically dysfunctional families.

The march presented Black fathers as life-sustaining agents of families under fire from adherents of anti-black ideology. If only for a moment, degrading stereotypes, orchestrated to erase Black men as engaged educators and agents of their children's successful socialization, met defeat. Proud Africana men, fathers with their children and other family members as well as supportive friends marched together, representing the truth of Black fatherhood, and projecting the fact that the Black family is, indeed, a strong, viable unit, "In It Together." Each step taken and every sign held emphasized the strength of Black families in a collective struggle wherein the man, the woman, and the child(ren) play out their roles in life for "harmony" and "the *ultimate* survival of the global community" (Hudson-Weems, *Africana Womanism,* 152, 19, 103).

That Sunday morning peaceful protestors exposed a revisionist American history, attempting to erase notions of human value from Black life and familial organization. The public appearance of Black men-in-charge, pushing baby strollers while holding the hand of older sons and daughters, highlighted an undeniable truth: Black fathers are not absent or uncaring. They are fundamental socializing agents in the lives of their children. That Sunday morning's challenge exposed stereotypes that blame victims of racial violence and social death for a physical absence executed through acts of murder both sanctioned and performed by American law enforcement.

The "March of Dads'" truth-reveal was only one of many social revelations disrupting assumptions, behaviors, and expectations the spring and summer of 2020. With unrelenting fury, the voice of God rumbled, making business as usual quite impossible everywhere. Health and social struggles in the form of disease and anti-blackness marked the beginning of a "new normal" in both the US and the world-at-large. The combined forces of the COVID-19 virus and anti-blackness took the breath of unsuspecting victims who died or fell ill, leaving behind families unprepared for exposure to "the real," as it emerged in the form of dual pandemics. It seems God's hand of correction "dropped a bomb" no one could ignore, although many tried to deny it, minimize it, and re-inscribe its meaning.

One such attempt occurred three mornings after *The Dad Gang's* march when Scottsdale Arizona City Councilman, Guy Phillips, held a COVID-19 anti-mask rally, during which he attempted to undermine awareness of anti-blackness in America. By appropriating the rally cry of the Black Lives Matters Movement (BLM), his use of double-voiced discourse (dual meanings) became evidence of how revisionist history undermines truth through ominous wordplay. While denying the threat of a deadly virus, Phillips rejected the safety precaution of mandated mask wearing. His attempt to transform mask-wearing into a violation of American civil liberty and choice achieved more than expected because of the double-voiced discourse his introductory comment generated.

As a greeting, Phillips appropriated the dying words of police murder victim George Floyd by unmasking and announcing sarcastically, "I can't breathe." At that moment, the anti-mask rally entered the annals of revisionist history. Acting as scaffolding for racial stereotypes that engorge anti-black sentiments in the US, Phillips' appropriation was a reminder that under the guise of White normativity, even air is contested property wherever Black lives matter. Much like the dismissive declaration that "all lives matter," Phillips' introductory words minimized the importance of Floyd's experience as a Black man dying beneath the knee of a Minneapolis police officer. Phillips' words generated fear in those who treated breath as the property of White American virtue and social rule. In this way, the rally gave anti-blackness buoyancy, positioning it as a necessary contagion, which civic-minded Americans should appreciate and endorse.

Although Phillips later denied his comment had any connection to George Floyd's cry of "I can't breathe," opponents denounced it as an attempt to do racist business as usual. The attempt failed miserably. It did not subvert the BLM rally cry, Floyd's dying words or his call to "Mama." Moreover, it did not minimize the horror of law enforcement's dismissal of Black people's need for something as essential to life as air. Nor did it fail to deflect the need for police reform or American accountability in brutal race-based acts of murder and social death. Instead, the sarcasm connecting Phillips' inability to breathe while wearing a removable, black mask failed because Black men, attempting to breathe while living Black, died.

Willie Ray Banks died in police custody December 2011; James Brown died in police custody July 2012; Eric Gardner died in police custody July 2014; Byron Williams died in police custody September 2019; and George Floyd died in police custody May 2020. These men and many others like them could not take off the mask of racial identity they wore and as a result died, crying "I can't breathe." The virus mirrored those deaths, stealing the breath of hundreds of thousands as it exposed racist hierarchies of human value and racialized health disparities. But most importantly, Phillip's revisionary history failed because Floyd's words registered in human minds and hearts, demanding acknowledgement of life-compromising harm condoned in a swell of White silence, hateful stereotypes, and self-aggrandizing moralism. Ultimately, Phillips' attempt at rewriting history and re-establishing anti-black rule failed because denying COVID-19 could not deny the reality of the pandemic or of being Black in an anti-black world.

Clearly something vile and deadly roamed the earth during the spring and summer of 2020—something proponents of anti-blackness could not dismiss, something without prejudice, something, "seeking whom it shall devour" (1 Peter 5:8 KJV). Anti-blackness as a vile and deadly force, was not newly born that year, however. In fact, its xenophobic assaults, aimed at extinguishing Black lives without fear of retribution or retaliation, have existed in America since slavery. So, it is no surprise that long before Daryl Curry and *The Dad Gang* marched in support of the Black family, Black men were stereotyped as an absent presence seen only as sub-human foils in the narrative of a dangerous, unruly, and pathological Black family matriarchy.

Daniel P. Moynihan, sociologist and then US Assistant Secretary of Labor, makes this charge in his 1965 report, *The Negro Family: The Case for National Action.* He and his colleagues presented the infamous report as a government sanctioned analysis of the pathology and financial devastation facing mid-twentieth century, African American families. In it, Moynihan blames Black women and their activities as wives, as mothers and, ultimately, as *emasculating* matriarchs for much of the Black family's socio-cultural and economic problems. If it were not for her, Black men, as patriarchs, and Black families, as legitimate socializing units, would be better positioned for success and longevity.

Instead of bringing life and strength to America, Moynihan's Black matriarch caused chaos by violating notions of family that affirm White patriarchal order. For Moynihan, Black mothering bodies (Black motherhood) were out of control, lost property, dooming Black families to inevitable pain, alienation, and financial failure. These dangerous and rule-corrupting bodies threaten chaos by dismantling the heteronormative, White nuclear family and denying its strength as a stabilizing force of American socialization, prosperity, and civic order. Countering these assumptions and conclusions, Hortense Spillers gives a thorough analysis of this report and the devastating effects of the history surrounding its claims in her 1987 essay, "Mama's Baby, Papa's Maybe," later included in her 2003 notable collection of essays in *Black, White, and in Color.*
Gender and sexualities specialist, Tiffany Lethabo King, places the stereotype in the context of urban unrest and describes the perceived danger this way:

> Read in the context of White civil societies' anxieties during the period of Black urban unrest, Black matriarchy has the potential to undo structures of property that undergird the integrity of the nuclear family and the nation. In addition to the threat they posed to the nuclear family as a unifying American ideal structured through property relations, the Black matriarch was imagined as a threat to the physical property of the urban landscape. ... In many ways the Black matriarch unhinges property relations from the categories of gender, sexuality, progeny and space. The Black matriarch—female flesh ungendered—becomes a threat to the social order. (80)

King's reading of the Black matriarch echoes and summarizes ideas motivating my approach to this chapter. In short, Moynihan's report, like Phillip's "I can't breathe" is nothing more than revisionary history. It is a tool in the White master narrative's symbolic arsenal aimed at corrupting truth, transforming perceptions of Black motherhood, and denying Black men's full partnership in family building and socialization. The report's act of denunciation armed anti-blackness silently, giving it strength to defeat the Black family by dividing its house against itself, bringing it to desolation, causing it to fall (Luke 11:17). Consequences of the report were multiple, including its hidden "divide and conquer" agenda. Reimagining Black men and women as pathological playmates and thorns in the American landscape rendered Black men invisible and Black mothers, loss. Their pathological behaviors contradict Africana womanists' belief in their roles as safe social agents and supporters of male and female prosperity. It also represented America's loss of urban spaces as sites of social order.

The divide and conquer strategy worked in many ways as some Black men, even today, cried "foul" and chastised Black women's strength, condemning it as abrasive and domineering—often turning from Black women for the promises of an *assumed* meeker, more easily controlled, White woman. Men who think like this do not consider the sniper behind Moynihan's complaint: the one who understands that without the Black woman, the Black man would not exist. He would have never been born. Was this the ultimate "cloak and dagger" intent of the report's assessment: to rid America of the Black man, his invasion of the moral space called home and the real property rights and urban spaces claimed only by true men (i.e., White men)? A man in violation of heterosexual normativity and property, like the feminized Black father of slavery (examined by Hortense Spillers in "Mama's Baby, Papa's Maybe") and its aftermath, had no place in America and neither was the product of his hand, his mind, and his loss progeny. Denying his partnership with Black women while crushing his attempts to breathe the free air of liberty was, and still is, anti-black strategy, making his separation from children, home and hearth, a strategic necessity.

What motivated this type of social control strategy? Can a source for this destructive approach to social change be identified? Considering the moralistic impulses of anti-black rhetoric, what role might Moynihan's Catholic faith have played in his interpretation of problems facing the Black family? Could it be that in order to avoid a rip in the fabric of White prosperity, social domination and the maintenance of a White moral contract, Moynihan channeled the unknown author of the biblical book of *Job*? The similarities demand attention.

Both the book of *Job* and the report (as well as Phillips' 2020 anti-mask rally) employ revisionist history to explain how men might avoid financial ruin and social death. Both blame the womb for all that defeats the hopes and prosperity of innocent men. Both offer a social analysis that confines, to the realms of violation and curses, unacceptable men and their relationship to "the womb" that birthed them.

Four verses after the mother of Job's children, his angry wife, demands he "curse God, and die" (Job 2:9), the protagonist himself, suffering the enmity of social death and economic defeat, curses the day of his birth, the darkness surrounding his conception and the womb that bore him:

> After this Job opened his mouth and cursed the day of his birth. Job said:
> "Let the day perish in which I was born,
> and the night that said,
> 'A man-child is conceived.'
> Let that day be darkness!
> May God above not seek it,
> or light shine on it.
> Let gloom and deep darkness claim it.
> Let clouds settle upon it;
> let the blackness of the day terrify it.
> That night—let thick darkness seize it!
> let it not rejoice among the days of the year;
> let it not come into the number of the months.
> Yes, let that night be barren;
> let no joyful cry be heard in it.
> Let those curse it who curse the Sea,
> those who are skilled to rouse up Leviathan.
> Let the stars of its dawn be dark;
> let it hope for light, but have none;
> may it not see the eyelids of the morning—
> because it did not shut the doors of my mother's womb,
> and hide trouble from my eyes. (*Job* 3:1-10 NRSV—See Table 1 for comparative translations).

Job's curses in these verses are tantamount to acts of revisionist history if not also the destruction of the created world. His desire to erase the truth of his body's conception, gestation, and birth revises how he came to be and denounces the value of a woman's role in that becoming. More essential to this reading, it condemns blackness as antithetical to a successful "becoming" and a profitable life. Moynihan's report suggests America faces a similar defeat as Black men fight to control a womb cloaked in blackness, a womb held prisoner by a dangerous and death-wielding matriarchy. Considering this, Moynihan's anti-black rhetoric positions the Black woman's womb as even more menacing than Phillip's mask-wearing breathlessness. Because it gives birth to the Black man, the Black woman's womb is a threat to not only White, masculine prosperity, but also to a desirable, patriarchal, and traditional "American" life. Hence, this, as Moynihan describes it, is a *national* problem in need of *national* action.

In reading through the lens of Job's curses and the use of metaphor in 3:1-10, "national action" should ensure that no night be received, nor should the Black woman's shouts of sexual ecstasy or joy be heard. Therefore, her ability to "rouse" the leviathan of phallic potency should be extinguished. And, if she should manage to "subdue the great sea monster," the doors of her womb should be shut and the night it conceives a boy child, cursed. With this in mind, "national action" aligns easily with disparaging notions of sons born beneath a curse of blackness and a rule-defying Black matriarchy.

The juxtaposition of the *Book of Job* and the Moynihan report, like the juxtaposition of COVID-19 and BLM, fascinates me and I desire to ascertain if my reading of their symbolic alignment has merit. Specifically, I explore *Job's* use of metaphor and symbolism as literary tools designed to condemn the womb, blaming both it and God for creating a man who suffers undeservedly. My commentary traces how the protagonist's opening lament positions darkness (and, by extension, blackness) as markers identifying the socially dead as well as a place where light and all things "good" created by God emerges in *Genesis* 1:2-4. In the Moynihan report, this light is the condition of White authority that must be preserved, defended against and given a place of superiority and preference over darkness and blackness.

Job's use of metaphor builds double-voice discourses that serve as testaments to women's power and creative authority in collaboration with God—with or without light. For the Moynihan report, this woman is a Black mother of Black children—especially Black boys—who, for the sake of White normativity and social rule, should reject the womb of Black "matriarchy," "curse God, and die." According to this reading, as her creative power dies, so does the pathology of the Black family and the suffering of innocent Black men, exiled or forced into isolation because of it. What is inferred here is that the "creative power" of the Black woman/mother, which in and of itself should be a positive, needs be terminated ultimately as an irredeemable negative force for the Black family—particularly for the Black male, and by extension the overall patriarchal system under White supremacy. Thus, according to the Moynihan Report, beginning with the root of a national problem threatening American life in general, the creative role of the Black mother/wife must be removed.

What follows in this chapter is a biblical exegesis, or close reading, of wordplay in *Job* that signals plausible actions wherein an unruly blackness undermines the natural and God-ordained power of women as participants in not only creation but also the rules of "good" (profitable), creative order. For the moment, then, I abandon my discussion of events occurring in the spring and summer of 2020 as well as the biblical text's relationship to the 1965 Moynihan report to offer an exegesis of my subject pericope (Job 3:1-10). The study returns to these opening discussions, offering an analysis of how women (particularly Black women) as mothers respond to moments of protest, injustice and social upheavals that threaten the very existence of Black people. The subject of that concluding section is the 2020 BLM Movement and the response of seven, living Black mothers of children murdered by law enforcement culminating in George Floyd's haunting call to his deceased "Mama."

## Part Two: Wordplay as Revisionist Incantation

"Whar did your Christ come from? From God and a woman! Man had nothin' to do wid Him!" (Sojourner Truth, "And Aren't I a Woman")

Biblical scholars consider *Job* a literary masterpiece originating in the ancient Near East. Its eponymous protagonist is a man from Uz, a land in that region. When we meet Job, he is a successful patriarch, a man of good character who despises sin and avoids it without compromise. The book introduces him by announcing his dedication to God, revealing the number of children born to him and enumerating the animal and human holdings of his immense wealth. These biographical facts alert the reader to matters of value that order Job's world: sinlessness, family, economic prosperity, and power over others (slaves). While Job focuses on these matters and the order they bring to his world, his children enjoy the fruits of his class status. They party incessantly, moving their feast day fun from one brother's home to the next with their sisters in attendance. After each cycle, Job calls them forth for sanctification and makes sin sacrifices to God, just in case the seven sons and three daughters have offended God with their robust celebrating, or worse, if they "cursed God in their hearts" (1:5 NRSV).

While this occurs on earth, in heaven the Divine Counsel meets "before the Lord," including the entity holding the title *Ha-Satan*, or the Satan (1:6). Seeing *Ha-Satan* at counsel, the Lord asks where he/she has been. The answer is one this character's official position (as the accuser) demands. *Ha-Satan* has returned from "going to and fro on the earth…walking up and down on it," perhaps seeking mischief to promote or sinners to accuse (1:7). Understanding this, the Lord offers his servant Job as a targeted consideration. *Ha-Satan* dismisses this suggestion because God protects Job from all harm and mischief. However, the Lord releases Job into the hands of *Ha-Satan* for the sake of a challenge. The Lord believes Job will remain faithful under any circumstance from the loss of family to the loss of prosperity and power while *Ha-Satan* believes Job will curse the Lord.

When the loss of children, property, and power does not cause Job to curse God, *Ha-Satan* gains permission to attack Job's body—but not take his life. Job loses his health. He is so tormented with sores, his wife suggests he do the unthinkable, "Curse [or bless] God, and die" (2:9). It is important to note the revisionist history employed by interpreters of the double-voiced discourse in the wife's words. Most give voice to the "curse" while silencing the blessing. Valerie Forstman Pettys of Brite Divinity School in Texas suggests in "Let There Be Darkness" that this statement engages in "euphemistic" wordplay by using בָּרַךְ instead of "traditional [Hebrew] verbs for cursing." Through it the text establishes "the impossibility of a real curse, but it has also provided an ominous foil for Job's poetic outcry" (Pettys, 94). In this condition, the once wealthy and successful patriarch faces the shock and pity of his friends who visit him and sit silently with him for seven days and nights, watching him suffer. The intensity of this final attack brings a curse to Job's lips; but, instead of cursing God, as his wife commands, Job speaks in 3:1-10 to curse the day he was conceived and born (this time using the more traditional verb קָלַל).

Job sees no reason, no fault of his own, for his suffering. He lives a righteous life, a life honoring God and following the rules Moses outlined in the book of Deuteronomy. Yet, he suffers great loss and compromised health. This subversion of the Deuteronomic Retribution Theory disorients Job, and he concludes that the moral order of the world is corrupted, out-of-balance—false. It is as Pettys describes— "a parody of divine order" (92). Job's curse expresses what biblical scholar David Clines calls "a psychic reaction to disorder" (loc. 2255). Michael Fishbane, scholar of Judaism and rabbinic literature, puts it this way: "Job, in the process of cursing the day of his birth (v. 1), binds spell to spell in his articulation of an absolute and unrestrained death wish for himself and the entire creation. [Much like the White supremacist, Job] assume[s] that the world both centered around and depend[s] upon him" (153).

Therefore, in the verses following this pericope, Job's psychic dilemma intensifies. He curses his mother's reception of him after birth, wishes for death and falls silent briefly as his friends, beginning with Eliphaz in Chapter 4, rebuke him for his spiteful words and contemplate reasons for his suffering. Job does not speak again until Chapter 6 where he raises his voice against his unjust, *out-of-order* situation, pleads for God to kill him and ultimately, much later, challenges God to justify God's actions in allowing a man to suffer unjustly.

Job's curse conjures images of both joy and gloom—gloom at masculine defeat and joy in sexual pleasure. Pleasure and "joyful cries" arise in Verse Seven as Job summons the ones who, in the next verse, "rouse" the image of phallic power called Leviathan (the monster who, when embattled, spews fire from its mouth [read *male genitalia*]). These spell-casters do as Job requests. As small "g" gods, they act (as do the mythological gods of the ancient Near East) to "subdue" it, "disable" it, release the energies necessary for life—spermatozoon—and thereby, as heroines, gain control of its creative force. Job, knowing conception cannot be reversed by man's desire, curses further rejoicing as the days and months of gestation in darkness occur. But, by acknowledging it and the darkness of the womb, he blesses the creative force of women as small "g" gods. Again, words double in semantic force beneath the text's surface as the bless/curse dichotomy of Job's wife's בָּרֵךְ command and linguistic "incantation" foil Job's intent. In the end, nothing Job says can curse without blessing the union of God and woman as co-creators. The morning, or birth, does come in Verse Nine because nothing could "shut the doors of [the] mother's womb [nor] hide trouble from [Job's] eyes" (Job 3:10 NRSV).

This pericope is a meditation on disorder that, in its opposition to the womb, highlights the creative and procreative authority of women as lovers and mothers. The repetition of darkness and blackness in the text brings with it a sensibility that spreads beyond that which hides or diminishes the activities of creation to invoke and envelop the womb itself. It is this darkness, this particularly menacing site of mystery, when owned by Black women, that has the power to "rouse" and then "disarm" *Leviathan*, a symbol in this reading of masculine power (Black and non-Black) and the spewing of procreation's "fire" from its "mouth."

Just as Job presents magic in a biblical text renowned as a centerpiece of the Wisdom Literature movement, Moynihan's report presents its *curse-incantation language* in a presidentially endorsed document. Furthermore, reading these texts as wordplay allies, speaking against the creative strength of women, we discover why Moynihan positions the Black matriarch as a threat to White normativity and socialization. As a matriarch who assumes masculine roles, even if living with a man, Black women are among the small "g" gods Job calls forth in the biblical text.

Black matriarchs are able to defeat Leviathan and release its fire of procreation. If Black women defeat it, its procreative potential is controlled by her. However, as gods and collaborators with the Supreme

Being, they not only have access to the Black man's reproductive abilities but also the capacity to release its potency as life giving energy for the benefit of social conformity or chaos. Without the oversight and control of a properly socialized (i.e., White) patriarchy, Black families and their viability are out-of-line and antithetical to the socio-cultural viability and economic security of plantation capitalism owned by those within Moynihan's "American," nuclear family. Hence, the consistent assignment of an intended-to-be derogatory terminology for the Black woman as matriarch, (and I say "intended to-be derogatory," for the term does not always hold a negative connotation in some cultures), is, therefore, a necessity for the racist position of the Moynihan report to be successful in destroying the image and the future of the Black family. In this way, the report renders the womb of every Black woman a potential force for destruction whether or not she takes the leadership role in her household.

Such name-calling sets a boundary separating her and the Black family from the Black male as leader and socializing agent. According to the White patriarchy, the boundary also prevents her access to an acceptable American identity. Her social death frees White authority and anti-blackness from being blamed for the unjust suffering of not only Black men, but also Black women and children. America has nothing to lose when charging her for every malady the Black race faces from economic collapse, to the role reversals that un-gender both men and women, to being stereotyped because her rule condemns her family to the realm of improperly socialized and disorderly bodies.

This reading exposes the damage revisionist mythologies, such as Moynihan's Black matriarchy, do to Black lives. It not only challenges normativity, it separates those it aims to destroy. When standing in opposition to the Black woman who controls the fire of Leviathan, the Black man loses the joy of his seed (as Job does) and his "fire" (his presence as civic proprietor and enforcer of justice as well as procurer of home and safety) is lost in America's racial chaos. However, in collaboration with her, as a "god-force" of creation, that "fire" becomes part of a creative whole—a human being with hope and a future, an empowered and, maybe even, prosperous being. Through respect for the Black mother's sacred duty—her strength as mother and partner, married or co-parenting— sociocultural chaos for the Black family subsides and, with God's leadership and blessings, inevitably and victoriously hope for the future rises.

## Part Three: "A Sacred Invocation"

A call to your mother is a prayer to be seen…it is a sacred invocation, a hedge against the people who don't see us. (Lonnae O'Neal, "Commentary" in *The Undefeated*, July 24, 2020)

A call to "Mama" is a call to the divine. It acknowledges the sacred charge given those who create and/or adopt children, assuring them of love, safety, and a home. Perhaps this is why George Floyd called out to his mama, Larcenia Jones Floyd, who died two years and five days prior to his murder. Absent of mental disablement, caused by the physical assault he was suffering, Floyd knew his mother was not able to reach out to him, not able to offer physical help. Perhaps he intended his call to be heard by her spirit, her "god-force" as partner with God, the Supreme Being, in creation.

This role and authority of "mama" was not overlooked by those in attendance at Floyd's Minnesota memorial. In his eulogy, Reverend Al Sharpton brought it to mind as he offered his interpretation of Floyd's call to mama. "Maybe he was calling his mama," Sharpton said, "because at the point he was dying, she was stretching [her] hands out, saying, "Come on George, I welcome you where the wicked will cease from troubling, where the weary will be at rest. There's a place where police won't put knees on your neck, George" (Olding, "Get Your Knee Off Our Necks"). Interestingly, Sharpton quotes the *Book of Job* 3:17 where the eponymous protagonist contemplates the role a "stillbirth" could have played in his (un)becoming:

There the wicked cease from troubling,
and there the weary are at rest.
There the prisoners are at ease together;
they do not hear the voice of the taskmaster.
The small and the great are there,
and the slaves are free from their masters. (*Job* 3:17-19)

Like many other Black males in America, Floyd was doomed to be a prisoner, a slave, beneath the knee of anti-black social, civic, and political rhetoric and violence. Also, like many other children of Black mothers and inheritors of slavery's denigration, he found mama's shield of protection soothing. He had rested his head against breasts where a mother's heart quiets rage and soothes woundedness with the salve of acceptance and compassion. He learned while in the arms of a mother's authority that "mama" would do everything she could to hold at bay the raging sea of anti-blackness. Floyd's mother did this and more for each of her children and any Black child in need. She was the bedrock of Christian faith and authority in Floyd's life until he emerged a fully-grown man with children and grandchildren of his own.

Floyd was not an absent, lazy or uncaring father as the stereotypes of Black fatherhood would have us believe. In fact, he moved to Minnesota to provide "better" for himself and his children. He was a father with a family, doing all he could to give them the same things his mother had given him—namely love, spiritual strength, and hope. By all accounts, he was an engaged Black father who valued his children (especially his youngest daughter) and was present for them, which is another way of saying he was an enemy of the state, struggling to succeed or just live peacefully, beneath a curse of death.

Job might say Floyd was the product of a womb condemned to bring misery and disorder to anyone birth through it or associated with it. Daniel P. Moynihan might say he was one of the undeserving victims of infamy and loss resulting from the chaos and unruly arrangements of Black mothering authority—an authority without "light," or, in other words, White masculine rule. In essence, both would probably say George Floyd should have never been born.

Floyd's murder, like that of Emmett Till in 1955, left the world wondering, what now? As Emmett Till expert, Clenora Hudson-Weems, observed, just as "the true ugliness of American racism staring us in the eye, symbolizing the bloated face of Emmett Till, catapulted us into the Civil Rights Movement of the 50s and the 60s," so did the brutal murder of Floyd, "an Emmett Till Continuum," ignite today's Civil Rights Movement. The mother of Emmett answered that question in 1955, agreeing with her advisor, Rayfield Mooty, by revealing the ugliness of racism that disfigured and killed her 14-year-old son. She put that distortion and ugliness on display as Emmett lay in an open casket for all of America and the world to see. Because of her actions, Rosa Parks was emboldened to demonstrate against prejudice and injustice by refusing to sit in the back of a city bus. In this way, Till's murder "set the stage for the year-long 1956 Montgomery bus boycott" occurring three months later, an event inaugurating the Civil Rights Movement (Hudson-Weems, *Africana Womanism*, 1993/2019; *Emmett Till*, 1994; and "The Civil Rights Movement, Then and Now," 2020).

Thoughts of Emmett Till's suffering gave Rosa Parks the courage and determination to protest injustice even if it meant she might suffer bodily injury. Although she had no children of her own, she read Mamie Till's actions as a national (and international) charge to action issued by one with the authority of Black motherhood ordained by God. It was a call to action for all—mothers, fathers, family, and community—a call Rosa

Parks answered. Similarly, Floyd's call to his deceased mama alerted all living mothers, particularly Black mothers of murdered children, to unite in "national action." This action, however, was not the same as that conjured by Moynihan's report. Mothers throughout the world united in defense of Black bodies, including the seven Black mothers of sons and daughters, greeted recently with death by the racist behavior of American law enforcement officers.

On July 13, 2020 *Good Morning America* hosted a discussion between the mothers of Ahmaud Arbery, Trayvon Martin, Botham Jean, Antwon Rose, Breonna Taylor, Eric Garner and Tamir Rice. Each of these young people were confronted by, assaulted by, and killed by police officers during this century. ABC news correspondent, Deborah Roberts, led the conversation—mentioning, as she did, her own fears and frustration as a Black mother (Roberts, "Their Painful Bond").

The mothers begin by recalling the emotional impact of losing their child, by remembering that two of those deaths occurred close to the victim's birthdays, and by giving God honor for the strength they rely upon each day. Each describes herself as the voice of their children and each views her fight as the responsibility and duty of a sacred charge. Wanda Cooper Jones, Ahmaud Arbery's mother, sums it up in a succinct and definitive way. "Fighting is what I am supposed to do as a mother," she said, "I've been fighting ... for my children ever since I had them. So, fighting is normal." Fighting, according to Jones, is nothing new for Black mothers; however, she maintains that the fight erupting around the death of George Floyd and the other murdered children during the spring and summer of 2020 is different. Indeed, this is a fight for legacy and life, justice and change—real, meaningful change—and, for these mothers, that is the only "national action" worth engaging.

As the video of the conversation progresses, the women share feasible solutions for ending the violence of anti-black hate. Their messages range from the impact of post-traumatic stress disorder (PTSD), to why participants in BLM protests should be careful of those who hold no serious and focused intent to achieve change, to how protests and legislative action must combine to achieve positive police reform. Gwen Carr, mother of Eric Garner, called out protestors who join BLM marches as a trendy thing to do during a summer of COVID-19 quarantines. Instead of engaging in protest behaviors distracting from the cause and premise that "black lives matter," Samaria Rice, calls for "righteous protests," a sentiment that echoes Hudson-Weems' point in her article, "Removal of Statues/Monuments Detracts from 'I Can't Breathe' Movement," posted a couple of days before the show. This means having a clear agenda that supplants chaos with arguments and initiatives in support of Black lives and nonviolent police interactions.

The image of George Floyd under attack by those sworn to "protect and serve" achieved the Africana womanist hope for touching hearts and minds in ways that move people to action through compassion. This, however, is only a first step (acknowledgement) of the "five-step equation" for addressing societal wrongs outlined by Hudson-Weems in her essay, "The Civil Rights Movement Then and Now." To make meaningful change, we need to address the other four steps: remorse, atonement, redemption and forgiveness. The mothers featured in the Roberts interview offer practical answers addressing the third step, atonement. Hudson-Weems deems atonement, a "pivotal element, with personal and civic accountability, going hand in hand with addressing systemic internal racist assumptions, undergirded by the internal racist mentality of whites toward Blacks, which manifests as external racist acts" (Hudson-Weems, "The Civil Rights Movement Then and Now," 2020). By consensus, the mothers directed protestors and others opposed to the brutality of anti-blackness in America to address systemic issues at the heart of the problem. They agreed that those opposed to anti-blackness should stand before governors, Congress, and the Supreme Court to demand legal action via legislation. Without legislation and a revaluation of behavioral and civic expectations, or atonement, change will not come. It is as the mother of Eric Garner said, "We must go from demonstration to legislation."

Sybrina Fulton, the mother of Trayvon Martin, does more than charge the system with responsibility for change. She charges every African American to unite as change agents. "The mere fact that you have children, or you have compassion for somebody else that [sic] has children…should compel you to get involved," she says, "You should not turn your face from what's going on right now. Your heart should not allow you to do so. You have to get involved." Her suggestions for being "involved" range from voting to writing letters to political officials and signing petitions to jury duty.

Allison Jean of Castries, St Lucia, speaks of her son, Botham's innocence, as he awaited the start of a televised sports event. She speaks to the hearts and minds of those listening when explaining that his murderer "blew out" his heart as he retired for the evening in his own home. Instead of spectacle centered around anger or a display of pain, she and the other mothers interviewed issued a strong warning to America, a warning spoken in the voice of one holding sacred power, a warning I read as an incantation for life amid tears. "If America does not shake up after all these incidents,"

Allison Jean says, "the tears we all shed as mothers will be the tears that will break America."

Moynihan saw the Black mother's leadership in the home as a threat to the concept of an American nuclear family. He saw it as a threat to the American way of life. His report, disturbing and flawed in so many ways, was right about one thing, however. Black mothers are powerful beings, capable of influencing the outcome of unjust behaviors that kill and cause suffering amongst her own, the innocent, whether the victim of harm comes in the form of an individual, a community, or a nation. Black women have the power to bless this nation or curse it. The choice is ours. We must stand together—men, women and children—in the genuine spirit of true Africana womanists who stand boldly and erect against anti-blackness just as they stand for Black motherhood. This means standing in the unmasked authority of a relationship, as co-creators, with the Almighty in life and in humanity's becoming.

Words are powerful. Name calling, potent. But there is no wordplay that undermines truth, no matter how hard one tries. There is no authority like that given by God. Black motherhood is a site of authority bestowed by a God who sees an image of God's *self* reflected in her. Often, we consider physical attributes the most viable interpretation of humanity's form as an image of God. This interpretation obscures the power of the reflection announced in Genesis 1:26 where God says, "Let us make humankind in our image, according to our likeness; and let them have dominion over the fish of the sea, and over the birds of the air, and over the cattle, and over all the wild animals of the earth, and over every creeping thing that creeps upon the earth" (NRSV). Theodore Runyon, Candler School of Theology Emeritus Professor, outlines three ways theologian and father of Methodism, John Wesley, defines *the image of God*. According to Wesley, the image of God means humanity is a reflection of God's natural image or spirit, God's political image, and God's moral image (14). These descriptions align with arguments presented in this chapter, which offer the image of God as a spirit of liberty, the benevolence of leadership, and love.

For Black mothers (and mothering others) facing the horrors of anti-blackness, the image of God is an image of authority. In this way, mothers are givers and sustainers of life, tasked to love as God loves, nurturing in leadership as God nurtures, and charged to challenge the politics of racism and *anti-blackness* as God would. The call for radical reform issued by the seven Black mothers discussed above, whether incantation or prophecy, is, then, a call of authority, a call that matters, a righteous call for unity in action—national action. It is a call to not only denied and maligned, Black fatherhood but to all who hear it. It is a call to listen and understand: "If America does not shake up after all these incidents, the tears we all shed as mothers will be the tears that will break America!"

Debra Walker King

**Table 1—Translations Job 3:1-10**

| Vs. | NRSV | KJV | NIV | JB1 | TNK2 | LXX3 |
|---|---|---|---|---|---|---|
| 1 | After this Job opened his mouth and cursed the day of his birth. | After this opened Job his mouth and cursed his day. | After this, Job opened his mouth and cursed the day of his birth. | In the end it was Job who broke the silence and cursed the day of his birth. | Afterward, Job began to speak and cursed the day of his birth. | After this Job opened his mouth and cursed his day, |
| 2 | Job said: | And Job spake, and said, | He said: | This is what he said: | Job spoke up and said: | saying: |
| 3 | "Let the day perish in which I was born, and the night that said, 'A man-child is conceived.' | Let the day perish wherein I was born, and the night *in which* it was said, There is a man child conceived. | "May the day of my birth perish, and the night that said, 'A boy is conceived!' | May the day perish when I was born, and the night that told of a boy conceived. | Perish the day on which I was born, And the night it was announced, "A male has been conceived!". | May the day perish in which I was born, and the night in which they said, 'Look, a man-child!' |
| 4 | Let that day be darkness! May God above not seek it, or light shine on it. | Let that day be darkness; let not God regard it from above, neither let the light shine upon it. | That day—may it turn to darkness; may God above not care about it; may no light shine on it. | May that day be darkness, may God on high have no thought for it, may no light shine on it. | May that day be darkness; May God above have no concern for it; May light not shine on it; | May that day be darkness! And may the Lord above not seek it, or light come to it. |

Call "Mama"

| | | | | | | |
|---|---|---|---|---|---|---|
| 5 | Let gloom and deep darkness claim it. Let clouds settle upon it; let the blackness of the day terrify it. | Let darkness and the shadow of death stain it; let a cloud dwell upon it; let the blackness of the day terrify it. | May darkness and deep shadow claim it once more; may a cloud settle over it; may blackness overwhelm its light. | May murk and deep shadow claim it for their own, clouds hang over it, eclipse swoop down on it. | May darkness and deep gloom reclaim it; May a pall lie over it; May what blackens the day terrify it. | But may darkness and deathly shadow seize it. May gloom come upon it. |
| 6 | That night—let thick darkness seize it! let it not rejoice among the days of the year; let it not come into the number of the months. | As for that night, let darkness seize upon it; let it not be joined unto the days of the year, let it not come into the number of the months | That night— may thick darkness seize it; may it not be included among the days of the year nor be entered in any of the months. | Yes, let the dark lay hold of it, to the days of the year let it not be joined, into the reckoning of months not find its way. | May obscurity carry off that night; May it not be counted among the days of the year; May it not appear in any of its months; | May that day and night be cursed; may darkness carry it away! May it not exist among the days of the year or be numbered among the days of the months. |
| 7 | Yes, let that night be barren; let no joyful cry be heard in it. | Lo, let that night be solitary, let no joyful voice come therein. | May that night be barren; may no shout of joy be heard in it. | May that night be dismal, no shout of joy come near it. | May that night be desolate; May no sound of joy be heard in it; | Rather, may that night be anguish, and may gladness and joy not come upon it. |

| | | | | | | |
|---|---|---|---|---|---|---|
| 8 | Let those curse it who curse the Sea, those who are skilled to rouse up Leviathan. | Let them curse it that curse the day, who are ready to raise up their mourning. | May those who curse days curse that day, those who are ready to rouse Leviathan. | Let them curse it who curse the day, who are prepared to rouse Leviathan. | May those who cast spells upon the day damn it, Those prepared to disable Leviathan; | Rather, may he who curses that day curse it—he who is about to subdue the great sea-monster. |
| 9 | Let the stars of its dawn be dark; let it hope for light, but have none; may it not see the eyelids of the morning— | Let the stars of the twilight thereof be dark; let it look for light, but have none; neither let it see the dawning of the day: | May its morning stars become dark; may it wait for daylight in vain and not see the first rays of dawn, | Dark be the stars of its morning, let it wait in vain for light and never see the opening eyes of dawn. | May its twilight stars remain dark; May it hope for light and have none; May it not see the glimmerings of the dawn— | May the stars of that night be dark; may it remain so and not be lit up, and may it not see the morning-star rising— |
| 10 | because it did not shut the doors of my mother's womb, and hide trouble from my eyes. | Because it shut not up the doors of my mother's womb, nor hid sorrow from mine eyes. | for it did not shut the doors of the womb on me to hide trouble from my eyes. | Since it would not shut the doors of the womb on me to hide sorrow from my eyes. | Because it did not block my mother's womb, And hide trouble from my eyes. | because it did not shut the gates of my mother's womb, for it would have put away trouble from my eyes. |

# Bibliography

Atler, Robert. "Job: Chapter Three" in *The Wisdom Books: Job, Proverbs, and Ecclesiastes*. New York: W.W. Norton & Co, 2010. Kindle Edition, Loc. 542- 626.

Attridge, Harold W. *HarperCollins Study Bible: New Revised Standard Version*. New York: HarperOne. Kindle Edition.

Berlin, Adele and Marc Zvi Brett, eds. *The Jewish Study Bible (Tanakh Translation)*. 2nd Ed., Oxford: Oxford University Press, 2004, 2014. Kindle Edition.

Boorstein, Michelle and Nick Anderson. "On Father's Day, Families Gather in D.C. to Celebrate Black Fatherhood and Challenge Stereotypes." *The Washington Post*. June 21, 2020. https://www.washingtonpost.com/local/on-fathers-day-families-gather-in-dc-to-celebrate-black-fatherhood-and-challenge-stereotypes/2020/06/21/f06f2ace-b26c-11ea-8758-bfd1d045525a_story.html. Accessed July 14, 2020.

Clines, David. "Job's First Speech" in *Word Biblical Commentary*: *Job 1-20*, vol. 17. Grand Rapids, Michigan: Zondervan, 1989. 2017. Kindle Edition, 75-114.

Cox, Claude E., Translator. *New English Translation of the Septuagint*. Vol. 28. New York: Oxford University Press, 2007, 2009, 2014. Electronic Edition. http://ccat.sas.upenn.edu/nets/edition/28-iob-nets.pdf. Accessed January 11, 2019.

Crenshaw, James L. "Introductory Commentary to Job" in *HarperCollins Study Bible: New Revised Standard Version*. Attridge, Harold W., General Editor. New York: HarperOne. Kindle Edition.

Fishbane, Michael. "Jeremiah IV 23-26 and Job III 3-13: A Recovered Use of the Creation Pattern," *Vetus Testamentum* 21, JSTOR Journals: E. J. Brill Publishing, 1971. 151-167. https://www-jstor-org.lp.hscl.ufl.edu/stable/1517281. Accessed January 12, 2019.

Flynn, Megan. "To Protest Face Masks, Arizona City Councilman Uses George Floyd's Words: 'I Can't Breathe.' " *The Washington Post*. June 25, 2020. https://www.washingtonpost.com/nation/2020/06/25/guy-phillips-mask-floyd/. Accessed July 14, 2020.

Fox, Michael V. "Behemoth and Leviathan." *Biblico* 93(2) Pontifico Institute, 2012. 261-267. https://www-jstor-org.lp.hscl.ufl.edu/stable/42615102. Accessed January 12, 2019.

Freedman, David Noel., editor-in-chief. *Anchor Bible Dictionary*. New York: Doubleday, 1992.

Gordon, Cyrus H. "Leviathan: Symbol of Evil" in *Biblical Motifs: Origins & Transformations*. ed. Alexander Altmann Cambridge, MA: Harvard University Press, 1966. 1-10.

Habel, Norman C. *Literary Criticism of the Old Testament (Guides to Biblical Scholarship Old Testament Series)* Philadelphia: Fortress Press, 1971. Kindle Edition.

Hudson-Weems, Clenora. "Africana-Melanated Womanism and the King-Parks-Till Connection" in *Africana Womanism: Reclaiming Ourselves*. Fifth Edition. London and New York: Routledge, 2020, 121-128.

Hudson-Weems, Clenora. *Emmett Till: The Sacrificial Lamb of the Civil Rights Movement*. Troy, MI: Bedford Publishers, 1994.

Hudson-Weems, Clenora. "Removal of Statues/Monuments Detracts from 'I Can't Breathe' Movement." *The Columbia Daily Tribune*. July 11, 2020. https://www.columbiatribune.com/opinion/20200711/commentary-removal-of-statuesmonuments-detracts-from-ldquoi-canrsquot-breatherdquo-movement

Hudson-Weems, Clenora. "The Civil Rights Movement, Then and Now: Anti-Racism to Stop the Emmett Till Continuum in a 5-Step Solution." *Columbia Daily Tribune*, June 20, 2020. https://www.columbiatribune.com/opinion/20200620/civil-rights-movement-then-and-now-anti-racism-to-stop-emmett-till-continuum-in-5-step-solution

Jones, Alexander, General Editor. *The Jerusalem Bible: Readers' Edition*. New York: Doubleday. 1968. http://mullumbimbycatholic.com.au/wp-content/uploads/2015/12/Jerusalem_Bible_Readers_Edition.pdf. Accessed Jan 14, 2019.

King, Tiffany L. "Black 'Feminisms' and Pessimism: Abolishing Moynihan's Negro Family. Theory & Event, 21(1), 2018, 68-87. https://login.lp.hscl.ufl.edu/login?url=https://search-proquest-com.lp.hscl.ufl.edu/docview/2157617464?accountid=10920. Accessed July 13, 2020.

Longman, Tremper et.al. *Dictionary of Biblical Imagery*. Illinois: InterVarsity Press, 1998.

Moynihan, Daniel P. "The Negro Family: The Case for National Action." Washington, D.C.: United States Dept. of Labor, Office of Policy Planning and Research, 1965. https://www.dol.gov/general/aboutdol/history/webid-moynihan. Accessed JAN 12, 2019.*New International Version of the Holy Bible: Giant Print Reference Bible*.

Grand Rapids, Michigan: Zondervan, 1990, 773-774.

Olding, Rachel. "'Get Your Knee Off Our Necks': Family Bids Farewell to 'Big Floyd' in Fiery Memorial Service." *The Daily Beast*, June 4, 2020. https://www.thedailybeast.com/rev-al-sharpton-delivers-fiery-eulogy-at-george-floyd-memorial-in-minneapolis. Accessed July 29, 2020.

O'Neal, Lonnae. "George Floyd's Mother Was Not There But He Used her as a Sacred Invocation" in *The Undefeated*. May 28, 2020. https://theundefeated.com/features/george-floyds-death-mother-was-not-there-but-he-used-her-as-a-sacred-invocation/. Accessed July 24, 2020.

Pettys, Valerie Forstmann. "Let There Be Darkness: Continuity and Discontinuity in the 'Curse' of Job 3," vol. 98, *Journal for the Study of the Old Testament*. New York: Continuum Publishing Group, 2002, 89-104.

Roberts, Deborah. "Their Painful Bond: Black Mothers Speak Out Together on Their Unimaginable Loss." *Good Morning America*. July 13, 2020. https://www.goodmorningamerica.com/news/video/painful-bond- black-mothers-speak-unimaginable-loss-71728823. Accessed July14, 2020.

Runyon, Theodore. "The Renewal of the Image of God" in *The New Creation: John Wesley's Theology Today*. Nashville: Abingdon Press, 1998, 13-25.

Spillers, Hortense. "Mama's Baby, Papa's Maybe: An American Grammar Book" in *Black, White, and in Color: Essays on American Literature and Culture*. Chicago: University of Chicago Press, 2003, 203-250.

Truth, Sojourner. "And Aren't I a Woman" in *Narrative of Sojourner Truth*. New York: Arno and *The New York Times*, 1968.

Wakeman, Mary K. *God's Battle with the Monster: A Study in Biblical Imagery*. Leiden: E. J. Brill, 1973.

Wolfers, David. *Deep Things Out of Darkness: The Book of Job*. Grand Rapids, Mich.: William. B. Eerdman, 1995.

# Notes

1   *The Jerusalem Bible.*

2   *The Jewish Study Bible: Tanakh Translation.*

3   *A New English Translation of the Septuagint.*

# 13

## CONCLUSION

## *CLENORA HUDSON (WEEMS), PHD* AND *VERONICA ADADEVOH*

We need our own Africana theorists, not scholars who duplicate or use theories created by others in analyzing Africana texts." (Hudson-Weems, "Africana Womanism & the Critical Need for Africana Theory & Thought," *The Western Journal for Black Studies BS* 79—1997).

From the above quotation, clearly the analytical participants in this 1st U.S. based edited volume on Africana Womanism are committed to authentic scholarship wherein they utilize and/or create authentic tools of analysis for assessing Africana life, encompassing materials, acts, and concepts. Moreover, in reading the interpretations herein, one sees that, in fact, Africana interpretive tools are firmly in place, providing the authenticity of each chapter, which naturally includes each writer as well. Thus, after reading, learning and, moreover, thoroughly enjoying the essence of Africana-Melanated Womanism, the assigned tool of analysis for each subject presented here, how best to articulate the true lived experiences of Africana people is the key question at hand.

*Africana-Melanated Womanism: In It Together* is a continuum for an important debate between Africana Womanism and Feminisms, and by extension Womanism as introduced and defined by Alice Walker. The 1st U. S. based edited volume on the theory of Africana Womanism, this comprehensive, all-inclusive edited volume spans the totality of life--the spiritual, historical, cultural, social, political, etc. It is a powerful compilation of theory, thought and practice, consisting of a select diverse group of contributors, all of whom embrace the challenges inherent in their specific areas of expertise. Their collective messages, demonstrating the urgency and the power of speaking truth and accuracy to Africana women and by extension, their entire families and the world at large, also offer plausible solutions for correcting societal ills. In addition to the perceptive, progressive voices of Africana women, this body of resolute contributors also men, thereby enhancing both objectivity and true diversity. In short, this manuscript represents the continuous dialogue on an evolving global concept, which shows how Africana-Melanated women in particular, and their male counterparts, prioritize race, class, and gender in the struggle against everyday racial dominance. In facilitating this goal, the 18 characteristics of Africana Womanism stand resolute, relative to a productive family-centered existence.

That said, this volume cannot close without serious contemplation and commentary on The Generational Gap for Africana people, evoking serious commentary on the on-going debate surrounding reparations as a plausible solution for correcting this historical, pervasive nemesis impeding Black wealth. And what better way than to have an accomplished representative from the Business world to speak to that very important and necessary goal. A successful entrepreneur and investor, this true Africana womanist personality has masterfully operated her own 30-year Business with one of the nation's major Insurance companies. She seals the economic deal in thought and in practice, for I am convinced that with an insistence upon Africana Womanism "**Collectivity**" for achieving our ultimate goals, we can radically change the trajectory of Africana life, thereby bringing to full fruition the long-deserved and overdue **Generational Wealth,** which includes Political Power, for our own, speaking truth to economically empowering Africana people as a mandate for real freedom and thus, true social justice for all! Her curt, though accurate, opening statement, indeed, a truism that Nobel Laureate Toni Morrison earlier articulated in her explanation as to why she spends virtually no time "explaining" Black life, says it all:

# Generational Wealth

It goes without saying that things understood do not have to be explained! But understand that there is a price to be paid for speaking your "Truth," not only in white or Corporate America, but in Black America as well. For Blacks, there is an additional price to be paid, primarily because of our status as man-made subjects. We are too often and for too long, left with no power to really own "Our Truths." Hence, we have continued to live a limited life, experiencing the loss of our initiatives to the other, the dominant culture, who callously control all aspects of the land and its people of many ethnicities, the result being those who expectantly look forward to Rising Up on our Backs as benefactors of our birthrights as fellow human beings.

Yes, there are spies among us, and we know it. Were it not so, I would not have said it. Just think about it for a moment. Too frequently we find ourselves at the bottom, which clearly does not add up, for we have had so little movement in our countless attempts to move forward. We are all Sacred Beings, longing to be Free. But unfortunately, what we have is in no way true Freedom. Per the Declaration of Independence, We are All created Equal with unalienable Rights, "that among these are Life, Liberty and the Pursuit of Happiness." Indeed, we are entitled to these Rights, for we have put our lives on the line in wars from the very beginning of the Colonies, some for Britain and others for America. Yet and still, we were relegated to the level of only three fifths human being.

Need I remind you that The Trail of Tears for Native Americans is still Our Trail of Tears today? Can you imagine how different our lives would be if we had received our promise of 40 Acres and a Mule? There would have been planting and harvest, as well as Acquisitions and compounding of interests, escalating into Generational Wealth and Legacies. Instead, we witness Power and Promise for the other, all tied up in their selfish and inhumane act of racial injustice. That is why Black men and women, in January of 1863, questioned Freedom without resources, despite the fact of the signing of the Emancipation Proclamation by President Abraham Lincoln on January 1, 1863, known by the Texans 2 and ½ half years later (1865). The defining question remains even today – Free to do what?

Freedom without resources is another type of enslavement. What does 40 Acres and a Mule represent in today's economy? It equates to forty million dollars at least in some cities in America, and one hundred million dollars plus if invested in stocks. This represents inconceivable potential if invested in Our People, such as more Historical Black Colleges and Universities (HBCUs), more Hamptons, more Martha's Vineyards, Hilton Heads and Beach Fronts properties for *us*. It represents more manufactures, inventions, and discoveries, made by *us*. Moreover, it represents less crimes, fewer jails, less guns and killings by and against us. What we are talking about for Africana people is changing the trajectory of our lives, which makes a huge difference. People don't really think about how valuable those resources would have been, which would have been automatically translated into Generational Wealth, and Political Power for us as well. In short, there would be less murders and poverty, and a host of other negatives.

So there we have it – a power-filled body of materials that succinctly represents the unimaginable woes, as well as joys of Africana people, with emphasis here on the African American, as we strive toward total freedom, which, with the help of God Almighty, we will achieve. The litany of Africana-Melanated Womanism perspectives articulated in this edited book speaks volume, indeed, to a profound comment by Nobel Laureate, Toni Morrison in an interview decades ago – "Given all that we've gone through, it's a wonder we're still alive!"

# EPILOGUE

## S. RENEE MITCHELL, EDD

I was first introduced to Africana Womanism by listening to Dr. Clenora Hudson-Weems on a podcast while waiting in a drive-through for a caramel latte, with light whipped cream. Her characterization of the cultural values that undergird how I, as a Black woman, should approach my work as an educator, a business owner, a scholar, and a visionary was like the first time someone had sprinkled salt on my mashed potatoes at the family cookout. It was the key ingredient I didn't know I was missing. Suddenly, I had the framework, the words to more deeply understand why feminism, including Black feminism, never tasted right on my tongue.

America's white supremacist society has used colonial undermining to strip us of the brilliant roadmap that can led to our own liberation. African Womanism, as outlined in this book, anchors that journey with authenticity and ancestral connection to Unbuntu values that center human dignity at the core of our actions, thoughts and values. African Womanism gives Black women and Black men a code of conduct for co-existence, as we work together for the benefit of Black children and the Black community. It allows Black women, as social-justice warriors, to be central to the cause of racial equality, without having to give up our femininity, our innate longing to nurture, protect and provide, or our right to stand with and not behind Black men – as the preferred option that white patriarchal allows – as we engage in the necessary work of repairing and uplifting our Black lineage. African Womanism doesn't require women to choose only ourselves and hope our children and Black men eventually catch up. Similar to Unbuntu, African Womanism provides an enlightened – and an endarkened, if you will – code of conduct that acknowledges our shared humanity, our oneness that requires us to care about the whole, rather than just the individual, or a particular gender.

Zora Neale Hurston, in her 1937 novel, *Their Eyes Were Watching God*, said that Black women are the mules of the earth. We have been conditioned so well to serve everyone else while putting ourselves last. However, Africana Womanism lifts the role of the so-called mule to an enlightened archetype who approaches the responsibility of holding up her community with a consciousness and purpose, as a visionary who can see the benefit of the bigger picture. Through the eyes of others, being a mule can be interpreted as a derogatory slight of a Black women's worth. Through Africana Womanism, the woman can embrace both her immutable strength – *and* her vulnerabilities – as virtues, and, therefore, purposefully defy the white gaze from interpretating her worth through confining, denigrating, and stereotypical terms.

Black women are not colored white women. History has shaped us differently, physically, emotionally, and spiritually.   Harriet Tubman knew it. Ida B. Wells knew it. Toni Morrison knew it.  All helped carry our community further by unapologetically stepping into their own power and interpreting it as a blessing to serve and uplift. They were aware of need to prioritize race, of the interconnectedness of our continuing struggle, and that Black men and Black children need Black women. Our dogged perseverance, our tender love of community and our innate creativity are collectively the salt that makes living with the perils of racism just a little bit more bearable, more hopeful.  Africana Womanism is the only social-justice framework that truly reminds Black people of what is possible when we finally and fully come home to ourselves.  The 18 tenants of Africana Womanism give us permission to lean in closer to a spiritual and sacred grace that holds space and time for the rest of our community to (re)member our ancestral resilience that held our community together through its darkest moments. Its concepts remind us to embrace our cultural wisdom and beauty, to pay homage to those, alive and deceased, who recognized that they were born Black for good reason, and then commit to live to fight another day to move us even closer toward for our collective humanity. Africana Womanism reminds us all that we must persevere to protect the futures of our precious and worthy children, living and yet unborn, by committing to the continued unfolding of our ancestors' wildest dreams.

# AFTERWORD

## *JAMES S. STEWART, PHD*
## AND *ANN STEINER, PHD*

This impressive collection of commentaries assembled by Dr. Clenora Hudson-Weems thoroughly documents the explanatory and liberatory power of Africana Womanism. As the volume's title suggests, African descended men, women, and children are inevitably conjoined in an ongoing struggle against the multi-faceted system of oppression emanating from the overarching ideology of white supremacy.

It is especially appropriate that the last contribution to the volume is entitled "Call 'Mama'--God, Family and the Un-Masked Authority of Black Motherhood." Recently the unparalleled power of Black motherhood was vividly demonstrated during George Floyd's life-and-death struggle with Minneapolis, Minnesota police.

As he fought to breathe with Derek Chauvin's knee pressed unrelentingly on his neck, Floyd called out for his mother, Larcenia Floyd. Larcenia Floyd, known affectionately as "Miss Cissy," died in 2018 in Houston. "Miss Cissy" was described as "the center of George Floyd's world" and her name was tattooed on his torso. His call out to Miss Cissy was a poignant reminder of the organic connection between Black men and their mothers that transcends mortal life. As Lonnae O'Neal has observed regarding Floyd's entreaty, "to call out to his mother is to be known to his maker. The one who gave him to her."[1] The timeless spiritual propinquity between Black men and their mothers is one of the most hermetic dimensions of male-female inter-connectedness emphasized within Africana Womanism.

Several musicians have joined the battle against police assassinations of Black citizens by producing songs featuring Floyd's, "I Can't Breathe" declaration. "MAMA I Can't Breathe!" by the Prodege Project is notable for its emphasis on George Floyd's supplication to his mother. This song features LV and Daddy Dizzie and the lyrics include the queries:

"Where Obama, Mama?
Where Maxine and Al Sharpton, Mama?
They ain't doing what they promised, Mama!"[2]

These queries can be seen as an indirect call for mothers to take an even more active role in the current phase of the liberation struggle, in effect to operationalize Africana Womanism. In fact, we are seeing evidence of what may be an emergent "Applied Africana Womanism." Recently, the mothers of Ahmaud Arbery, Breonna Taylor, Botham Jean, Eric Garner, Tamir Rice, Antwon Rose and Trayvon Martin – who have all lost a son or a daughter, came together for a conversation with ABC News' Deborah Roberts to discuss their shared bond in mourning, and their journeys and sacrifices as Black mothers in America.[3]

Indeed, Black mothers are organizing across the country to confront epidemic police violence plaguing Black communities. **Mothers In Charge, Inc.**, based in Philadelphia, advocates for families affected by violence and provides counseling and grief support services when a loved one has been murdered. The organization collaborates with elected officials, community leaders and other community and faith-based organizations on legislation and solutions to support safe neighborhoods and communities for children and families.[4] Dallas based, **Mothers Against Police Brutality (MAPB) describes itself as** "*the voice for justice for victims of police brutality and deadly force.*"5 *MAPB is attempting to unite mothers nationwide to fight for civil rights, police accountability, and police reform.*

And then there is more! Other Black women in relationships with Black male victims, such as wives, significant others, and mothers of their children, are also raising their voices in support of Black men. They are left with the responsibility of answering to their children, who join them in their unimaginable and unspeakable new reality, heaped upon them with the numbing absence of the male companions in the Black family. They are left devastated, as the male for centuries has served as the protector of his family, indeed, an overall male tradition of all races. What, then, is the mother to do or say to her children, who are now forced to share with her the feeling of absolute annihilation? These children, now fatherless, find themselves in an endless state of helplessness, confused and conflicted, defeated and devastated with the unlawful death, or the careless removal of their fathers, whose status too often has been radically altered by legal channels. These husbands and fathers are daily ripped from their homes and sent off to their final resting places or to prisons, where they are left with long, lonely and cold years of residency within the walls of the Prison Industrial System. Oftentimes too many of them have been charged with such crimes as "a joint," marijuana, now not so criminal after all, as it is now a legalized substance, bringing millions to many, now being sold for medical or medicinal purposes. The big question now is, why have not victims of these particular drug crimes been immediately released? Instead, they continue to live out their sentences of 30, or 40, or more years of incarceration as if no change in the statue of the crime has taken place. While we are not exonerating all criminal acts, such as those reflected in serious drug problems we see in the streets every day with perpetrators who should be sent to rehabilitation centers to assist in their possible success in "kicking" the drug dependency, we must point out that many, though not all, have taken this route, this form of employment, if you will, because of myriad inopportunities for Blacks, sadly rooted in insensitive and selfish racial discrimination.

Notably, women who are mothers of the children of these Black men are now beginning to step up and speak out in a firm demand for justice for their entire Africana family—men, women and children. As Africana Womanism represents, this is a family thing; we are "all in it together," which is how Dr. Hudson-Weems opened up her poem, "Africana Womanism: I Got Your Back, Boo," written and dedicated to all Africana people shortly after the Inauguration of Barack Obama in 2009, during her travel to the 2nd National Africana Womanism Symposium in Pittsburg, PA.

Don't you know by now, girl, we're all *In It Together*!
Family-Centrality--that's it; we're going nowhere without the other.
That means the Men, the Women, and Children, too,
Truly collectively working—*"I got your back, Boo."* . . .

The movement is escalating, particularly visible during the 2020 Presidential election process, when a number of Black women publicly rejected on television assumptions and conclusions that a given female leader represents the voice of all Black women. They announced that no one candidate for any given position necessarily represents *all Black women*. It's the privilege of each and every one as citizens of these United States of America to choose what side he/she chooses. And for many, we see those who stand side-by-side with their male counterparts, many of whom were, in fact, "hardworking husbands and fathers who got no recognition. . . . overlooked in the historical perspective but are now [like many Black women] coming to the forefront" (Hudson-Weems 44).

The efforts of organizations and these individual supporters can be strengthened through in-depth engagement of the wealth of material presented, authored by committed scholar-activists in this volume. Conversely, ongoing efforts to build upon the theoretical foundations of Africana Womanism can benefit from dialogue with the mothers and wives and significant others as well, who, albeit unknowingly, are practicing a budding form of Applied Africana Womanism.

# Notes

1 Lonnae O'Neal, "George Floyds mother was not there, but he used her as a sacred invocation," *nationalgeographic.com.* URL: https://www.nationalgeographic.com/history/2020/05/george-floyds-mother-not-there-he-used-her-as-sacred-invocation/ (May 30, 2020).

2 The Prodege Project, "MAMA I Can't Breathe!" URL: https://music.apple.com/us/album/mama-i-cant-breathe-feat-lv-daddy-dizzle-single/1522595497

3 Sabina Ghebremedhin, Joel Lyons, Nicole Pelletiere, Lauren Sher, and Lesley Messer, "Their painful bond: Black mothers speak out together on their unimaginable loss," *abcnews.com.* URL: https://abcnews.go.com/GMA/News/painful-bond-black-mothers-speak-unimaginable-loss/story?id=71626874 (July 13, 2020).

4 "Mothers in Charge." URL: https://www.mothersincharge.org

5. "Mothers Against Police Brutality." URL: https://mothersagainstpolicebrutality.org/2020-about/

6 Hudson-Weems, C. *Africana Womanism* 120.

7 Hudson-Weems, C. *Africana Womanism* 44

# ABSTRACTS

## Part I: Theory: Africana-Melanated Womanism

## 1

## The Significance of an Authentic Africana Womanism Paradigm: Collectivity and Interconnectedness for Social Justice

### *Clenora Hudson (Weems), PhD*

### Abstract

Chapter I offers a comprehensive overview of a global family centered concept, Africana Womanism, which validates the critical need for an authentic paradigm for all Africana people, prioritizing race, class and gender. Prior to developing this paradigm, Nobel Laureate, Toni Morrison, in her commentary in "What the Black Woman Thinks about Women's Lib" (1971), openly challenges white women's position, which excludes the race factor, addressing the problem of gender exclusivity for Africana women. Fourteen years later, in 1985, I took up this challenge, bent on naming and defining a paradigm more accurate for the Africana woman, insisting that proper terminology is essential and thus, "feminism" is, in fact, inappropriate for describing the lives and works of Africana women/people:

> Most women outside and some inside academe have found the terminology problematic, since any and all brands of feminism sees female empowerment as their collective priority. (Hudson-Weems, "The African American Literary Tradition" in *The African American Experience*, 135, 2001)

The term, "intersectionality," too, is problematic, for Africana women represent the interconnected nature of all things relative to our everyday lives and our on-going fight against racial dominance.

## 2

## Contrastive Analysis of Africana Womanism, Black Feminism and African Feminism

### *Ama Mazama, PhD*

### Abstract

This essay undertakes a contrastive analysis of three theories, Black feminism, African feminism, and Africana Womanism. The development and main tenets of each of those theories are surveyed, leading to the inescapable conclusion that given the historical and cultural origins of feminism among European women, feminism, whether labeled "black" or "African" is inherently incapable of leading African women out of the chaos and confusion created by white supremacy. Much to the contrary, the imposition of European theories on African people under the guise of universalism, is part and parcel of the colonization process set up and maintained by white supremacy. Africana Womanism, on the other hand, as a theory grounded in African cultural values and mindful of the current predicament in which African people find themselves worldwide, emerges as an indispensable tool in the African struggle for liberation and relevance.

## 3

## Africana Womanism as an Antidote to Mainstream Black Feminisms

### *Mark Christian, PhD*

### Abstract

This chapter, Africana Womanism: An Antidote to Mainstream Black Feminisms, boldly challenges the proliferation of Black Feminism in the academy, which appears to be sweeping all other ways of thinking about gender relations aside. In other words, if one is not ingratiating oneself to Black feminisms (plural because Black feminists, according to Black psychologist, Julia Hare, find it difficult to agree upon "a true core definition" for the term), it can mean one is advocating patriarchal society and misogyny.   As incredulous as this may seem, this negative generalization is rather evident in academia, especially in the era of "Me-Too-ism," which tends to cancel out anyone who stands erect within the context of Black manhood. Focusing on Africana Womanism, as espoused and theorized by Dr. Clenora Hudson-Weems, this chapter engages an authentic, workable paradigm of gender relations that offers the distinct empowerment of Black women of African heritage, while at the same time allowing her male counterpart to live in harmony and equality as well. Indeed, it is not idealistic to think of a woman and a man of African heritage to find equilibrium in their lives. And, of course, this is only the beginning of the many benefits of a positive relationship between an Africana woman and her male counterpart, particularly its relevancy to race empowerment, which includes a cooperation between both men and women as a top priority for human rights.

# Part II: Securing Our Legacy and Mission via Africana Texts

## 4

## Reclaiming Africana-Melanated Women: The Future of the Africana Family and the Power of the Media

*Marquita M. Gammage, PhD*

### Abstract

The unique positioning of Africana-Melanated womanist voices in the 21st century media has birthed a return to cultural truths that embrace womanhood as central to the family and the wellbeing of Africana peoplehood. As owners, producers and writers of Africana stories, Africana women continue to activate their creative energies to produce media imagery that is natural and uplifting to the Africana family. Through these media productions, Africana womanists weave together cultural conventions—Africana family values and social justice—serving as a fundamental precept to the reclamation of the Africana image in the media, which should be authentically identified, as opposed to being assigned, via naming, their presence outside of their cultural reality. Hence, studying these media productions from an authentic perspective, Africana-Melanated Womanism, will thereby demonstrate the power of restorative justice in the media via recognizing the long-standing practice of authentic existence for the ultimate advancement of the Africana family.

## 5

## Our Children, Too, Need Models: A Letter to Aunt Daisy: The Spirit of an Africana Womanist

### *Alice Faye Duncan*

### Abstract

The Africana womanist is committed to the art of mothering and nurturing, her own children in particular and humankind in general. The Africana woman comes from a legacy of fulfilling the role of supreme Mother Nature—nurturer, provider and protector. (Hudson-Weems, *Africana Womanism*, 48)

Hudson-Weems aptly asserts that true Africana womanists play a key role in the making of beautiful, happy, secure beings, who must one day assume a similar role, needing positive images in their literature to reflect their true reality. Impacting upon their impressive minds, mother figures lovingly motivate their imaginations, thereby creating precious moments, while guiding them ultimately toward future possibilities and responsibilities. Everything has its beginning; for humankind it begins with our love and trust in God, who in turn gives to us the child. In this Open Letter to Aunt Daisy, one experiences the 1st signs of love and self-esteem, ensuring a positive and healthy life, imbued with a purpose and a commitment.

**6**

# Africana Womanism: The Importance of Religion & Politics in Africana Life

## *April C. E. Langley, PhD*

### Abstract

Africana women have long demonstrated their understanding that religion and politics operate in tandem. That is, they have simultaneously celebrated faith and spirituality through the sacred call to fulfill the secular demands for global, national, and local civic response to our shared struggles and triumphs. They have, in short, rigorously sought to make manifest a biblical mandate for a better world "on earth, as it is in heaven." As such Africana women, who have all too often been mis-characterized or considered "the least of them" in this world, have labored to lift and liberate themselves and others, as they exercise free will and existential power in a myriad of contexts. From the enslaved poetic genius of the devout Christian, Phillis Wheatley, who asserts that a God-given "Love of Freedom . . . impatient of Oppression [yearning] for Deliverance" is a "principle' [that] lives in [all of] us," to Maya Angelou's reminder of our where we've been, where we are and most important, who we are: "past that's rooted in pain . . . Welling, swelling [and] bear[ing] in the tide . . . Into a daybreak that's wondrously clear . . . Bringing the gifts that my ancestors gave"—We rise. This piece will explore the significance of Africana women's spirituality that prays, works, and imagines the power of a people, thriving through the remembrance and respect of their past, acknowledgment of the present, and future, fully embracing the power of faith to inspire change, and chart their future.

7

# Nobel Laureate Toni Morrison: Model Africana Womanist Literary Crusader for Social Justice

## *Clenora Hudson (Weems), PhD*

## Abstract

"I am really happy when I read something, particularly about black people, when it is not so simple minded . . . when it is not set up in some sociological equation where all the villains do this and all the whites are heroes, because it just makes black people boring; and they are not. I have never met yet a boring black person. All you have to do is scratch the surface and you will see. And that is because of the way they look at life." (Samuels and Hudson-Weems, *Toni Morrison* 1)

The above quotation, which appears in the 1st critical study of the works of Nobel Laureate Toni Morrison, is Morrison speaking on the focus she gives to her writings, particularly in probing her characters' "relationship to . . . society" and concluding that they are not "bigger than life," . . . but [rather] "as big as life," (Samuels and Hudson-Weems 1). Their lives and works represent the on-going liberation struggle of Africana people worldwide, wherein I am able to connect the dots between Morrison, the literary crusader for social justice, and Ida B. Wells-Barnett, the anti-lynching crusader for social justice, both of whom spent a lifetime fighting for Social Justice for Africana people. It was quite appropriate that Rust College, Ida B. Wells' Alma Mater, would host a special event in honor of Morrison, "Remembering Toni Morrison: A Tribute," for which I served as Distinguished Lecturer, with a presentation on Morrison as a model Africana Womanist.

# Part III: Generational Wealth and Moral Responsibility --An Africana Womanism

## 8

### Pre-Africana Womanist, Ida B. Wells-Barnett: The Embodiment of the Principles of Africana Womanism

*Hilda Booker Williams, EdD* and *Charles Williams, PhD*

### Abstract

This chapter will focus on Ida B. Wells-Barnett--educator, entrepreneur, investigative journalist, social worker, social justice/civil rights advocate, and activist--who was the supreme embodiment of the interconnectedness and prioritization of race, class, and gender as advanced in Hudson-Weems' theory of Africana Womanism. During the late 1800s and the early 1900s, Wells-Barnett, a model pre-Africana Womanist, reigned as a forerunner and an early practitioner of several principles identified in Africana Womanist Theory, long before Clenora Hudson-Weems codified the theory in the mid-1980s during her defining years at the University of Iowa as theorist. As co- writers of this dialogue, which highlights the political activities of Ida B. Wells-Barnett as Anti- Lynching Crusader for Social Justice, we will explore and discuss her personal and private life and works in relation to the following seven (7) of the eighteen (18) distinct Africana Womanism principles as identified by Hudson-Weems: Self-Naming, and Self- Definition, Females working In Concert with Males in the Liberation Struggle, Role Flexibility Family Centeredness, Adaptability, and Spirituality.

## 9

# From Public/Private School to the Academy: Africana Womanism--Interconnectivity & the Family

## *Tammy S. Taylor, Dissertator*

## Abstract

Dr. Clenora Hudson-Weems, progenitor of the concept of Africana Womanism, identified the elevation and empowerment of the Africana race and community as the center of consciousness for the Africana Womanist. She postulates that Africana men, women, and children share a unique connection, allowing the triumvirate to garner strength from each other, realizing that they are far better together than either of the three could ever be apart from one another. As an Academician, she has spent her life challenging the status quo; her legendary work, identifying Emmett Till as the catalyst of the modern Civil Rights Movement, positioned her as an authority on the Black Community. However, her careful examination and presentation of Africana Womanism as a theoretical construct has confirmed her as an expert and authority not only in the Black Community, but also in the system that represents – Institutions of Higher Education (The Academy) across the globe.

Unlike Dr. Hudson-Weems, I am a principal, and a practitioner in the PK-12 public school system. I personally find Dr. Hudson-Weems' work to be fascinating and timely, as the coronavirus pandemic has seemingly created an even greater gap in the trajectory of students' matriculation from the PK-12 education system into higher education. As an educator and practitioner, I understand the magnanimity of pedagogically communicating the 5 Ws to a listening or reading audience. As such, this chapter will explain the **Who, What, When, Where**, and **Why** relative to life in general.

## 10

# Today's Civil/Human Rights Movements: Africana Men & Women against Racism & Till Continuums in a 5-Step Solution

### *Clenora Hudson (Weems), PhD*

## Abstract

According to Mark Christian in the Afterword to *Contemporary Africana Theory, Thought and Action*, "for liberation to become a reality, and not just a mere goal, the next generation of Africana scholars will require the varied [Africana] tools offered [for both] Academic excellence and social responsibility." (463-4). As for the scholar-activist, critically respecting and embracing social responsibility, the true Africana Womanist must be represented as the counterpart to her male companion in the on-going struggle for Human/Civil Rights. The Civil Rights Movement, then (its true inception was established in my 1988 Ford doctoral dissertation), was ignited by the 1955 lynching of a 14-year-old, who naively violated an American taboo, the sexual indiscretion of a Black male lusting for a white female. The saga culminates in the interconnectedness of all surrounding the subsequent injustices suffered by African Americans, including key participants, a trilogy of a sort—Dr. Martin Luther King, the father of the Movement; Rosa Parks, its mother; and Emmett Louis Till, the child of the Movement. "Successfully orchestrated via inclusivity," the fight would continue 'til good ensues (Hudson-Weems, *Africana Womanism*, 122). However, now we find ourselves continuing to witness more victims, representing the Emmett Till Continuums, which makes for an urgent call—A 5-Step Solution to End Racial Dominance. But what must be included first is the debunking of racism, achieved via dispelling the myth that Blacks have contributed nothing to this civilization, that we are an ill intelligent race of people who have no vision and, thus, not meritous of life's rewards/bonuses, traditionally passed on by whites, constituting Generational Wealth for them only. The chapter closes with today's greatest example of righting an historical wrong via returning property to the rightful heirs of Willa and Charles Bruce, Marcus and Derrick, great grandsons, thus, exemplifying Generation Wealth for Blacks.

# 11

## Social & Racial Justice in Teacher Education:
## An Africana Womanist Mandate

### *Lasana D. Kazembe, PhD* and *Tambra O. Jackson, PhD*

### Abstract

This essay discusses the concept of social and racial justice in teacher education in tandem with core tenets drawn from Hudson-Weems' theorizing on Africana Womanism: *spirituality, respect for elders, family centeredness, mothering.* As Africana people continue to grapple with reverberating crises within education, it is increasingly clear that we need to embrace and articulate a theoretical lens, philosophical stance, and praxis rooted in Africana perspectives and in the centrality of our culture in order to move us toward mental and cultural liberation. Aside from parents, educators represent the largest group of socializing agents who directly and consistently impact the lives of children and youth. Thus, if Black educators operate from a colonized ontology and epistemology, then Black children are likely to be seen as empty vessels in need of fixing. In order for our social and racial justice project to flourish, it is critical that we engage in a constant shedding (i.e. unlearning/relearning) of non-Africana knowledge hierarchies while simultaneously re-orientating and re-rooting ourselves in liberating paradigms and practices drawn from Africana culture and traditions of educational excellence. The result is a restorative approach to teacher education, informed by the liberatory theoretical vision and generative possibilities of Africana Womanism.

# 12

# Call "Mama": God, Family and the Un-Masked Authority of Black Motherhood

## *Debra Walker King, PhD*

## Abstract

Chapter 12, "Call 'Mama': God, Family and the Unmasked Authority of Black Motherhood", offers an Africana Womanist reading of the 1965 *Moynihan Report* via an exegesis of *The Book of Job* 3:1-10, focusing on Job's curse against the day of his birth, as well as his denunciation of the womb that bore him. This Africana Womanist reading culminates in an insightful discussion of a few challenges, rooted in historical perceptions, which have continued, and, hence, now face 21st century Black families and communities as they (we) build strength, in spite of racism's hostile curses and spiritual wounding. It celebrates our legacy of perseverance and resilience as we continue until our promise from God is realized.

# ABOUT THE BOOK

*Africana-Melanated Womanism: In It Together,* the 1st U.S. based edited volume on the theory, also introduces two highly talked about phenomena today—Closing the gap between the high school, college and university readership, and Generational Wealth for Blacks. A comprehensive, interdisciplinary book that spans the totality of life, with perceptive writers, embracing inherent challenges in their fields via the Africana Womanist lens, it speaks truth to Africana women and their families, while offering plausible solutions for correcting historical and current societal ills. It shows how Africana women prioritize race, class and gender, within a family-centered paradigm, in combatting daily racial dominance, utilizing the 18 distinct characteristics of Africana Womanism.

The following makes a commentary on the power of Africana Womanism within the parameters of academic and social responsibilities via scholarship and activism:

> The first African American woman intellectual to formulate a position on Africana Womanism is Clenora Hudson-Weems, author of the 1993 groundbreaking study *Africana Womanism: Reclaiming Ourselves.* Taking a strong position that black women should not pattern their liberation after Eurocentric feminism but after the historic and triumph woman of African descent, Hudson-Weems has launched a new critical discourse in the Black Women's Literary Movement. (Hill, general editor, *Call & Response: The Riverside Anthology of the African American Literary Tradition* 1735.)

# About the Editor and Contributors

**Veronica Adadevoh**—Entrepreneur; Owner of a highly successful 30-Year Business; Realtor

**Molefi Kete Asante, PhD**—Professor/Chair, Department. of Africology and African American Studies, Temple University. Leading proponent of the theory of Afrocentricity; Founding and Current Editor, *Journal of Black Studies*; Author of *The Afrocentric Idea* and *The Afrocentric Manifesto*

**Mark Christian, PhD**—Professor/Former Chair, Department of Africana Studies, City University of New York; Author of *The 20th Century Civil Rights Movement: An Africana Studies Perspective*

**Alice Faye Duncan**--Children's Books Author; 2019 Coretta Scott King Honor Medal Award; Author of *Memphis, Martin & the Mountaintop*

**Marquita M. Gammage, PhD**--Professor, Africana Studies, CAL State U-Northridge; Author of *Representations of Black Women in the Media*

**Clenora Hudson (Weems), PhD**—Conceptualizer--*Africana Womanism*; Establisher of Till as Catalyst of the Civil Rights Movement; Ida Beam Distinguished Visiting Professor (2021-2022), African American Studies, University of Iowa; English Professor, U of MO; Film Writer/Producer; Author of original *Africana Womanism* (4) and *Emmett Till* (4) books

**Rev. Deborah Jackson, D.Min**— Dean, Foisie Business School, Worcester Polytechnic Institute; Author of *Meant for Good: Fundamentals of Womanist Leadership*

**Tambra O. Jackson, PhD**--Dean and Professor, Indiana University-Purdue University, Indianapolis; Editor of *Black Mother Educators: Advancing Praxis for Access, Equity, and Achievement*

**Lasana D. Kazembe, PhD**—Assoc Publisher & Executive Director, Third World Press; Assist. Professor, Indiana U Purdue U-Indianapolis; Editor of *Keeping Peace: Reflections of Life, Legacy, Commitment & Struggle*

**Debra Walker King, PhD**--Professor of English & UF Term Professor--2019-2022, University of Florida; Author of *African Americans and the Culture of Pain*

**April C. E. Langley, PhD**—Director, African American Studies Program, Associate Professor of English and African American Studies, U of South Carolina; Author of *The Black Aesthetic Unbound: Theorizing the Dilemma of Eighteenth-Century African American Literature*

**Ama Mazama, PhD**—Managing Editor, *Journal of Black Studies*; Associate Professor, Department of Africology and African American Studies, Temple University; Editor of *The Afrocentric Paradigm*

**S. Renee Mitchell, EdD**--Award-Winning 25-year Former Newspaper Journalist and two-time nominee for the Pulitzer Prize, she is the visionary for the national award-winning and research-based program—I AM M.O.R.E. (Making Ourselves Resilient Everyday), which empowers Black youth to move from being spirit-murdered to being emotionally emancipated from racial trauma.

**Anne Steiner, PhD**--Associate Vice President (ret.) and Professor Emerita, Department of English, Central State University

**James B. Stewart, PhD**—Senior Fellow, New School's Institute on Race, Power & Political Economy & Dir, The Black Economic Research Center for the 21st Century; Past Pres.—NEA, NCBS, ASALH; V. Provost & Prof. Emeritus, School of Labor & Employment Relations, Penn State U; author of *Intro to African American Studies, Transdisciplinary Approaches & Implications*

**Tammy S. Taylor, Dissertator** (University of South Carolina)—South Carolina Public School Principal; Co-Founder of Create & Educate

**Gretel Thornton, Dissertator**--Department of English, Auburn U

**Charles Williams, PhD**--Director, Ida B. Wells-Barnett Institute, Rust College; author of *African American Life & Culture in Orange Mound*

**Hilda Booker Williams, EdD**—Associate Professor of English, Rust College; author of *Ida B. Wells-Barnett: Answering the Call to Serve*

# APPENDIX

## AFRICANA-MELANATED WOMANISM
### SYLLABUS—*ZOOM/In-Person*

Africana-Melanated Womanist Writers—4420 & 7420
Class: Tues/Thurs—12:30-1:45 pm
Instructor: Dr. Clenora Hudson (Weems), Professor of English

https://english.missouri.edu/people/hudson-weems
https://en.wikipedia.org/wiki/Africana_womanism
https://en.wikipedia.org/wiki/Clenora_Hudson-Weems

### Course Description, Rationale, Goals and Objectives

Africana Womanism/Africana-Melanated Womanism is an Undergraduate (4420) and Graduate (7000 Level) Course specifically designed to broaden one's scope from a family-centered perspective in the area of issues, recurring themes and/or trends in modern Africana-Melanated women fiction, highlighting its applicability to our everyday lives worldwide. A study of the lives and selected works by 4 leading Africana women writers—Pre-Africana Womanist, Zora Neale Hurston (*Their Eyes Were Watching God*); Nobel Prize-Winning author, Toni Morrison (*Beloved*); Popular Cultural Novelist, Terry McMillan (*Disappearing Acts*); and 21st century Award-winning novelist, Angie Thomas (*The Hate U Give*) --will be enhanced by careful readings of two (2) theory books from the Africana Womanism Trilogy— *Africana Womanism: Reclaiming Ourselves, 5th* Edition and *Africana Womanist Literary Theory*--as well as readings of scholarly selections by and about the various authors. We will be highlighting the prioritization of Race, Class & Gender, a major cornerstone of this paradigm, committed to the empowerment and equality of all.

For Part I of the course, students will be introduced to an authentic Africana theoretical concept, Africana Womanism, and for Part II, they will be applying it to the 4 Africana-Melanated womanist novels as they reflect our daily lives throughout the world. Together, the primary and secondary reading materials, and other media materials, will enhance students' understanding of critical current issues, particularly as they relate to

Africana-Melanated women and their families and communities.

The ultimate objective of the course, then, is to enhance one's knowledge and appreciation of Africana-Melanated women and their interconnection with their families (men and children) in particular, and Africana life and culture (historically and currently) in general. Its purpose is to introduce students to a relatable theoretical construct, as a possible antidote to some of the other female-base theories, such as feminisms. Africana Womanism is an authentic Africana paradigm designed specifically for all women of African descent, and by extension, for all men and women in general, as it demonstrates that we are after all IN IT TOGETHER!

# TEXTBOOKS AND COURSE MATERIALS
## PRIMARY SOURCES (REQUIRED)

Hudson (Weems), Clenora—*Africana-Melanated Womanism: In It Together* (Cambridge Scholars Publishing 2022)

Hudson-Weems, Clenora—*Africana Womanism Reclaiming Ourselves*, Fifth Edition (Routledge Press 2019-2020)

Hudson (Weems), Clenora—*Africana Womanist Literary Theory* (Africa World Press 2004)

Hurston, Zora Neale—*Their Eyes Were Watching God* (U of Illinois Press)

McMillan, Terry—*Disappearing Acts* (Knopf)

Morrison, Toni—*Beloved* (Alfred A. Knopf)

Thomas, Angie3—*The Hate U Give* (Balzer +Bray)

## Secondary Sources
### (Selections from these Selections are required):

Bonetti, Kay—*The American Audio Prose Library*--Interview with Toni Morrison (1980s); Interview with Clenora Hudson-Weems (1995)

Samuels, Wilfred & Clenora Hudson-Weems, *Toni Morrison* (Prentice-Hall, 1990)

**1 *YouTube* Video**—"Africana Womanism: A Global Paradigm for Human Survival"—Bowdoin College, 2015 & YouTube Videos on *Africana Womanism*—CHW

**3 Videos (Use either of my website Links at top of Syllabus Page)**
*Africana Womanism* and *Emmett Till*--Southern Utah U, 2007
*Africana Womanism vs Black Feminism*--Barbara Christian & Clenora Hudson-Weems (Lincoln U, June 1993
*The Issue Is*--St. Thomas, U.S. Virgin Islands, June 1994

## Handouts--Syllabus, Key Engagements, etc.
### —On Canvas under **Announcements**

# Grade Determination:

3 + unexcused absences result in lower class grade, a minimum of 1 grade level.*
*(If you anticipate barriers related to the format or requirements of this course, if you have emergency medical information to share with me, or if you need to make arrangements in case the building must be evacuated, please let me know as soon as possible.)*

- —Class Participation—15 %
- —Oral Report (10 Minutes)—15 %
- —Pop Quizzes (2-3)—20 %
- —Mid-Term—25 %
- —Annotated Bibliography (5-7 pages) or Research Paper (7-8 pages)—25 %

# Weeks 1-15

1.  *Student Introduction*—Name, Home, Classification, Major, Interest in Course; Expectations & Things you wish to contribute from your particular experiences or observations.

*Course Overview*—Course Requirements—Class Participation; Oral Reports; Pop Quizzes; Mid-Term Exam; Annotated Bibliography or Research Paper (Proper Documentation), etc.

Details for **Oral Report(s)**—What is expected, i.e. Format & Content

**Annotated Bibliography/Research Paper**—Follow **MLA** Style Sheet

Selections—to be read before scheduled class period for discussions.

**Video**—Interview—Dr. Barbara Christian & Dr. Clenora Hudson-Weems—Black Feminism/Africana Womanism (1995)—On Webpage (View before class, followed by class discussion)

2.  Chapter 1, "Africana-Melanated Womanism: Authenticity/Collectivity for Social Justice" from *Africana Paradigms* (**Handout**)

**YouTube**—"Africana Womanism" (Bowdoin College, 2015)

Part I—*Africana Womanism: Reclaiming Ourselves*, 5th Edition:
Preliminary Materials: Endorsements; Forewords, Preface, Introduction

and Afterword

3. Chapter 1—"Africana Womanism" (10-20)
   Chapter 2—"Cultural & Agenda Conflicts in Academia" (21-27)
   Chapter 3—"Africana Womanism: A Theoretical Need" (28-34)

4. Chapter 4—"The Agenda of the Africana Womanist" (35-49)

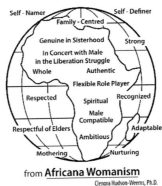

from **Africana Womanism**
Clenora Hudson-Weems, Ph.D.

—Conclusion—*Africana Womanism* (129-30)

5. **Video**—*The Issue Is*—St. Thomas, US Virgin Island (Class Discussion)

   *Africana Womanist Literary Theory (AWLT)*—Preliminaries
   Chapter I—"*Nommo*—Self-Naming, Self-Definition" (1-21)
   Chapter III—"Africana Womanism: The Authentic Agenda" (33-50)

6. **Video**--Southern Utah U Convocation Address—Africana Womanism
   Chapter IV—"Proud Africana Women Activists" (51-63)
   Chapter V—"Genuine Sisterhood or Lack Thereof" (65-77)
   Chapter VI—"Africana Male-Female Relationships & Sexism" (79-97)

7. Chapter X—Conclusion; Epilogue; Afterword (pp. 131-139)

   Chapter 10—"Authenticating & Validating Africana-Melanated Womanism: A Global Paradigm for Human Survival" (from *Africana Womanism*, 94-105)

Chapter 11—"Africana Womanism's Race, Class and Gender: Pre-Intersectionality" (*Africana* Womanism, 106-112)

- **Mid-Term Exam**

**8.** —*Africana-Melanated    Womanism:    In    It    Together*—Preliminary Info—Foreword, Preface, Intro, Conclusion, Epilogue, Afterword & Endorsements

> **Part 1**—Africana-Melanated Womanism: Theory

> Chapter1—"The Significance of an Africana Womanism Paradigm"

> **Oral Report(s)**—Chapter 2 and/or 3

**9.   Part II**—Literary Texts: Films and Novels

> Chapter 7—"Nobel Laureate, Toni Morrison: Model Africana Womanist Literary Crusader for Social Justice"

> **Oral Report(s)**—Chapter 4—Reclaiming Africana-Melanated Women: The Future of Africana Family/The Power of the Media"

> **Part   III**—"Africana Womanist Perspectives on Moral Responsibility and Generational Wealth

> Chapter 8—"Pre-Africana Womanist, Ida B. Wells-Barnett: Embodiment of Africana Womanism Principles"

> Chapter 10—"Today's Civil/Human Rights: Generational Wealth & Africana Men and Women Together Against Racism & Emmett Till Continuums—A 5-Step Solution"

**10.**   Application of Theory to Literary Texts—from *Africana Womanism* (Novels-- Part II, 51-53)

> Zora Neale Hurstons' *Their Eyes Were Watching God*

**Oral Report(s)**

Chapter 5—"Hurston's *Their Eyes Were Watching God*: Seeking Wholeness" (From *Africana Womanism*, 54-60)

11. Cont. Hurston's *Their Eyes*

Toni Morrison
Samuels/Hudson-Weems' *Toni Morrison*
Chapter One—"As Big As Life"
**Quiz** on Morrison
Chapter Six in *Toni Morrison* – "Ripping the Veil" (1-30)

12. **Oral Report(s)**—*Beloved*
"Morrison's *Beloved*: All Parts Equal," Chapter 8 (*AW*, 115-126)
*Beloved*: From Novel to Movie, Chap IX (*AWLT* 127-30)

Terry McMillan's *Disappearing Acts*
**Quiz**—*Disappearing Acts*
**Oral Report(s)**

13. "McMillan's *Disappearing Acts*: In it Together"–Chap 9--86-91

Angie Thomas's *The Hate U Give*
**Quiz**—*The Hate U Give*
**Oral Report(s)**

14. **Oral Report(s)**—*The Hate U Give*
Discussion on these novel & previously discussed novels as Africana-Melanated Womanist Novels

15. Course Wrap-Up and Final Project (Due):

—**Annotated Bibliography** for Africana Womanism (5 to 7 pages)
—**Research Paper** (6 to 8 pages)—**Suggested Topic**s:

a. The Need for an Africana Paradigm
b. Africana-Melanated Womanist Reading(s) of Africana Novel(s)
c. Africana Womanists Characters in Action in Literature
d. Interconnectivity versus Intersectionality
e. Collectivity for Ultimate Victory

## *Africana Womanism: "I Got Your Back, Boo" (CHW--FEB 2009)*

Don't you know by now, girl, we're all In It Together.
Family-Centrality--that's it; we're going nowhere /out the other.
That means the men, the women, and children, too,
Truly collectively working—"I got your back, Boo."

*Racism* means the violation of our constitutional rights,
Which creates on-going legal and even physical fights.
This 1st priority for humankind is doing what it must do.
Echoing our 1st lady, Michelle—"I got your back, Boo."

*Classism* is the hoarding of financial privileges.
Privileges we must all have now in pursuit of happiness.
/out a piece of the financial pie, we're doomed to have a coup.
Remember--protect the other—"I got your back, Boo."

*Sexism*, the final abominable sin of female subjugation,
A battle we must wage right now to restore our family relations.
All forms of sin inevitably fall under 1 of the 3 offenses.
A. W.— "I got your back, Boo," —corrects our common senses

# INDEX

Academy/academia/academe viii,
    xvi, 3, 13, 14, 19, 39, 128, 129,
    130, 131, 142, 143, 212, 216,
    217
Acknowledgement of the crime 156
Activism 33, 61, 73, 86, 92, 95, 100,
    101, 118, 119, 123, 125, 151,
    167, 168, 171, 173, 220
Adadevoh, Veronica viii, xvii, 201,
    223
Adaptable xi, 104, 130, 141, 163,
    168
Affirmative Action Set Asides 21
African American/African
    Americans xi, xii, xvi, xviii, xix,
    3, 4, 6, 8, 10, 23, 24, 25, 39, 44,
    45, 47, 48, 50, 53, 54, 60, 64,
    65, 68, 69, 70, 71, 72, 73, 74,
    77, 78, 79, 89, 92, 94, 97, 99,
    100, 103, 117, 121, 122, 126,
    146, 148, 151, 153, 154, 156,
    158, 159, 160, 162, 164, 165,
    174, 175, 176, 178, 181, 192,
    203, 210, 218, 220, 221, 222
African American Literary Tradition
    3, 4, 23, 24, 25, 210, 220
African Feminism vii, 10, 27, 30,
    34, 35, 39, 40, 41, 42, 132, 211
Africana family vii, viii, xv, xvi, 4,
    19, 48, 58, 59, 73, 92, 128, 129,
    133, 138, 172, 208, 212, 213
Africana-Melanated Womanism vii,
    ix, x, xiii, xv, xvi, xxi, 2, 14, 23,
    101, 106, 110, 151, 162, 199,
    201, 203, 213, 221, 223,
Africana Men viii, 6, 9, 15, 16, 17,
    49, 87, 107, 128, 130, 133, 134,
    140, 150, 178, 216, 217

*Africana Paradigms, Practices, and
    Literary Texts* 5, 14
Africana people vi, xii, xiii, xv, xvi,
    xvii, xviii, 2, 4, 5, 6, 13, 15, 16,
    17, 22, 40, 58, 61, 62, 64, 66,
    73, 74, 87, 88, 90, 95, 98, 101,
    102, 104, 107, 108, 109, 113,
    129, 131, 132, 134, 137, 143,
    147, 150, 156, 158, 160, 161,
    162, 163, 164, 165, 166, 167,
    168, 170, 201, 202, 203, 208,
    210, 212, 215, 218
Africana Studies 2, 3, 7, 8, 9, 24, 25,
    26, 42, 45, 77, 111, 129, 148,
    162, 175, 221
Africana Womanism vii, viii, x, xi,
    xii, xiii, xv, xvi, xviii, xix, xx,
    xxi, 2, 3, 4, 5, 6, 7, 8, 9, 10, 11,
    12, 13, 14, 15, 16, 17, 18, 19,
    23, 24, 25, 26, 27, 31, 34, 38,
    40, 41, 43, 47, 49, 51, 54, 55,
    56, 58, 60, 68, 78, 83, 84, 85,
    86, 89, 91, 95, 96, 97, 98, 101,
    102, 104, 105, 106, 107, 108,
    109, 110, 112, 113, 114, 115,
    116, 117, 118, 120, 122, 125,
    126, 128, 129, 130, 131, 132,
    134, 137, 138, 139, 140, 141,
    141, 144, 145, 146, 148, 149,
    151, 161, 162, 163, 167, 168,
    169, 170, 171, 172, 173, 175,
    179, 190, 199, 201, 202, 204,
    205, 206, 207, 208, 209, 210,
    211, 212, 213, 214, 215, 216,
    218, 219, 220, 221, 223, 224
*Africana Womanism: Reclaiming
    Ourselves* 2, 3, 7, 10, 18, 24, 25,
    26, 56, 78, 97, 102, 106, 126,
    128, 162, 175, 199, 220, 223

Africana womanist vii, viii, xi, xii,
xiii, xvi, xviii, 3, 5, 7, 8, 9, 10,
11, 12, 13, 14, 15, 17, 18, 21,
22, 23, 24, 25, 26, 38, 58, 73,
80, 83, 95, 101, 102, 103, 104,
105, 106, 107, 108, 110, 111,
112, 113, 126, 128, 131, 140,
145, 146, 148, 162, 163, 167,
169, 172, 174, 175, 182, 191,
192, 193, 202, 212, 213, 214,
215, 216, 217, 218, 219, 220,
223
*Africana Womanist Literary Theory*
xii, xx, 1, 2, 3, 4, 5, 6, 7, 10, 11,
12, 13, 14, 15, 17, 18, 19, 20,
22, 23, 25, 40, 52, 53, 56, 58,
59, 62, 64, 73, 86, 87, 88, 89,
92, 94, 95, 96, 100, 102, 113,
131, 133, 140, 163, 166, 167,
168, 169, 170, 201, 210, 212,
214, 220, 223
Africana women xii, xx, 1, 2, 3, 4,
5, 6, 7, 10, 11, 12, 13, 14, 15,
17, 18, 19, 20, 22, 23, 25, 40,
49, 52, 53, 56, 58, 59, 62, 64,
73, 86, 87, 88, 89, 92, 94, 95,
96, 100, 102, 113, 131, 133,
140, 163, 166, 167, 168, 169,
170, 201, 210, 212, 214, 220,
223
Afrocentric xix, 2, 6, 11, 13, 20, 26,
38, 41, 42, 131, 174, 176, 177,
223, 224
Afrocentricity xv, 5, 174, 223
Agenda 5, 10, 11, 12, 13, 17, 18, 19,
20, 25, 30, 35, 38, 40, 46, 49,
56, 62, 71, 87, 108, 130, 144,
146, 167, 176, 182, 191
Aldridge, Delores P. 3, 7, 8, 24,
131, 148
Alternative xvi, xviii, 3, 4, 8, 10, 12,
14, 23, 40, 66
Ambitious xi, 104, 130, 141, 142,
158, 163
American Democracy 155, 158

American Descendants of Slavery
(ADOS) 156, 162
Anderson, Talmadge 9, 24
Angelou, Maya 89, 92, 94, 100, 214
anti-blackness 69, 112, 179, 180,
182, 189, 192, 193
anti-racism 91, 97, 109, 162, 199
apartheid 25, 164, 165
Aptheker, Bettina 24
Asante, Molefi Kete vii, xv, xix, 5,
6, 11, 13, 18, 24, 27, 34, 41,
146, 148, 155, 162, 168, 174,
223
Assimilation 23, 105, 150
Atonement 155, 156, 157, 192
Authentic vii, xi, xiii, xv, xvi, 2, 3,
4, 5, 6, 7, 10, 11, 16, 51, 58, 60,
61, 62, 63, 64, 68, 72, 73, 102,
104, 105, 107, 108, 130, 131,
146, 163, 168, 201, 210, 212,
213, 223, 224
Authenticity xiii, 6, 25, 60, 138,
146, 160, 161, 201, 204

Baby Boy 65, 66, 79
Baldwin, James 56
Bassard, Catherine Clay 90, 97, 99,
100
*Beloved* xiii, 60, 61, 78, 102, 103,
105, 106, 107, 111, 223
Beyoncé 95, 97
"Beyond Bra Burning" 8, 9
Birthright 5, 6, 11, 103, 109, 146,
155, 202
Black fatherhood 112, 179, 190,
193, 198
Black Feminism vii, xvii, 3, 6, 7, 10,
12, 14, 27, 30, 31, 33, 39, 40,
41, 42, 43, 45, 47, 49, 53, 54,
55, 99, 126, 204, 211, 212
Black Liberation 50, 51, 52, 123,
134
Black Lives Matter 50, 56, 71, 73,
87, 91, 124, 179, 180
Black male bodies xvii
Black manhood 43, 212

Black media 61, 62, 64, 68, 69, 71
Black motherhood viii, 178, 181,
    182, 190, 193, 206, 219
Black women owned media 62
Black Women's Literary Movement
    3, 10, 220
Blueprint xix, 7, 12, 13, 19
Brazil 164
Bruce, Anthony, Marcus, Derrick,
    Willa and Charles 158, 159,
    160, 218
Bruce, Aubrey 152
Bryant, Carolyn 150, 157
Burke, Tarana 86, 87, 97, 98

*Call and Response* 2, 3, 10
Caribbean 167
Carnell, Yvette 156
Celebrations of Blackness 58, 63, 73
Chambliss, Jr., Alvin O. 153
characteristics of Africana
    Womanism xiii, 89, 105, 116,
    141, 163, 201, 220
Cherish the Day 67, 77
Children vii, xi, xiii, xvi, xviii, 4,
    15, 16, 29, 34, 36, 59, 61, 65,
    72, 75, 80, 81, 83, 84, 92, 94,
    103, 104, 108, 110, 114, 116,
    141, 142, 143, 145, 146, 149,
    152, 161, 165, 166, 167, 168,
    188, 189, 190, 191, 192, 193,
    204, 205, 206, 207, 208, 213,
    216, 218, 221, 224
Christian, Mark vii, xvi, 12, 13, 18,
    24, 43, 56, 76, 77, 113, 126,
    129, 148, 162, 212, 219, 223
Christianity29, 87, 88, 99, 164
Civil Rights 30, 31, 53, 54, 71, 83,
    96, 105, 108, 114, 119, 120,
    121, 124, 125, 128, 129, 133,
    134, 139, 143, 148, 150, 151,
    152, 153, 154, 156, 157, 161,
    162, 190, 192, 199, 207, 216,
    217, 221
Classrooms xvii, 85, 166, 175, 176

Collectivity vii, 2, 5, 16, 24, 25,
    34,126, 160, 161, 202, 211
Community xiii, xv, xvi, xviii, xx,
    2, 11, 16, 19, 21, 33, 35, 37, 39,
    44, 46, 48, 49, 54, 64, 65, 66,
    67, 69, 70, 74, 77, 86, 88, 97,
    102, 104, 105, 106, 107, 114,
    116, 117, 118, 119, 128, 129,
    130, 131, 132, 134, 138, 141,
    142, 146, 153, 154, 168, 169,
    171, 172, 177, 178, 179, 190,
    193, 204, 205, 207, 216, 217
Complementarity xix, 40
Connectivity/Interconnectivity viii,
    16, 17, 128, 134, 138, 144, 217

Contemporary Africana Theory,
    Thought and Action 3, 12, 13,
    25, 26, 77, 107, 111, 129, 148,
    162, 175, 219
Cooper, Anna Julia 13, 31, 125, 169
Covid-19/coronavirus x, 83, 115,
    129, 133, 134, 179, 180, 184,
    191, 217
Crenshaw, Kimberlé 41
Cuba 164

Davis, Angela 47, 48, 52
Defining Quotes 10, 11, 12, 13, 14,
    15
Dred Scott Decision 152, 157
Douglass, Frederick xii, 23, 42, 117,
    121, 122, 133, 137
Duplicate 11, 12, 13, 201
DuVernay, Ava 62, 63, 64, 67, 69,
    70, 71, 77

economic exploitation 150
education viii, xvii, 46, 47, 50, 56,
    82, 114, 116, 118, 129, 130,
    131, 132, 134, 135, 139, 140,
    143, 144, 146, 149, 155, 156,
    160, 163, 164, 165, 166, 167,
    168, 169, 170, 171, 172, 173,
    174, 175 176, 177, 217, 218,
    219

elders xi, 66, 67, 104, 130, 141, 163, 168, 169, 170, 173, 218
evolution 2, 13, 19, 114

family, family centered xi, 64, 117, 118, 119, 125, 130, 170, 171, 173, 210, 216, 218
female compatible 104
feminism xii, xvi, xx, 3, 4, 5, 6, 7, 9, 10, 12, 14, 16, 17, 18, 20, 22, 23, 24, 28, 29, 30, 34, 35, 38, 39, 40, 41, 42, 43, 45, 48, 49, 53, 54, 130, 201, 204, 210, 211, 224
five steps to ending racism 155
Floyd, George x, 51, 71, 83, 109, 125, 137, 179, 180, 185, 189, 190, 191, 192, 198, 200, 206, 209
Forgiveness 139, 155, 157, 162, 192
future generations xvii, 53, 150

Generational Wealth viii, xvi, xvii, 112, 150, 160, 202, 203, 216, 219, 222
genuine sisterhood 49, 104
God viii, xiii, xiv, xvi, 84, 88, 92, 93, 95, 96, 98, 100, 103, 104, 106, 109, 110, 119, 120, 132, 137, 144, 145, 155, 157, 178, 179, 183, 184, 185, 186, 187, 188, 189, 190, 191, 193, 195, 200, 203, 204, 206, 213, 214, 219, 223

Hahn, Janice 159, 160
Hare, Julia 12, 212
Harper, Frances Watkins xii, 89, 91, 97, 135, 136, 149
Harris, Jr, Robert L. 9, 14, 24
Higher education 46, 47, 50, 56, 129, 130, 131, 144, 176, 217
Hill, Lauryn 89, 93, 94, 97
Hill, Patricia Liggins 3, 10, 24
historical wrongs 23, 157, 160
Holy Spirit 83

*Home* xvii, xviii, 19, 66, 80, 82, 83, 92, 103, 105, 107, 108, 138, 172, 182, 185, 188, 189, 192, 193, 205, 207
hooks, bell 56, 78
Hudson-Weems, Clenora vii, viii, x, xi, xii, xiii, xv, xvi, xvii, xviii, xix, xx, xxi, 2, 3, 4, 5, 6, 8, 9, 10, 11, 12, 13, 15, 17, 18, 19, 20, 22, 25, 38, 39, 40, 41, 43, 47, 48, 49, 52, 53, 54, 56, 60, 61, 73, 76, 78, 83, 84, 85, 88, 91, 96, 97, 101, 102, 103, 104, 105, 106, 107, 108, 110, 111, 114, 116, 118, 125, 126, 128, 129, 130, 131, 132, 134, 137, 138, 143, 144, 145, 146, 148, 151, 153, 155, 157, 161, 162, 163, 168, 169, 171, 172, 173, 175, 179, 190, 191, 192, 199, 201, 205, 207, 209, 210, 211, 213, 214, 216, 218, 219, 220, 222, 223
human rights, human/civil rights viii, 14, 21, 88, 107, 108, 150, 154, 157, 212, 217

*I Got Your Back, Boo* xxi, 15, 16, 25, 84, 129, 208
*I Want My Boo Back* 16
Inclusive xi, xii, 14, 15, 18, 20, 51, 68 69, 110, 139, 145, 201
Interconnectedness vii, xii, 2, 16, 17, 18, 22, 23, 70, 93, 95, 113, 114, 134, 205, 210, 216, 217
Interconnectivity viii, xvi, 16, 128, 134, 138, 144, 216
Intercultural 17, 24
International Africana Womanism Conference 5
intersectionality/pre-intersectionality 12, 16, 17, 18, 19, 20, 21, 22, 23, 30, 31, 32, 33, 40, 41, 42, 48, 50, 114, 210
interweaving 21, 94, 114

Jackson, Deborah vii, x, xv, 109, 221
Jason's Lyric 65, 66, 78
Jim Crow laws 116, 152
Johnson, James Weldon xiv
*Journal of Black Studies* 2, 174, 176, 221, 222

Kazembe, Lasana D. viii, xvi, 163, 220, 223
King, Debra Walker vii, xvi, 112, 178, 220, 224
King, Martin Luther, Jr. 53, 71, 108, 151, 153, 156, 218

Legacy vii, xvi, xvii, 2, 8, 17, 18, 20, 23, 25, 35, 52, 53, 58, 70, 72, 86, 89, 92, 94, 95, 97, 103, 106, 108, 109, 111, 122, 160, 172, 191, 212, 213, 219, 221
Legendary 128, 140, 144, 146, 153, 156, 160, 162, 216
Liberation xi, xiv, xviii, xix, xx, 2, 3, 4, 9, 10, 11, 20, 21, 25, 30, 34, 39, 46, 49, 50, 51, 52, 54, 88, 104, 107, 113, 114, 122, 123, 134, 137, 145, 146, 165, 167, 168, 170, 172, 173, 204, 207, 211, 215, 216, 217, 218, 220
Life, Liberty and the Pursuit of Happiness 155, 158, 202
"Lift Every Voice and Sing" xiv
Lincoln, C. Eric 9, 150, 151
literary warrior 108
lived experiences xii, xiv, 73, 201
Love Jones 65, 66, 79
Lorde, Audre 11, 45, 47, 54, 89, 97
Lynching xii, 83, 101, 103, 109, 116, 117, 119, 126, 143, 151, 152, 154, 172, 215, 216, 217

Madondo, Gracious 5, 15, 25, 34, 41
Malcolm X 53, 108, 154, 156, 157
male-female relationships 6, 68, 107
Manhattan Beach 158, 159

Mazama, Ama vii, viii, ix, xvi, 2, 6, 11, 12, 25, 26, 27, 113, 126, 211, 222
Media vii, x, xvi, 20, 58, 59, 61, 62, 63, 64, 65, 68, 69, 70, 71, 72, 73, 74, 75, 76, 77, 78, 103, 212, 213, 221, 223
Mobley, Mamie Till 139, 154, 190
Mompati. Ruth 11
Moore, Atty. Antonio 156, 162
Mootry, Maria 6, 7
Morrison, Toni viii, xii, xx, 11, 17, 24, 60, 68, 78, 96, 101, 102, 103, 104, 105, 106, 108, 109, 111, 151, 153, 155, 202, 204, 206, 211, 216, 215
Moses 94, 98, 136, 148, 186
Mothering xi, xiii, 104, 114, 115, 118, 125, 126, 130, 139, 163, 171, 172, 173, 181, 190, 193, 213, 218
Moynihan, Daniel P. 63, 78, 181, 190, 200
Mujuru, Honorable Joice 5
Muwhati, Itia 5, 14, 119, 203

Naming/Self-Naming xi, 4, 6, 13, 18, 23, 38, 39, 88, 95, 99, 104, 105, 121, 210
Newson-Horst, Adele S. 3, 12, 14, 26, 107, 111
Ntiri, Daphne 8, 13, 25, 26
Nurturing xi, 19, 104, 130, 139, 163, 166, 167, 168, 171, 172, 193

*Out of the Revolution* 7, 8, 10, 24, 25

Paradigms 5, 8, 17, 23, 25, 76, 89, 146, 161, 162, 165, 173, 219
Parks, Rosa 73, 77, 116, 151, 154, 190, 191
Pedagogy 166, 168, 169, 170, 173, 174

PK-12 129, 130, 131, 132, 143, 144, 146, 217
politics, political viii, xvi, 9, 11, 17, 34, 36, 41, 42, 70, 77, 78, 86, 95, 96, 97, 115, 134, 143, 155, 193, 214
post-civil rights 96
praxis 163, 165, 167, 168, 169, 173, 175, 176, 218, 221
prioritize xviii, 20, 62, 87, 104, 110, 113, 134, 201, 205, 220
prioritization 12, 15, 16, 18, 20, 22, 34, 68, 91, 95, 113, 114, 216, 223
*pro-bono* 157
*Psalms* 93, 98

*Queen Sugar* 62, 67, 78
Queer 33, 34, 41, 44, 45, 46, 47, 48, 49, 50, 51, 54, 56

Racism viii, xvi, xxi, 4, 7, 15, 20, 22, 24, 30, 31, 33, 44, 45, 48, 49, 54, 56, 57, 63, 67, 69, 70, 71, 72, 76, 77, 86, 87, 91, 97, 102, 104, 105, 108, 109, 116, 122, 123, 135, 150, 151, 152, 153, 155, 156, 157, 158, 160, 162, 171, 190, 193, 199, 205, 217, 218, 219
Rae, Issa 62, 64, 79
Reciprocity xx
Reckoning x, 100, 109, 134, 196
Redemption 90, 93, 139, 155, 157, 162, 192
Religion viii, xvi, 42, 86, 89, 93, 95, 99, 100, 109, 121, 155, 164, 214
Remorse 155, 156, 157, 160, 192
Reparations 156, 160, 162, 202
resistance to patriarchy xx
respect xi, 21, 22, 36, 40, 67, 74, 89, 102, 104, 109, 131, 138, 141, 145, 152, 168, 169, 170, 171, 173, 188, 214, 218

Samuels, Wilfred D. xxi, 104, 111

Self-Made: Inspired by the Life of Madam C.J. Walker 73, 74, 77
self-esteem 81, 106, 213
sexism xxi, 7, 16, 20, 48, 53, 54, 86, 87, 95, 116
Sister Sledge 80
social justice vii, viii, xii, xvi, xvii, 2, 17, 25, 63, 68, 69, 70, 72, 75, 76, 86, 88, 89, 94, 95, 99, 100, 101, 103, 105, 108, 109, 119, 120, 124, 125, 138, 144, 146, 149, 154, 161, 162, 165, 166, 172, 173, 202, 210, 212, 214, 215, 216
Sofola, 'Zulu 11, 131, 149
Spiritual, Spirituality 42, 86, 88, 89, 93, 95, 97, 99, 104, 114, 119, 125, 164, 166, 167, 168, 171, 173, 215, 217, 219
Stereotypes xvi, 19, 59, 69, 102, 178, 179, 180, 190, 198
Stewart, James B. ix, xv, 2, 11, 26, 28, 42, 113, 126, 207, 224
Stewart, Maria W. xii
Strong xi, 3, 6, 10, 11, 18, 19, 24, 51, 103, 123, 124, 125, 130, 133, 139, 143, 145, 149, 154, 161, 163, 179, 192, 220
Survival xiii, xviii, 15, 17, 35, 42, 87, 94, 96, 102, 104, 107, 109, 110, 129, 150, 164, 173, 179

Taylor, Breonna x, 71, 191, 207
teacher education viii, 163, 165, 166, 168, 169, 175, 176, 218, 219
terminology 4, 7, 10, 12, 17, 19, 22, 188, 210
The African Heritage Study Association 6
The American Dream 63, 158
The Association for the Study of African American Life and History 6
The College Language Association 6

The National Council for Black
  Studies 2, 6, 7
*The Bluest Eye* 105, 111
*The Dad Gang* 112, 178, 179, 181
*The New York Times* xx, 200
The Photograph 66, 78
Till, Emmett Louis viii, xiii, 53,
  109, 128, 139, 143, 148, 150,
  151, 152, 157, 162, 190, 199,
  216, 218, 221
Trajectory 48, 68, 74, 120, 129, 144,
  202, 203, 217
true cultural diversity xiii,
truth xvi, 5, 32, 45, 68, 70, 92, 102,
  108, 118, 122, 125, 134, 145,
  147, 153, 158, 161, 178, 179,
  182, 183, 193, 201, 202, 220
Truth, Sojourner xii, 21, 135, 144,
  145, 185, 200
Tubman, Harriet 108, 135, 136, 137,
  138, 148, 205

United States x, xi, 5, 24, 28, 40, 49,
  91, 115, 118, 119, 130, 133,

137, 152, 154, 155, 162, 164,
  165, 175, 200, 208
University of Zimbabwe 5
Uplifting xi, 94, 123, 205, 214

Victimization 103, 150
Victory xiv, xvi, 23, 152, 160, 161

Walker, Alice xii, 4, 99, 201
*We Are Family* 80, 82, 83, 84, 85
Wells-Barnett, Ida B. viii, xii, xvi,
  53, 101, 103, 104, 108, 109,
  113, 114, 115, 117, 119, 122,
  124, 125, 126, 127, 154, 172,
  205, 215, 216, 222
West, Cornell 156
*Western Journal of Black Studies* 5,
  7, 8, 9, 20, 25, 26, 49, 56, 60,
  78, 144, 148
Wheatley, Phillis 89, 90, 91, 94, 95,
  97, 99, 100, 214
Whitten, John, Jr. 157

Young, Charlene 7

# PRAISE FOR THE BOOK

"*Africana-Melanated Womanism* is a tremendous contribution that provides an authentic understanding of the complementary roles Africana women and men have played and must continue in our ongoing quest for liberation and abundant life. As collectivity is a powerful force uniting Africana men and women, our legacy of survival ensures our victory. From the academy to the community, it provides an Africana liberatory lens, conceptual framework, and significant tools for analysis and synthesis."
—**Chike Akua, PhD**, Professor of Educational Leadership, Clark-Atlanta U; author of *Education for Transformation: The Keys to Releasing the Genius of African American Students*

"While a student in Dr. Hudson-Weems' class a decade ago, she put words to what I had felt as a Black woman who couldn't find her home in feminism. In this book, she marries unapologetic demands for Black women's equality & celebration, and a partnership of Black men in our struggle. She also highlights the need for us to self-determine our own frameworks for equality & traces how Black women throughout history have defied the "strong Black woman" trope that has done more harm than good. We must lift each other as we climb & strive for all to flourish, never compromising our true values, indeed, just what today's social movements need to succeed."
—**Laura Faith Kebede**, Distinguished Journalist in Residence, Institute for Public Service Reporting, U of Memphis; coordinator of Civil Wrongs, a project for journalism and history students to connect America's racial past to the present; author of some 1200 journalistic articles

"With a family history of activism, guided by the presence of God in our everyday lives, I can truly appreciate this valuable book, which demonstrates the applicability of Africana-Melanated Womanism for virtually any field of interest, as presented by the diverse contributors in this timely volume. This is so important today as we ponder, seeking strategies to replace racial discrimination with justice for Black men, women, children, families, and communities worldwide."
—**Alveda C. King, PhD**, Evangelist and Niece of Dr. MLK, Jr., Chairman, America First Policy Institute (AFPI) Center for the American Dream;

author of *King Rules: Ten Truths for You, Your Family, and Our Nation to Prosper*

"This book, informed by the liberating lens of Africana Womanism, is rooted in African cultural values and perspectives. It reveals how global Africana people continue their fight for peace and restorative justice. Appropriately, the 1st International Africana Womanism Conference was hosted by the U of Zimbabwe (2010), whose presenters, like these in this book, unraveled our ongoing experiences in their call for genuine dialogues between men and women as an effective strategy to solve global racism. It offers hope for a more just world for the dignity of Africana men, women and children."

—**Zifikile Makwavarara, PhD**, Professor, Department of African Languages & Literature, U of Zimbabwe; Co-Editor of *Rediscoursing African Womanhood in Search for Sustainable Renaissance: Africana Womanism in Multi-Disciplinary Approaches*